Round Hall Annotated Legislation Series

NATIONAL ASSET MANAGEMENT AGENCY ACT 2009

Dr Noel McGrath
Lecturer-in-Law, Dublin City University

and

Morgan Shelley
Barrister-at-Law

Note: The contents of this book have been substantially extracted from the
Irish Current Law Statutes Annotated (ICLSA),
Round Hall, Dublin, 2009.

ROUND HALL

THOMSON REUTERS

Published in 2011 by
Thomson Reuters (Professional) Ireland Limited
(Registered in Ireland, Company No. 80867.
Registered Office and address for service:
43 Fitzwilliam Place, Dublin 2, Ireland)
trading as Round Hall

Typeset by
Gough Typesetting Services
Dublin

Printed by
CPI, Antony Rowe, Chippenham, Wiltshire

ISBN 978-1-85800-635-2

A catalogue record for this book
is available from the British Library

PREFACE

Since its creation was initially announced in April 2009, the National Asset Management Agency (NAMA) has been the subject of much controversy and public debate. The essence of the scheme was summarised by the Divisional High Court in *Dellway Investments v NAMA* [2010] IEHC 364 at [4.3]:

> The purpose of NAMA itself is, in general terms, to obtain the best achievable financial return for the State. In so doing, NAMA is to contribute to the achievement of the purposes of the Act ... by expeditiously acquiring eligible assets from participating institutions, thus removing uncertainty about those assets and the effect of that uncertainty on credit institutions. In addition, NAMA is to deal with those assets and to protect or otherwise enhance the value of those assets, in the interests of the State.

The establishment of NAMA has been a central part of the State's response to the financial and economic crisis experienced in Ireland from 2008 onwards. In view of the severity of the conditions leading to its establishment, it is not surprising to find that the Oireachtas has conferred wide-ranging powers on NAMA, many of which are controversial in nature.

Given the long-term horizon on which NAMA is designed to operate, the sheer scale of the assets which it has acquired and the economic uncertainty which Ireland faces at the time of writing, it will not be possible to adequately asses NAMA's successes or failures for many years to come. Instead, this volume provides a section-by-section analysis of the legislation underpinning NAMA. In doing so, it aims to identify the scope of NAMA's powers and functions, to provide an account of the legislative vision of NAMA's operation and to identify areas of difficulty.

During the process of writing this book, we have had cause to become indebted to a wide range of people for their very kind assistance, and would like to take this opportunity to thank them.

First, we wish to express our appreciation to the staff at Round Hall. Particular thanks are due to commissioning editor, Frieda Donohue, and editorial manager, Martin McCann, for their help in bringing this text to completion. We were also particularly fortunate to have had the benefit of the insight and expertise of Professor Robert Clark on various aspects of the text and we are very grateful for his input.

At an individual level, Noel McGrath would like to express his appreciation to his colleagues at the School of Law and Government at Dublin City University for their ongoing advice and support. He would also like to record his gratitude to David Kenny of the School of Law at Trinity College, Dublin for a number of illuminating discussions of the *Dellway Investments* litigation.

Morgan Shelley would like to express his gratitude to Eoghan Fitzsimons SC, Benedict Ó Floinn BL and Séamus Clarke BL for their years of advice and guidance.

Finally, we would like to thank our families for their support, encouragement and affection, for which we could never adequately express our gratitude.

We have endeavoured to state the law as it appears from the materials available to us as of April 30, 2011. Parts 1–9 of the Act were annotated by Noel McGrath and Morgan Shelley annotated Parts 10–15. Any errors or omissions are those of the authors, though no liability is accepted for them and the usual disclaimers apply.

Noel McGrath
Morgan Shelley
Dublin; April 30, 2011

NATIONAL ASSET MANAGEMENT AGENCY ACT 2009

(2009 No. 34)

ARRANGEMENT OF SECTIONS

PART 1

PRELIMINARY

PART 2

NATIONAL ASSET MANAGEMENT AGENCY

CHAPTER 1

Establishment, Functions and Powers

CHAPTER 2

Membership of Board and Related Matters

CHAPTER 3

Chief Executive Officer

CHAPTER 4

NAMA's Relationship with NTMA

CHAPTER 5

Contracted Service Providers

PART 3

FINANCE, PLANNING, ACCOUNTABILITY AND REPORTING

PART 4

DESIGNATION OF CREDIT INSTITUTIONS AS PARTICIPATING INSTITUTIONS AND DESIGNATION OF ELIGIBLE BANK ASSETS

CHAPTER 1

Designation of Participating Institutions

CHAPTER 2

Designation of Eligible Bank Assets

PART 5

VALUATION METHODOLOGY

PART 7

REVIEW OF DECISIONS RELATING TO ACQUISITION

CHAPTER 1

Expert Reviewer

CHAPTER 2

Review of Valuations

PART 8

RELATIONSHIP BETWEEN NAMA AND PARTICIPATING INSTITUTIONS

PART 9

POWERS OF NAMA IN RELATION TO ASSETS

CHAPTER 1

Definitions

CHAPTER 2

General Powers of NAMA in Relation to Assets

CHAPTER 3

Statutory Receivers

CHAPTER 4

Vesting Orders

SCHEDULE 1

POWERS OF STATUTORY RECEIVERS

SCHEDULE 2

REDRESS FOR CONTRAVENTION OF *SECTION 223(3)*

SCHEDULE 3

AMENDMENTS OF OTHER ACTS

PART 1

AMENDMENT OF BUILDING SOCIETIES ACT 1989

PART 2

AMENDMENT OF CENTRAL BANK ACT 1942

PART 3

AMENDMENT OF COMPANIES ACT 1963

PART 4

AMENDMENTS OF COMPANIES (AMENDMENT) ACT 1990

PART 5

AMENDMENT OF FINANCE ACT 1970

PART 6

AMENDMENTS OF LANDLORD AND TENANT (AMENDMENT) ACT 1980

PART 7

AMENDMENTS OF NATIONAL TREASURY MANAGEMENT AGENCY ACT 1990

PART 8

AMENDMENT OF PLANNING AND DEVELOPMENT ACT 2000

PART 9

AMENDMENT OF STAMP DUTIES CONSOLIDATION ACT 1999

PART 10

AMENDMENTS OF TAXES CONSOLIDATION ACT 1997

PART 11

AMENDMENTS OF VALUE-ADDED TAX ACT 1972

An Act—

To address a serious threat to the economy and to the systemic stability of credit institutions in the State generally by providing, in particular, for the establishment of a body to be known as the National Asset Management Agency for the purposes of—

(*a*) the acquisition by that agency of certain assets from certain persons to be designated by the Minister for Finance,

(*b*) effecting the expeditious and efficient transfer of those assets to that agency,

(*c*) the holding, managing and realising of those assets by that agency (including the collection of interest and capital due, the taking or taking over of collateral where necessary and the provision of funds where appropriate),

(*d*) the taking by that agency of all steps necessary or expedient to protect, enhance and better realise the value of assets transferred to it,

(*e*) the performance by that agency of such other functions, related to the management or realisation of those assets, as provided in this act or as directed by the Minister, and

(*f*) the facilitation of restructuring of credit institutions of systemic importance to the economy, and

To provide for the valuation of the assets concerned and the review of any such valuation,

To give the National Asset Management Agency certain powers and other functions in respect of land or an interest in land acquired by that agency, including powers relating to the development of land,

To provide for the issuing of debt securities by the Minister for Finance and by that agency in the performance of its functions under this Act,

To provide for certain legal proceedings relating to assets acquired by that agency, to amend the Central Bank Act 1942, and to provide for related matters.

[*22nd November*, 2009]

Acts Referred to

Acquisition of Land (Assessment of Compensation) Act 1919	9 & 10 Geo. 5, c. 57
Agricultural Credit Act 1978	1978, No. 2
Bankers' Books Evidence Act 1879	42 & 43 Vict., c. 11
Bankruptcy Act 1988	1988, No. 27
Bills of Sale (Ireland) Acts 1879 and 1883	
Borrowing Powers of Certain Bodies Act 1996	1996, No. 22
Building Societies Act 1989	1989, No. 17
Capital Gains Tax Acts Central Bank Act 1942	1942, No. 22
Central Bank Act 1997	1997, No. 8
Central Bank Acts 1942 to 2001	
Central Bank and Financial Services Authority of Ireland Act 2003	2003, No. 12
Central Bank and Financial Services Authority of Ireland Act 2004	2004, No. 21
Civil Service Regulation Act 1956	1956, No. 46
Companies Act 1963	1963, No. 33
Companies Act 1990	1990, No. 33
Companies Acts Companies (Amendment) Act 1982	1982, No. 10
Companies (Amendment) Act 1983	1983, No. 13
Companies (Amendment) Act 1990	1990, No. 27
Competition Act 2002	2002, No. 14
Comptroller and Auditor General (Amendment) Act 1993	1993, No. 8
Conveyancing Act 1634	10 Chas. 1 sess. 2, c. 3
Conveyancing Act 1881	44 & 45 Vict., c. 41
Corporation Tax Acts Courts Act 1981	1981, No. 11
Credit Institutions (Financial Support) Act 2008	2008, No. 18
Data Protection Acts 1988 and 2003	
Ethics in Public Office Act 1995	1995, No. 22
European Communities Act 1972	1972, No. 27
European Parliament Elections Act 1997	1997, No. 2
Family Home Protection Act 1976	1976, No. 27
Finance Act 1970	1970, No. 14
Health Contributions Act 1979	1979, No. 4
Housing Act 1966	1966, No. 21
Income Tax Acts Industrial and Commercial Property (Protection) Act 1927	1927, No. 16
Interpretation Act 1937	1937, No. 38
Investment Funds, Companies and Miscellaneous Provisions Act 2005	2005, No. 12
Investment Funds, Companies and Miscellaneous Provisions Act 2006	2006, No. 41
Land and Conveyancing Law Reform Act 2009	2009, No. 27
Lands Clauses Acts Land Clauses Consolidation Act 1845	8 & 9 Vict., c. 18
Landlord and Tenant (Amendment) Act 1980	1980, No. 10
Local Government Act 2001	2001, No. 37
Markets in Financial Instruments and Miscellaneous Provisions Act 2007	2007, No. 37
National Treasury Management Agency Act 1990	1990, No. 18
Netting of Financial Contracts Act 1995	1995, No. 25
Official Languages Act 2003	2003, No. 32
Patents Act 1992	1992, No. 1
Planning and Development Act 2000	2000, No. 30
Planning and Development Acts 2000 to 2007	
Prevention of Corruption Act 1906	6 Edw. 7, c. 34
Prevention of Corruption Acts 1889 to 2001	
Public Bodies Corrupt Practices Act 1889	52 & 53 Vict., c. 69
Redundancy Payments Act 1967	1967, No. 21
Registration of Deeds and Title Act 2006	2006, No. 12
Registration of Deeds and Title Acts 1964 and 2006	
Registration of Title Act 1964	1964, No. 16
Safety, Health and Welfare at Work Act 2005	2005, No. 10

Social Welfare Consolidation Act 2005	2005, No. 26
Stamp Duties Consolidation Act 1999	1999, No. 31
Statutory Instruments Act 1947	1947, No. 44
Tax Acts Taxes Consolidation Act 1997	1997, No. 39
Trade Marks Act 1996	1996, No. 6
Unfair Dismissals Acts 1977 to 2005	
Value-Added Tax Act 1972	1972, No. 22

Associated Secondary Legislation

National Asset Management Agency Act 2009 (Commencement) Order 2009 (S.I. No. 545 of 2009)

National Asset Management Agency (Determination of Long-term Economic Value of Property and Bank Assets) Regulations 2009 (S.I. No. 546 of 2009)

National Asset Management Agency Act 2009 (Establishment Day) Order 2009 (S.I. No. 547 of 2009)

National Asset Management Agency (Designation of Eligible Bank Assets) Regulations 2009 (S.I. No. 568 of 2009)

National Asset Management Agency (Determination of Long-Term Economic Value of Property and Bank Assets) Regulations 2010 (S.I. No. 88 of 2010)

Guidelines Issued Under Section 210(1) of the National Asset Management Agency Act 2009 Regarding Lending Practices and Procedures and Relating to the Review of Decisions of Participating Institutions to Refuse Credit Facilities (S.I. No. 127 of 2010)

GENERAL NOTE

The creation of the National Asset Management Agency (NAMA) was announced by the Minister for Finance, Brian Lenihan TD in his budget speech to Dáil Éireann on April 7, 2009 (679 *Dáil Debates* Col.679). The National Asset Management Agency Bill 2009 was first published in draft form on July 31, 2009, and was initiated in the Dáil on September 8, 2009. The National Asset Management Agency Act 2009 received the signature of the President on November 22, 2009, and was commenced by December 21, 2009 by the National Asset Management Agency Act 2009 (Commencement) Order 2009 (S.I. No. 545 of 2009). On January 26, 2011, the National Asset Management Agency (Amendment) Bill 2011 was introduced into Dáil Éireann. The Bill purposes substantial amendments to the Act, including the insertion of Pt 6A to facilitate the acquisition of an additional tranche of bank assets by NAMA. The additional class of assets are credit facilities which entered the balance sheet of a Part 6A participating institution before December 31, 2008, and where the total amount outstanding on the relevant credit facility is less than €20,000,000. No order for second stage had been made by the time of the dissolution of Dáil Éireann on February 1, 2011. As at the time of writing, the Bill has not been restored to the order paper following the general election of February 2011.

Parts 1–3 of the Act establish the National Asset Management Agency (NAMA) as a statutory corporation operating in close co-operation with the National Treasury Management Agency. Parts 4–7 deal with the designation of participating institutions by the Minister and the acquisition by NAMA of eligible assets from those institutions. Payment for eligible assets is to be made in the form of senior and subordinated bonds issued by NAMA and the Minister for Finance under Pt 4 of the Act. The level of payment provided for each individual asset is to be determined by NAMA in accordance with the valuation methodology set out in Pt 5. These elements of the NAMA scheme received State aid approval from the European Commission in February 2010 (See Communication regarding State Aid N725/2009 Ireland of February 26, 2010, C(2010)1155 final).

Parts 8 and 9 of the Act provide NAMA with extensive powers to manage bank assets acquired under the scheme. Under Pt 8, NAMA may engage participating institutions to service acquired bank assets. Part 9 provides NAMA with extensive powers to enforce security interests and other rights associated with bank assets. These include a right to appoint a statutory receiver with powers set out in Appendix 2 to the Act and a right to compulsorily acquire ransom strips connected with bank assets.

Part 10 is concerned with litigation under the Act. Notable provisions in this part include restrictions on the scope of judicial review of decisions of NAMA and restrictions on certain appeals to the Supreme Court. Part 11 permits disclosure of certain information to NAMA by participating institutions and provides for the protection of confidential information in the hands of NAMA.

Part 12 of the Act provides powers for the Minister for Finance and the Central Bank to effect restructuring in participating financial institutions. These powers must now be read in light of the Credit Institutions (Stabilisation) Act 2010. Parts 13–15 deal with miscellaneous matters, including amendments to other enactments.

A number of aspects of the Act were considered by the High Court in *Dellway Investments v National Asset Management Agency* [2010] IEHC 364, where a property developer with extensive interests, both inside and outside Ireland, sought leave to bring judicial review proceedings of NAMA's decision to acquire loans made to him and a number of companies owned or controlled by him. Five issues were raised for determination in the High Court:

(a) whether NAMA had taken the decision to acquire the relevant assets before or after the NAMA Act came into effect ("the timing issue");

(b) whether NAMA had taken all the appropriate considerations into account when making its decision to acquire the loans ("the relevant considerations issue");

(c) whether plaintiff was entitled to be heard by NAMA when making the decision to acquire its loans ("the fair procedures issue");

(d) whether the NAMA Act amounted to an unconstitutional interference with the plaintiff's rights ("the constitutional issue"); and

(e) whether NAMA's decision to acquire non-impaired as well as impaired bank assets amounted to a breach of State aid rules ("the State aid issue").

The application for leave for judicial review was heard in a "telescoped hearing" before a divisional High Court (Kearns P., Kelly and Clark JJ.). Argument was heard both in relation to the application for leave as well as the substance of the judicial review itself in order to facilitate a speedy decision. The court refused leave for judicial review in respect of all the issues with the exception of the fair procedures issue.

In relation to the timing issue, the High Court noted that the decision to acquire the relevant loans had been taken by an interim team of officials on December 11 and 14, 2009. The court rejected arguments that a legal basis for that decision could be found in s.17 of the Interpretation Act 2005 or in a direction of the Minister for Finance under s.4 of the National Treasury Management Agency Act 1990. The court held that the decision of December 11 and 14, 2009 had been implicitly adopted by the Board of NAMA at its inaugural meeting on December 23, 2009 and by the agency's subsequent conduct.

In relation to relevant considerations issue, counsel for the applicant suggested that the decision to acquire the relevant loans had been taken without having due regard to six factors connected to the solvency of the underlying debtors, and the fact that no default in payment had been made on the relevant loans. The High Court noted that under s.84(1) of the Act, NAMA has a discretion as to which eligible loans it chooses acquire. Adopting the approach of the High Court of Australia in *Peko-Wallsend v Minister for Aboriginal Affairs* (1986) 162 CLR 24, the court held that NAMA is not required to have regard to the strength or otherwise of the underlying loans when exercising its discretion under s.84(1).

The fair procedures issue was the only issue for which the High Court granted leave for judicial review. The applicant had argued that the acquisition of the relevant loans impacted on four classes of constitutionally protected rights and that accordingly an entitlement to fair procedures arose. The classes of right identified were the equities of redemption in the properties used as security for the loans, the right to earn a livelihood, contractual and quasi-contractual rights in the applicant's relationships with their banks and reputational rights. The court found that these arguments raised a substantial issue justifying leave for judicial review; however, in no case had the applicant established the existence of an interference with his constitutionally protected rights, and accordingly the reliefs sought were refused.

Arguments on the State aid issue centred on whether the Commission's decision approving the NAMA scheme had the effect of limiting NAMA's power to acquire bank assets, such that only non-performing assets could be acquired. The court rejected this argument. The applicant then sought to rely on a letter sent by a Commission official to Senator Eugene Regan which was said to support the applicant's interpretation of the Commission's decision. The court held that the letter was not admissible and that even if it were to be admitted it did not appear to support the applicant's case.

Finally, the court considered the constitutional issue. The court reiterated its finding that the applicant had not identified any interference with its constitutionally protected rights. The court went on to consider whether the NAMA legislation could be said to be overbroad or disproportionate. In both cases, the court rejected the applicant's contentions and leave to seek judicial review was refused.

In a subsequent decision ([2010] IEHC 375), the High Court granted leave to appeal its decision on the fair procedures ground to the Supreme Court.

The appeal was heard by a seven judge Supreme Court (Murray C.J., Denham, Hardiman, Fennelly, Macken, Finnegan, McKechnie JJ.). The court gave judgment on two of the issues which arose before the High Court. The decision of the Supreme Court ([2011] IESC 4) was given on February 3, 2011. The first judgment, delivered by Murray C.J., the court reversed the High Court's decision on the timing issue. Murray C.J. noted that "it is axiomatic that NAMA could not make any decision before it came into existence … [i]t follows that the decision of the interim team … was, in law, at the time when it was made, a nullity and had no legal effect".

The judgment went on to note that the NAMA Act contains no equivalent to s.37 of the Companies Act 1963, which permits a private company to ratify pre-incorporation contracts entered into on its behalf. Notwithstanding this, it would have been open to the Board of NAMA to take a fresh decision either as a result of its own deliberations or by adopting the work done by the interim team. On an examination of the affidavit evidence, the court held that it was satisfied that no fresh decision had been taken.

A second judgment, which also attracted the unanimous support of the court was handed down by Fennelly J. This judgment deals with the State aid issue which the court felt was not affected by its decision in relation to the timing issue. In dismissing the appeal, Fennelly J. held that the Commission's decision could not have imposed a condition on the acquisitions of eligible assets by NAMA. This followed from the fact that the Commission made a decision "not to open the formal investigation procedure under Article 108(2)" of the Treaty on the Functioning of the European Union. The court noted that where the Commission decides not to invoke the formal investigation procedure it cannot impose any conditions on the implementation of a notified State aid. As such the applicant's appeal failed. At para.[49] of the judgment, Fennelly J. expressed his agreement with the High Court decision not to have regard of the letter to Senator Regan.

In an *ex tempore* judgment on February 9, 2011, the Supreme Court held that in light of its first judgment, the relevant considerations issues were moot. The court delivered its judgments on the constitutional issue and the fair procedures issues on April 12, 2011. It should be noted that the following summary has been written based on unapproved copies of the judgments delivered by various judges of the court.

An agreed judgment of the court on the constitutional issue was delivered by Murray C.J. The judgment focused exclusively on a single constitutional argument—that s.69 of the Act confers such a broad discretion on NAMA to acquire bank assets as to amount to an interference with constitutionally protected property rights. The court upheld the constitutionality of the section. Murray C.J. noted that the power to acquire eligible bank assets can only be exercised where necessary or desirable for achieving the purposes of the Act. In such circumstance, the court concluded that the Oireachtas was entitled, as a matter of policy, to define eligible bank assets in very board terms. Further consideration of this judgment can be found in the notes to s.69.

Six judgments were delivered on the fair procedures issue. The fair procedures issue can be broken into two questions: First, what is the threshold of interference with a person's rights above which the right to fair procedures will be triggered? Second, does the acquisition of bank assets by NAMA fall above or below the threshold? The High Court took the view that there must be "be a real risk that a party's rights will be interfered with in the event that there is an adverse decision" (at para.[7.14]) and went on to hold that the acquisition of loans by NAMA did not affect any constitutionally protected rights of the applicants.

All of the judgments in the Supreme Court rejected the High Court's approach to the first question, but the judgments delivered differ significantly in their treatment of the issue. Murray C.J. held that the right to fair procedures is a constitutional right which arises wherever a statutory power "materially affects rights vested in them or impose (sic) obligations". Section 84 "must be interpreted as meaning that NAMA must permit persons whose rights may be adversely affected or on whom liabilities are imposed, as a consequence of a decision to acquire an eligible asset to make representations before such a decision is made". Denham J. adopted a similar approach in treating the right to fair procedures as a general feature of decision-making by statutory bodies, citing the decision of McCarthy J. in *State (Irish Pharmaceutical Union) v Employment Appeals Tribunal* [1987] I.L.R.M. 36 at 40, as authority for the proposition that statutory bodies must create and carry out fair procedures where these are not provided in their governing legislation.

Hardiman J. adopted the most radical approach to the first question. His judgment suggests that the right to fair procedures arises whenever a person's interests are "affected" by the decision of a public body. The necessary effect does not, it seems, have to amount to an interference with an identified constitutional or indeed legal right of the applicant. Instead, according to Hardiman J. the right to fair procedures is itself constitutional in nature whenever "matters of serious significance to a citizen are in question".

Fennelly J. (with Finnegan J. concurring on this point), rejected the High Court's "real risk to a constitutionally protected right" standard. In the view of Fennelly J., the real risk formulation is unduly narrow and must be qualified so as to recognise a right to fair procedures wherever there are "material and practical effects on the exercise and enjoyment of [rights]". Moreover, he rejected the suggestion that the right to fair procedures is predicated on an interference with "a specific and identifiable legal right".

Macken J. expressed agreement with the decision of Hardiman J. and suggested that the following factors might, among others, be relevant when determining whether the right to fair procedures has been triggered: "(a) the nature of the decision; (b) the nature of the statutory scheme; (c) the importance of the decision to the person invoking the right—in this case—to be heard; and (d) the choice of procedure, if any, adopted by the decision-maker."

All of the judgments on the fair procedures issue conclude that a decision to acquire the loans of the McKillen companies would amount to a sufficiently serious interference with their rights and interests that NAMA would have to observe fair procedures in making such a decision. The key judgment in this respect is that of Finnegan J. whose opinion was cited with approval by all the other members of the court. He held that the acquisition of a bank asset by NAMA has a significant impact on the rights of the borrower. Having considered the provisions of Pt 10 relating to NAMA's exercise of the mortgagee's power of sale, NAMA's right to obtain a vesting order under ss.152 and 153 of the Act, and the restrictions on the enforcement of certain representations to borrowers under ss.101 and 139 of the Act, Finnegan J. concluded that NAMA is in a different, and more powerful, position when dealing with borrowers than would have been the case had the borrower been dealing with his or her own bank. The details of this judgment are considered further in the notes to the relevant sections.

Be it enacted by the Oireachtas as follows:

PART 1

PRELIMINARY

Short title, commencement and collective citation

1.—(1) This Act may be cited as the National Asset Management Agency Act 2009.

(2) This Act comes into operation on such day or days as the Minister may appoint by order or orders either generally or with reference to a particular purpose or provision and different days may be so appointed for different purposes

or different provisions.

(3) An order under *subsection (2)* may, in respect of the amendments of Acts set out in *Part 15* and *Schedule 3*, appoint different days for the amendment of different Acts or different provisions of them.

(4) The Central Bank Acts 1942 to [2010], the Central Bank and Financial Services Authority of Ireland Act 2003, the Central Bank and Financial Services Authority of Ireland Act 2004, this subsection, *section 232*, and *Part 2* of *Schedule 3* may be cited together as the Central Bank and Financial Services Authority of Ireland Acts 1942 to 2009.

NOTES AND COMMENTARY

Associated secondary legislation

The Act was signed into law by the President on November 22, 2009. The legislation was brought into force by the Minister for Finance on December 21, 2009 under the National Asset Management Agency Act 2009 (Commencement) Order 2009 (S.I. No. 545 of 2009).

Subsequent amendments

Section 15 of the Central Bank Reform Act 2010 changed the collective citation of the Central Bank Acts to read Central Bank Acts 1942 to 2010.

Purposes of this Act

2.—The purposes of this Act are—

(*a*) to address the serious threat to the economy and the stability of credit institutions in the State generally and the need for the maintenance and stabilisation of the financial system in the State, and

(*b*) to address the compelling need—

(i) to facilitate the availability of credit in the economy of the State,

(ii) to resolve the problems created by the financial crisis in an expeditious and efficient manner and achieve a recovery in the economy,

(iii) to protect the State's interest in respect of the guarantees issued by the State pursuant to the Credit Institutions (Financial Support) Act 2008 and to underpin the steps taken by the Government in that regard,

(iv) to protect the interests of taxpayers,

(v) to facilitate restructuring of credit institutions of systemic importance to the economy,

(vi) to remove uncertainty about the valuation and location of certain assets of credit institutions of systemic importance to the economy,

(vii) to restore confidence in the banking sector and to underpin the effect of Government support measures in relation to that sector, and

(viii) to contribute to the social and economic development of the State.

NOTES AND COMMENTARY

Section 2 should be read together with the Preamble, s.10 and s.11 of the Act, all of which seek to provide an account of the functions of NAMA. The inclusion of s.2 is an unusual feature of the NAMA legislation. The normal approach in Irish legislative drafting is to set out the purposes and context of legislation in the long title. The inclusion of the section may raise difficult issues of interpretation since the long title and s.2 differ, both in form and content, in their recitation of the purposes of NAMA. In *Re McGrath and Harte* [1941] I.R. 68 at 72, Gavan Duffy J. held that there was no need to set out the purpose of an act in the main body of an enactment when this was done in the long title. How the courts would deal with a conflict between the two appears not to be covered by authority.

Regulatory functions not affected

3.—Nothing in this Act—
   (*a*) prevents the performance by [the Governor or the Central Bank] of functions in relation to any credit institution or other person authorised or regulated in the State, or
   (*b*) affects any obligation arising under—
        (i) the treaties governing the European Communities, or
        (ii) the ESCB Statute.

NOTES AND COMMENTARY

Amendment History

Section 15(11) Sch.2, Pt 11, of the Central Bank Reform Act 2010 amends the reference to "the Governor, the Central Bank of the Regulatory Authority" to refer to "the Governor or the Central Bank".

Comments

For the functions of the Governor and the Central Bank see Central Bank Acts 1942–2010.

Interpretation

4.—(1) In this Act—
"acquire", in relation to a bank asset, shall be construed in accordance with *subsection (2)*;
"acquired bank asset" means a bank asset that NAMA or a NAMA group entity has acquired, and in which NAMA or a NAMA group entity retains an interest;
"acquired portfolio", in relation to a participating institution, means all the bank assets specified in a completion notice that have been acquired from the participating institution;
"acquisition schedule" has the meaning given by *sections 87* and *89*;
"acquisition value", in relation to a bank asset, means the value determined by NAMA in accordance with the valuation methodology;
"applicant credit institution" means a credit institution that is applying or has applied under *section 62* to be designated;
"appointed member", in relation to the Board, has the meaning given by *section 19*;
"associated debtor" has the meaning given by *section 70*;

"bank asset" includes—
    (*a*) a credit facility,
    (*b*) any security relating to a credit facility,
    (*c*) every other right arising directly or indirectly in connection with a credit facility,
    (*d*) every other asset owned by a participating institution, and
    (*e*) an interest in a bank asset referred to in any of *paragraphs (a)* to *(d)*;

"Board" means the Board of NAMA referred to in *section 19*;

"borrow" includes the raising of money in any manner (including, in particular, borrowing by the creation and issue of bonds, debentures and debt securities, whether subordinated or not);

"Central Bank" means the Central Bank […] of Ireland;

"Chairperson" means the appointed member nominated under *section 25*;

"charge" includes—
    (*a*) a mortgage, judgment mortgage, charge, lien, pledge, hypothecation or other security interest or encumbrance or collateral in or over any property,
    (*b*) an assignment by way of security, and
    (*c*) an undertaking or agreement by any person (including a solicitor) to give or create a security interest in property;

"Chief Executive Officer" means the Chief Executive Officer appointed under *section 37* or *40(3)*, and includes—
    (*a*) in relation to any function of NAMA that the Chief Executive Officer has authorised an officer of NAMA to perform, that officer, and
    (*b*) any officer of NAMA designated by the Board under *section 38(4)*;

"company" means—
    (*a*) a company within the meaning of the Companies Acts, or
    (*b*) a body established under the laws of a state other than the State and corresponding to a body referred to in *paragraph (a)*;

"completion notice" means a notice referred to in *section 97*;

"confidential information" has the meaning given by *section 202*;

"Court" means the High Court;

"credit facility" includes every kind of financial accommodation (including a loan facility, a line of credit, a hedging facility, a derivative facility, a bond, a letter of credit, a guarantee facility, an invoice discounting facility, a debt factoring facility, a deferred payment arrangement, a leasing facility, a guarantee, an indemnity and any other financial accommodation giving rise to a payment or repayment obligation) provided to a debtor or associated debtor, whether alone or together with another person or persons and whether as part of a syndicate or otherwise;

"credit facility documentation" in relation to a credit facility means the documents, contracts, instruments and agreements containing or evidencing the terms or conditions applicable to, or that otherwise govern or regulate, any aspect of the credit facility or any associated arrangement or transaction entered into in connection with it, including any document issued or entered into by any person that directly or indirectly creates or provides or is expressed to create or provide any security, guarantee or surety or other benefit or collateral in connection with the credit facility or the associated arrangement or transaction;

"credit institution" has the same meaning as it has in the Central Bank Act 1997;

"debtor" means a person who is or was indebted or obligated to a participating institution under or in connection with a credit facility;

"debt security" means a note, bill, bond or similar financial instrument;

"designated bank asset" means a bank asset specified in an acquisition schedule that has been served on a participating institution in accordance with *section 87* or *89*;

"development land" means land wherever situated (regardless of its zoning or its status under the Planning and Development Acts 2000 to 2007 or any other enactment or applicable law)—

    (*a*) in, on, over or under which works or structures were or are to be constructed, or

    (*b*) where it was intended to make a material change in the use of the land,

that was intended to be sold or otherwise exploited;

"eligible bank asset" has the meaning given by *section 69(4)*;

"ESCB Statute" has the meaning given by section 2 of the Central Bank Act 1942;

"establishment day" means the day appointed by the Minister under *section 8* to be the establishment day;

"European Communities" has the meaning given by section 1 of the European Communities Act 1972;

"financial year", in relation to NAMA, means—

    (*a*) the period commencing on the establishment day and ending on 31 December 2010, and

    (*b*) each subsequent period of 12 months ending on 31 December in any year;

"functions" includes powers and duties, and references to the performance of functions include, with respect to powers and duties, references to the exercise of the powers and the carrying out of the duties;

"Governor" has the same meaning as in the Central Bank Act 1942;

"guarantor" means a person who has entered into a guarantee or indemnity in connection with a bank asset;

"interest", in relation to a bank asset, means—

    (*a*) the whole or any part or fraction of the bank asset,

    (*b*) any other estate in, right or title to or interest in, the bank asset (whether legal or beneficial), or

    (*c*) any interest, other than a legal or beneficial interest;

"land" has the same meaning as in the Land and Conveyancing Law Reform Act 2009, but also includes any right or interest in or over land;

"legal proceedings" includes any form of binding dispute resolution, and in particular includes arbitration;

"local authority" has the same meaning as in the Local Government Act 2001;

"Minister" means the Minister for Finance;

"NAMA" means the National Asset Management Agency;

"NAMA group entity" means—

    (*a*) a subsidiary of NAMA (within the meaning given by section 155 of the Companies Act 1963), or

    (*b*) any other body corporate and any trust, partnership, arrangement for the sharing of profits and losses, joint venture, association, syndicate or other arrangement formed, registered, incorporated or established by NAMA for the purpose of performing any of its functions under this Act;

"non-performing", in relation to a bank asset, has the meaning given by *subsection (3)*;

"NTMA" means the National Treasury Management Agency;

"officer of NAMA" means—

    (*a*) the Chief Executive Officer of NAMA, and

    (*b*) any person assigned to NAMA in accordance with *section 42*;

"participating institution" means a credit institution that has been designated by the Minister under *section 67*, including any of its subsidiaries that is not excluded under that section;

"performing asset" means a bank asset that is not a non-performing asset;

"quarterly report" means the report to the Minister under *section 55*;

[…]

"security" includes—

    (*a*) a charge,

    (*b*) a guarantee, indemnity or surety,

    (*c*) a right of set-off,

    (*d*) a debenture,

    (*e*) a bill of exchange,

    (*f*) a promissory note,

    (*g*) collateral,

    (*h*) any other means of securing—

        (i) the payment of a debt, or

        (ii) the discharge or performance of an obligation or liability, and

    (*i*) any other agreement or arrangement having a similar effect;

"statutory receiver" means a receiver appointed by NAMA pursuant to *section 147*;

"subsidiary" means a subsidiary (within the meaning given by section 155 of the Companies Act 1963) or a subsidiary undertaking (within the meaning given by the European Communities (Companies: Group Accounts) Regulations 1992 (S.I. No. 201 of 1992));

"surety" means a person who has provided a security in connection with the repayment by a debtor of a credit facility or in connection with a guarantor's obligations under a guarantee or indemnity;

"tax clearance certificate" has the meaning given by whichever of section 1094 or 1095 of the Taxes Consolidation Act 1997 applies in the particular case;

"total portfolio acquisition value", in relation to an acquired portfolio of a participating institution, means the total of all the acquisition values for the acquired portfolio of the participating institution and any of its subsidiaries that are also participating institutions;

"the treaties governing the European Communities" has the meaning given by section 1 of the European Communities Act 1972;

"valuation methodology" means the valuation methodology set out in *Part 5*.

(2) A reference in this Act to acquisition, in relation to a bank asset, includes—

    (*a*) any form of legal or beneficial transfer, including a vesting by operation of law,

    (*b*) a succession by operation of law,

    (*c*) a synthetic transfer,

    (*d*) a risk transfer,

    (*e*) the imposition of a trust,

    (*f*) the creation of a trust interest,

    (*g*) a novation,

    (*h*) an assignment,

    (*i*) an assumption,

    (*j*) sub-participation,

    (*k*) sub-contracting, and

    (*l*) any other form of transfer, acquisition, assumption or vesting recognised by the law applicable to the bank asset.

(3) For the purposes of this Act, a bank asset is non-performing if—

    (*a*) it is in the course of being foreclosed or otherwise enforced,

    (*b*) principal or interest or both are in arrears,

    (*c*) interest is being or has been capitalised or otherwise deferred otherwise than in accordance with its terms,

    (*d*) payments are not being, or have not been, met,

    (*e*) its covenants are not being, or have not been, complied with, or

    (*f*) other obligations are not being or have not been complied with.

NOTES AND COMMENTARY

Amendment History

In subs.(1), in the definition of "Central Bank" the words "and Financial Services Authority" were deleted by s.15(11), Sch.2 Pt 11 of the Central Bank Reform Act 2010 (No.23 of 2010).

In subs.(1), the definition of "Regulatory Authority" was deleted by s.15(11), Sch.2 Pt 11 of the Central Bank Reform Act 2010 (No.23 of 2010).

Comments

Interpretation sections are a standard feature in all Irish legislation and s.4 is typical in this regard. It is worth noting that the section does not provide guidance on the meaning of the terms "principal" and "interest" used in the definition of a non-performing bank asset in subs.(3). These terms will therefore have their natural and ordinary meaning (*Inspector of Taxes v Kiernan* [1981] I.R. 117 at 121). Interest, in this context presumably means the interest charged on a loan or credit facility while principal refers to the capital sum owing on such facilities.

Regulations

5.—(1) The Minister may make regulations to do anything that appears necessary or expedient for bringing this Act into operation.

(2) Where a provision of this Act requires or authorises the Minister to make

regulations, such regulations—

> (*a*) may make different provision for different circumstances or cases, classes or types, and
>
> (*b*) may contain such incidental, consequential or transitional provisions as the Minister considers necessary or expedient for the purposes of this Act.

NOTES AND COMMENTARY

The inclusion of a power to make regulations is a regular feature of Irish primary legislation. A similar example is to be found in s.37 of the Anglo Irish Bank Corporation Act 2009 which was drafted shortly before the NAMA legislation. It should be noted that there is no requirement for the Minister to engage in consultation or to lay drafts of the proposed regulations before the Houses of the Oireachtas before exercising his powers under s.5.

Section 5 confers a reserve power to make regulations, several other provisions confer specific power on the Minister to issue regulations to deal with specific matters arising under the legislation (see for example s.1(2), s.8, s.11 etc.). The power is only exercisable within the constitutional limits on delegated legislative powers set out by the Supreme Court in *Cityview Press Ltd v An Chomhairle Oiliúna* [1980] I.R. 381 and subsequent case law.

Expenses of Minister and NTMA

6.—(1) The expenses incurred by the Minister in the administration of this Act shall be paid out of money provided by the Oireachtas.

(2) The expenses incurred by the NTMA under this Act shall be paid out of the Central Fund and the growing produce of that Fund.

(3) The expenses incurred by the NTMA in relation to NAMA since 7 April 2009 shall be paid out of the Central Fund and the growing produce of that Fund.

NOTES AND COMMENTARY

April 7, 2009 was the date on which the Minister announced the proposal to establish NAMA under the auspices of the NTMA in a statement to the Dáil (679 *Dáil Debates* Col. 679).

Notwithstanding, subs.(1), Pt V of Sch.III amends the Finance Act 1970 to provide that the Minister's expenses arising from ordinary banking transactions associated with his functions under the Act are to be charged to the Central Fund. Byrne and McEntagart suggest that there is a discrepancy between subs.(1) and the amendments in Sch.III; however the wording of the amendment to the Finance Act makes clear that the Minister is only entitled to charge expenses relating to ordinary banking transactions to the Central Fund. (See H.B. Byrne and L. McEntagart, *The National Asset Management Agency Act 2009: Annotations and Commentary* (Dublin: Bloomsbury Professional, 2010), p.25). The policy significance of the distinction is not clear.

Subsection (3) is designed to provide retrospective authority for the NTMA to recoup its costs prior to the establishment of NAMA.

Offences

7.—(1) A person on whom an obligation is imposed by or under *section 202(2)* and who intentionally does not comply with the obligation commits an offence.

(2) A person who intentionally, recklessly or through gross negligence provides false or inaccurate information to NAMA commits an offence.

(3) A person commits an offence if the person—

    (*a*) intentionally withholds information from NAMA in breach of an obligation to provide that information imposed by or under this Act, and

    (*b*) does so with the intention of having a material impact upon—

        (i) the manner in which NAMA deals with a bank asset,

        (ii) a decision by NAMA to refrain from dealing with a bank asset, or

        (iii) the value that NAMA determines for a bank asset.

(4) A person who intentionally withholds information from NAMA in breach of an obligation to provide that information imposed under this Act commits an offence if the withholding of the information has a material impact upon—

    (*a*) the manner in which NAMA deals with a bank asset,

    (*b*) a decision by NAMA to refrain from dealing with a bank asset, or

    (*c*) the value which NAMA determines for a bank asset.

(5) A credit institution that commits an offence under this section is liable—

    (*a*) on summary conviction, to a fine not exceeding €5,000, or

    (*b*) on conviction on indictment, to a fine not exceeding €20,000,000.

(6) A person other than a credit institution who commits an offence under this section is liable—

    (*a*) on summary conviction, to a fine not exceeding €5,000 or imprisonment for a term not exceeding 12 months or both, or

    (*b*) on conviction on indictment, to a fine not exceeding €5,000,000 or imprisonment for a term not exceeding 5 years or both.

(7) Where an offence under this section—

    (*a*) has been committed by a body corporate, and

    (*b*) is proved to have been committed with the consent or connivance of, or to be attributable to any wilful neglect on the part of, a person—

        (i) who is a director, manager, secretary or other officer of the body corporate, or

        (ii) purported to act in any such capacity,

that person as well as the body corporate shall be taken to have committed an offence and is liable to be proceeded against and punished as if he or she were guilty of the first-mentioned offence.

(8) Where the affairs of a body corporate are managed by its members, *subsection (7)* applies in relation to the acts and defaults of a member in connection with his or her functions of management as if he or she were a director or manager of the body corporate.

NOTES AND COMMENTARY

This section creates four offences and sets out associated penalties both for individual and corporate offenders. The first offence concerns the disclosure of confidential information which is governed by s.202 of the Act. Section 202 requires a person not to disclose, or use for the direct or indirect advantage of themselves or another, information obtained while acting as a member of the board of NAMA, providing services to NAMA, acting as an officer of NAMA or the NTMA or in the course of dealing with NAMA under s.199(2).

Confidential information is defined very broadly in s.202. Section 202(4) provides a rebuttable that a person is aware that information is confidential if that person ought to have known that it was confidential information. Section 202(5) provides exceptions where confidential information is disclosed to NAMA, a NAMA group entity, the NTMA, the Minister or their agents. There is an additional exception for witnesses giving evidence before the courts or before an Oireachtas committee. Section 202(6) provides for certain categories of protected disclosure to law enforcement agencies. In order to come within the subs.(6) exception, the person must act in good faith. In addition, the information must be such as gives rise to a suspicion that a participating institution, an employee or agent thereof or a debtor in respect of a bank asset has committed a criminal offence or has contravened company, tax, financial services or competition law.

The second offence is one of intentionally, recklessly or grossly negligently providing inaccurate information to NAMA. The offence is committed regardless of whether the person giving the information to NAMA was under a duty to do so and regardless of the impact which the information has on NAMA or its operations. In *People (Attorney General) v Dunleavy* [1948] 1 I.R. 95, the Supreme Court held that the proper test for gross negligence in the context of a manslaughter charge was that the defendant acted with reckless disregard to human life. It suggested that in the NAMA context a person who gave information in the knowledge that it was probably inaccurate or who chose to disregard a very substantial likelihood of inaccuracy would be caught by the offence in subs.(2).

The third and fourth offences are closely related. Under subs.(3), a person who, being obliged to give information to NAMA, intentionally withholds it with the further intention of materially impacting on specified NAMA operations commits an offence. Subsection (4) is also concerned with intentionally withholding information which the accused is obliged to hand over to NAMA. In a prosecution under subs.(4) however, there is no need for the prosecutor to prove that the information was withheld with an intent on the part of the accused to materially impact on NAMA's operations.

Subsections (5) and (6) set out the penalties which may be imposed on conviction. Prosecution of a credit institution would require that the relevant corporation be attributed the appropriate mens rea. For a general review of corporate criminal liability see The Law Reform Commission, *Report: Corporate Killing* (LRC 77-2005) pp.27–40).

Under s.18 of the Interpretation Act 2005, the definition of person is not confined to individuals but extends to corporations sole and aggregate as well as to unincorporated associations. Subsections (7) and (8) provide that where a body corporate commits an offence under s.7 and that offence is proved to have been committed with the consent or connivance of, or is attributable to wilful neglect by any person who is a director, manager, secretary or other officer of the body corporate then that person shall be taken to have committed an offence.

PART 2

NATIONAL ASSET MANAGEMENT AGENCY

CHAPTER 1

Establishment, Functions and Powers

Establishment day

8.—The Minister shall by order appoint a day as the establishment day for the purposes of this Act.

NOTES AND COMMENTARY

Associated secondary legislation

The National Asset Management Agency Act 2009 (Establishment Day) Order 2009 (S.I. No. 547 of 2009) appoints December 21, 2009 as the establishment day for NAMA. This is the same date on which the legislation was commenced under the National Asset Management

Agency Act 2009 (Commencement) Order 2009 (S.I. No. 545 of 2009).

Establishment of NAMA

9.—(1) There is established, on the establishment day, a body to be known as the National Asset Management Agency (in this Act referred to as "NAMA"), to perform the functions assigned to it by this Act.

(2) NAMA shall be a body corporate with perpetual succession. NAMA has power to sue and be sued in its corporate name and to acquire, hold and dispose of land or an interest in land, and to acquire, hold and dispose of any other property.

(3) Except where otherwise provided by this Act, NAMA is independent in the performance of its functions under this Act.

NOTES AND COMMENTARY

Sections 9(1) and (2) establish NAMA as a statutory corporation which has a separate legal personality to that of the State, the NTMA and the Minister for Finance. Virtually identical provisions are to be found in the enactments establishing many public bodies. See, for example, s.150 of the Residential Tenancies Act 2004 (establishment of the Private Rental Tenancies Board); ss.6(1)–(2) of the Inland Fisheries Act 2010 (establishment of Inland Fisheries Ireland); and s.13 and Sch.1 of the Charities Act 2009 (establishment of the Charities Regulatory Authority).

Section 9(3) provides NAMA with independence in the performance of its functions save where the Act otherwise provides. This provision is also regularly found in the enactments establishing public bodies, see s.2 of the Prosecution of Offences Act 1974 (independence of the Director of Public Prosecutions); s.24 of the Broadcasting Act 2009 (independence of the Board of the Broadcasting Authority of Ireland); s.7 of the Consumer Protection Act 2007 (independence of the National Consumer Agency).

Purposes of NAMA

10.—(1) NAMA's purposes shall be to contribute to the achievement of the purposes specified in *section 2* by—
  (*a*) the acquisition from participating institutions of such eligible bank assets as is appropriate,
  (*b*) dealing expeditiously with the assets acquired by it, and
  (*c*) protecting or otherwise enhancing the value of those assets, in the interests of the State.

(2) So far as possible, NAMA shall, expeditiously and consistently with the achievement of the purposes specified in *subsection (1)*, obtain the best achievable financial return for the State having regard to—
  (*a*) the cost to the Exchequer of acquiring bank assets and dealing with acquired bank assets,
  (*b*) NAMA's cost of capital and other costs, and
  (*c*) any other factor which NAMA considers relevant to the achievement of its purposes.

NOTES AND COMMENTARY

This section operates in conjunction with s.2 and ss.11–12 of the Act. Taken together these sections delineate the boundaries of NAMA's powers and functions. Section 10(1) provides NAMA with authority to undertake the acquisition and management of eligible bank assets.

This authority is limited in two respects. First by reference to the objectives set out in s.2. It would seem that acquisition of an asset for any other purpose would be ultra vires NAMA.

The second limitation is confined to NAMA's role in managing bank assets once they are acquired. Here subs.(2)(c) makes clear that the agency must endeavour to maximise the value of those assets. The language originally used in subs.(2)(c) in the consultation version of the Bill was altered to omit reference to long-term economic value, leaving the concept of value undefined in this section of the Act. Somewhat surprisingly, the Explanatory Memorandum accompanying the Bill when it was introduced in the Dáil did not reflect this change. It seems logical, however, that the reference to value in s.10(2)(c) is a reference to long term economic value as defined in s.72(2)(c). While the validity of considering the text of an explanatory memorandum as an aid to statutory interpretation is unclear in the aftermath of the Supreme Court's decision in *Crilly v T & J Farrington Ltd* [2001] 3 I.R. 251, explanatory memoranda are still referred to by the courts as an aid to the interpretation of statutes, for instance in *VU v Refugee Applications Commissioner* [2005] 2 I.R. 537.

Section 10(2) requires NAMA to "obtain the best achievable financial return for the State" in the performance of its functions. This language reflects the concerns expressed in the Parliamentary and public debate on the Act. While the wording clearly commits NAMA to the protection of taxpayers' interests, it should be noted that the section does not tie the Agency to any particular course of conduct, nor is it prescriptive in setting out matters which the Agency must consider in performing its functions.

Dr Martin Manseragh TD suggested that s.10 had the effect of ensuring that the principal aim of NAMA was to obtain the best possible financial result for the taxpayer. (See 198 *Seanad Debates* Col. 82 (Committee Stage)).

Functions of NAMA

11.—(1) In order to achieve its purposes, NAMA shall perform the following functions:

  (*a*) acquire, in accordance with *Part 6*, such eligible bank assets from participating institutions as it considers necessary or desirable for achieving its purposes;

  (*b*) hold, manage and realise acquired bank assets (including the collection of interest, principal and capital due, the taking or taking over of collateral where necessary and the provision of funds where appropriate);

  (*c*) perform such other functions, related to the management or realisation of acquired bank assets, as the Minister directs pursuant to *section 14*;

  (*d*) take all steps necessary or expedient to protect, enhance or realise the value of acquired bank assets, including—

    (i) the disposal of loans or portfolios of loans in the market for the best achievable price,

    (ii) the securitisation or refinancing of portfolios of loans, and

    (iii) holding, refinancing, realising and disposing of any relevant security.

(2) In the exercise of its functions NAMA shall have regard to the need to avoid undue concentrations or distortions in the market for development land.

(3) The Minister may confer on NAMA, by order, such additional functions connected with the functions for the time being of NAMA as he or she thinks necessary for the achievement of its purposes, subject to such conditions (if any) as may be specified in the order.

(4) An order under this section may contain such incidental, supplemental

and consequential provisions as are, in the opinion of the Minister, necessary to give full effect to the order.

(5) An order under *subsection (3)* shall be laid before each House of the Oireachtas as soon as may be after it is made and, if a resolution annulling the order is passed by either such House within the next 21 days on which that House has sat after the order is laid before it, the order shall be annulled accordingly, but without prejudice to the validity of anything previously done thereunder.

(6) NAMA shall act in a transparent manner in carrying out its functions under this Act to the extent that to do so is consistent with the proper and efficient and effective discharge of those functions.

NOTES AND COMMENTARY

Associated secondary legislation

Under the National Asset Management Agency (Conferral of Additional Function) Order 2010 (S.I. No. 505 of 2010) NAMA acquired an additional function of:

> "the additional function of taking, in accordance with Part 6…all necessary steps to acquire, as expeditiously as possible, such eligible bank assets from such participating institutions as it considers necessary or desirable for achieving the purposes of the Act, subject to such amended or varied terms and conditions as it thinks fit."

Notes

Subsection (1) confers power on NAMA to achieve its purposes by carrying on a wide range of banking and financial functions. It is worth noting that the Act does not define the terms "principal" and "interest" or "collateral" used in the definition of a non-performing bank asset in subs.4(3). These terms will therefore have their natural and ordinary meaning (*Inspector of Taxes v Kiernan* [1981] I.R. 117 at 121). Interest in this context presumably means the interest charged on a loan or credit facility while principal seems to refer to the capital sum owing on such facilities. The term collateral is more difficult. The *Oxford English Dictionary*, 2nd edn (Oxford: OUP, 1989) provides a number of definitions for the word "collateral" including a number of entries grouped under the heading "law". The most apposite of these definitions refers to collateral as "any property or right of action given as additional to the obligation of a contract or the like".

The natural and ordinary meaning of the term therefore seems to refer to property given as security for a debt. There may however be an ambiguity in the meaning of the term collateral. The reason for this is that Irish law adopts a formalist approach to the definition of security and distinguishes between formal real security interests created by grant (e.g. a chattel mortgage) and arrangements which create functional equivalents to security interests, such as reservation of title clauses. On a narrow reading of the term, only property over which a real security interest has been created by grant would come within the meaning of the term collateral.

Where a term is ambiguous, s.5 of the Interpretation Act 2005 requires the court to give "a construction that reflects the plain intention of the Oireachtas…where that intention can be ascertained from the Act as a whole." Given the broad powers, functions and objectives conferred on NAMA by the legislature and the wide functionalist definition of security in s.4(1), it is submitted that a court would be justified in giving a broad meaning to the term collateral.

Subsection (2) requires NAMA to have regard to the need to avoid excessive concentrations in the market for development land. No guidance is given on how NAMA is to identify a concentration in the market or how it is to judge when such a concentration becomes excessive. In the Seanad, Dr Martin Manseragh TD stated that the subsection had been included "because it is important that the property market develops on a sustainable basis" (198 *Seanad Debates* Col. 82 (Committee Stage)) Similar remarks were made by the Minister for Finance during the Committee Stage debates in the Dáil.

Subsections (3)–(5) provide the Minister with a power to make regulations which extend the functions of NAMA. It should be noted that the Minister's powers are limited by reference to the purposes of NAMA set out in s.10. The Minister must lay a copy of proposed regulations before the Houses of the Oireachtas which may annul them by a negative resolution. Similar resolution procedures are to be found elsewhere in the statute book, e.g. s.469 of the Taxes Consolidation Act 1997 (as inserted by s.6 of the Finance Act 2010); s.25 of the Criminal Justice (Psychoactive Substances) Act 2010. The annulment procedure leads to the potentially anomalous consequence of a legally valid action being taken by NAMA under regulations which are later declared to be annulled by a vote of either House of the Oireachtas. The constitutionality of the provision is doubted by Byrne and McEntagart (See H.B. Byrne and L. McEntagart, *The National Asset Management Agency Act 2009: Annotations and Commentary* (Dublin: Bloomsbury Professional, 2010), p.36) and by J. Casey, *Constitutional Law in Ireland* 3rd edn (Dublin: Round Hall, 2000), pp.226–227. The validity of such provisions has never been tested before the courts.

Subsection (6) imposes an obligation on NAMA to act in a transparent manner to the extent to which this is consistent with its functions. No guidance is given as to the meaning of transparency or as to how it is to be achieved.

Powers of NAMA

12.—(1) NAMA has all powers necessary or expedient for, or incidental to, the achievement of its purposes and performance of its functions.

(2) Without prejudice to the generality of *subsection (1)*, NAMA may—

    (*a*) provide equity capital and credit facilities on such terms and conditions as NAMA thinks fit,

    (*b*) borrow on any terms and conditions that NAMA thinks fit,

    (*c*) secure the payment of money in any manner, including on the assets of NAMA or on any particular property and rights, present or future, of NAMA,

    (*d*) initiate or participate in any enforcement, restructuring, reorganisation, scheme of arrangement or other compromise,

    (*e*) enter into contract options and other derivative financial instruments (including instruments expressed in currencies other than the currency of the State), whose purposes include—

        (i) eliminating or reducing the risk of loss arising from changes in interest rates, currency exchange rates or other factors of a similar nature, or

        (ii) eliminating or reducing the costs of raising funds or borrowing or the cost of other transactions carried out in the ordinary course of business,

    (*f*) guarantee, with or without security, the indebtedness and performance of obligations of others (whether or not NAMA receives any consideration for, or direct or indirect advantage from, the giving of the guarantee),

    (*g*) draw, accept and negotiate negotiable instruments,

    (*h*) distribute assets *in specie* to the Minister,

    (*i*) accept any security, guarantee, indemnity or surety,

    (*j*) enter into contracts of insurance, and insure and selfinsure, in relation to any of its activities and property,

    (*k*) enforce any security, guarantee or indemnity,

    (*l*) compromise any claim,

    (*m*) open and maintain bank accounts, including accounts in currencies other than the currency of the State, and carry out necessary banking transactions,

(*n*) form a NAMA group entity for the purpose of performing any of its functions,

(*o*) give security for any debt, obligation or liability of a NAMA group entity,

(*p*) enter into a partnership or joint venture for the purpose of performing any of its functions,

(*q*) establish a trust or participate in a trust as trustee or beneficiary,

(*r*) borrow, lend or transfer debt securities, including, (but not limited to) equity and debt instruments,

(*s*) acquire and dispose of property,

(*t*) purchase, by agreement, bank assets that are not eligible bank assets where in NAMA's opinion it is necessary to do so in the interests of the proper performance of its functions,

(*u*) invest its funds as the Board determines,

(*v*) vest property in any other person on behalf of, or for the benefit of, NAMA with or without declaring a trust in NAMA's favour,

(*w*) sell or dispose of the whole or any part of the property or investments of NAMA, either together or in portions, for such consideration and on such terms as the Board thinks fit,

(*x*) discharge any debt, obligation or liability,

(*y*) purchase, hold and sell any licence,

(*z*) make any planning application in relation to land, and intervene in any planning application made by another person,

(*aa*)make any application to develop minerals on land,

(*ab*)undertake development for the purpose of realising the full value of any asset,

(*ac*)carry on any business that NAMA considers can be conveniently carried on in connection with any of its functions or is calculated directly or indirectly to enhance the value of or facilitate the realisation of or render profitable any of NAMA's property or rights,

(*ad*)benefit from any carbon credits acquired by it, and

(*ae*)do all such other things as the Board considers incidental to, or conducive to the achievement of, any of NAMA's purposes under this Act.

(3) A reference in another provision of this Act to a power or the exercise of a power conferred by this section does not limit by implication the operation of this section unless the contrary intention is expressed.

(4) NAMA may exercise any of its powers or carry out any of its functions—

(*a*) within, or anywhere outside, the State,

(*b*) alone or in conjunction with others, and

(*c*) by or through an agent, NAMA group entity, contractor, factor, or trustee.

(5) NAMA may use its seal outside the State.

(6) NAMA may exercise any of its powers for the benefit of a NAMA group entity.

(7) Nothing in this Act authorises NAMA, when exercising any of its powers or carrying out any of its functions in any place, to act otherwise than in compliance with the law of that place.

(8) In exercise of its powers under *paragraphs (s), (z), (ab)* and *(ac)* of *subsection (2)*, NAMA shall have regard to proper planning and sustainable development as expressed in Government policy and in any relevant regional planning guidelines (within the meaning of the Planning and Development Act 2000) and development plans (within the meaning of that Act).

NOTES AND COMMENTARY

Subsections (1) and (2) set out the express powers of NAMA. Subsection (1) confers a general power on NAMA to do any act necessary for the achievement of its purposes and the performance of its functions. As a result the powers listed in subs.(2) are merely illustrative examples of NAMA's powers. In terms of determining NAMA's legal capacity, the important sections of the Act will be s.10 which sets out the purposes of NAMA and s.11 which sets out its functions. The various powers listed in subs.(2) (including (ae) which appears to be a legislative version of a "*Bell Houses* clause" (see T. Courtney, *Law of Private Companies* 2nd edn (Bloomsbury Professional, 2002), p.346) give a clear indication of legislative intent to confer a wide range of powers on NAMA. This point is further underlined by subs.(3) which states that other provisions of the Act are not to be interpreted as limiting the powers of NAMA by implication. Any reservations on the capacity of NAMA must be expressly provided for in the legislation. It would seem from the text of the Act that NAMA may only exercise its powers for the purposes and objectives set out in ss.10 and 11. Presumably this limitation would endure where NAMA exercised its powers for the benefit of a NAMA group entity.

Subsections (4) and (5) have the effect of authorising NAMA to Act extra-territorially in the exercise of its powers. Subsection (7) limits NAMA's capacity to Act outside the state by requiring it to act in compliance with the law of any place in which it is operating.

Subsection (8) contains the only substantial limit on the powers of NAMA contained in this section. It requires that NAMA have regard to Government policy and certain planning guidelines when exercising its powers to acquire land, apply for planning permission or engage in property development. It should be noted that NAMA is not required to comply with government policy or regional planning guidelines, merely that these should be considered in its decision making processes. The scope of "Government policy" is not entirely clear. Presumably it would embrace documents such as the National Development Plan 2007–2013 and the National Spatial Strategy.

Minister's powers to issue guidelines to NAMA

13.—(1) The Minister may issue guidelines in writing to NAMA for the purposes of this Act and, in so far as any such guidelines relate to issues within the Governor's remit, the Minister shall consult with the Governor before doing so.

(2) In particular, and without prejudice to the generality of *subsection (1)*, the Minister may issue guidelines in relation to the purposes mentioned in *subparagraph (viii)* of *section 2(b)*.

(3) In performing its functions under this Act, NAMA shall have regard to any guidelines issued by the Minister under this section.

(4) As soon as practicable after issuing guidelines, the Minister—

    (*a*) shall cause the guidelines to be published in *Iris Oifigiúil*, and

    (*b*) shall lay a copy of the guidelines before each House of the Oireachtas.

This section, taken together with s.14, enables the Minister for Finance to exercise an influence over the activities of NAMA. These sections would appear to be derogations from the principle established in s.9(3) that NAMA is independent in the performance of its functions. Under s.13 the Minister is permitted to issue guidelines to NAMA. Compliance with these guidelines is not required though NAMA must take them into account when performing its functions and under s.55(5)(a), NAMA must give a report to the Minister on its compliance with the guidelines on a quarterly basis.

Subsection (1) requires the Minister to consult the Governor of the Central Bank in advance of making any guidelines under this section. There is no statutory definition of the term "remit". The responsibilities of the Governor are set out in s.19A of the Central Bank Act 1942. The remit of the Governor would presumably embrace the Governor's role within the European System of Central Banks under the ESCB Statute and the Treaty of Rome.

Under subs.(4) the Minister is required to publish guidelines in *Iris Oifigiúil* and to lay copies of the guidelines before the Oireachtas. The Oireachtas has no role in approving the guidelines.

Minister's powers of direction

14.—(1) The Minister may give a direction in writing to NAMA concerning the achievement of the purposes of this Act.

(2) In particular, and without prejudice to the generality of *subsection (1)*, the Minister may give directions in relation to the purposes mentioned in *subparagraph (viii)* of *section 2(b)*.

(3) NAMA shall comply with a direction given by the Minister under this section.

(4) As soon as practicable after giving a direction to NAMA, the Minister—

    (*a*) shall cause the direction to be published in *Iris Oifigiúil*, and

    (*b*) shall lay a copy of the direction before each House of the Oireachtas.

This section, taken together with s.13, enables the Minister for Finance to exercise an influence over the activities of NAMA. These sections would appear to be derogations from the principle established in s.9(3) that NAMA is independent in the performance of its functions. Under s.14 the Minister is permitted to issue directions to NAMA. Unlike Section 13 guidelines, compliance with a direction is mandatory. Under s.55(5)(b), NAMA must give a report to the Minister on its compliance with the guidelines on a quarterly basis.

There is a surprising lacuna in the drafting of subs.(1) in that the Minister is under no obligation to consult the Governor the Central Bank prior to making a direction in an area which impacts on the Governor's area of operation. Such a requirement to consult is found in s.13(1) in relation to guidelines. Given that s.14 provides the Minister with a stronger power to interfere with the operation of NAMA, it is difficult to understand why the Minister would have to consult on a guideline but not on a direction to NAMA.

Under subs.(3) NAMA is required to comply with a direction from the Minister; however the Minister is not provided with any specific enforcement mechanism.

At least two directions have been made under this section. Appendix B to the NAMA Quarterly Report of June 30, 2010 (see s.55) contains a copy of a Section 13 direction from the Minister for Finance dated May 14, 2010. On October 22, 2010, the Minister for Finance directed NAMA to complete the acquisitions of eligible assets from participating institutions as expeditiously as possible.

Under subs.(4) the Minister is required to publish guidelines in *Iris Oifigiúil* and to lay copies of directions before the Oireachtas. It should be noted that Oireachtas has no role in approving the directions.

No shadow or *de facto* directorship

15.—(1) When discharging a function under this Act, none of the persons mentioned in *subsection (2)* shall be taken, only because of discharging that function, to be a shadow director (within the meaning given by section 27(1) of the Companies Act 1990) nor a *de facto* director nor a person discharging managerial responsibilities of—

  (*a*) any participating institution,

  (*b*) any person that is a debtor, guarantor or surety in relation to an acquired bank asset, or

  (*c*) a person that is an associated debtor of a debtor referred to in *paragraph (b)*.

(2) The persons are—

  (*a*) the Minister,

  (*b*) NAMA,

  (*c*) any appointed member of the Board,

  (*d*) the Chief Executive Officer of NAMA,

  (*e*) an officer of NAMA,

  (*f*) the NTMA,

  (*g*) any employee of the NTMA,

  (*h*) the Chief Executive of the NTMA,

  (*i*) the Governor,

  (*j*) a [member of the Commission] of the Central Bank,

  (*k*) an employee of the Central Bank,

  (*l*) [...]

  (*m*) a NAMA group entity,

  (*n*) a director of a NAMA group entity, and

  (*o*) an officer of, a consultant or adviser to, or a person employed by or under or acting on behalf of, any person, body or authority mentioned in *paragraphs (a)* to *(n)*.

(3) For the purposes of this section, a *de facto* director is a person who is determined to have been a director of a company although not formally or validly appointed to the position.

NOTES AND COMMENTARY

Amendment History

  In subs.(2), (j) the reference to "director" was substituted for "member of the Commission" by s.15(11), Sch.2 Pt 11 of the Central Bank Reform Act 2010 (No.23 of 2010).

  In subs.(2), (l) the reference to "a member of the Regulatory Authority" was deleted by s.15(11), Sch.2 Pt 11 of the Central Bank Reform Act 2010 (No.23 of 2010).

Comments

  Section 2(1) of the Companies Act 1963 defines a director as including "any person occupying the position of director by whatever name called". In *Re Lynrowan Enterprises Ltd,* unreported, High Court, O'Neill J., July 31, 2002, the High Court held that the test of whether a person is a de facto director depends on whether a person is engaged in directing the affairs of the company either alone or in company with others holding a formal appointment as director. Section 27 of the Companies Act 1990 establishes the concept of a shadow director. A shadow director is a person "in accordance with whose instructions the directors are accustomed to act…unless the directors are accustomed so to act by reason only that they do so on advice given [by the person] in a professional capacity." As a matter of company law, both de facto and shadow directors can be treated as directors for various purposes including the imposition of personal liability for the debts of the company in various circumstances (for further details see T. Courtney, *Law of Private Companies*, 2nd edn (Bloomsbury Professional, 2002), Chs 8 and 10).

The NAMA Act provides NAMA with extensive powers to interfere with the affairs of participating institutions. Section 15 is designed to protect various persons associated with NAMA and the NTMA from the risk of being held liable as a director of a participating institution by reason of their involvement in NAMA.

Prevention of corruption

16.—(1) To avoid doubt, the provisions of the Prevention of Corruption Acts 1889 to 2001 apply to—
   (*a*) every officer of NAMA,
   (*b*) the Chief Executive Officer,
   (*c*) the other members of the Board, and
   (*d*) every director of a NAMA group entity.

(2) Where in any proceedings against a person who performs functions for or on or behalf of NAMA, or who performs functions connected to the valuation of eligible bank assets, for an offence under the Public Bodies Corrupt Practices Act 1889 or the Prevention of Corruption Act 1906 it is shown that—
   (*a*) any gift, consideration or advantage has been given to or received by the person, and
   (*b*) the person who gave the gift, consideration or advantage or on whose behalf the gift, consideration or advantage was given was—
        (i) a person who is a debtor in relation to an eligible bank asset, or
       (ii) an associated debtor of such a person,
the gift or consideration or advantage shall be taken, unless the contrary is proved, to have been given and received corruptly as an inducement to or reward for the person performing or omitting to perform any of those functions.

<small>NOTES AND COMMENTARY</small>

Section 1 of the Prevention of Corruption Act 1906, as amended, applies the prevention of corruption legislation to various public officials and "any other person employed by or acting on behalf of the public administration of the State". The Acts also apply to various officials of foreign governments. Subsection 16(1) specifically applies the prevention of corruption legislation to the various categories set out therein. Interestingly the legislation omits reference to persons engaged by NAMA as service providers under s.45. It is unclear whether such persons would fall within s.1 of the 1906 Act.

Subsection (2) seems to envisage proceedings under the Prevention of Corruption Act 1906 or the Public Bodies Corrupt Practices Act 1889 being brought against persons who are performing functions on behalf of NAMA or who have a role in the valuation process. Presumably this category would embrace persons who are not officers or members of the Board of NAMA.

Subsection (2) provides for a presumption that a gift received from the debtor of an eligible bank asset is to be presumed to have been received corruptly as an inducement or reward for the person performing or omitting to perform their functions or any of them. This presumption does not apply to gifts given by a participating institution. Nor does it apply outside the context of criminal proceedings under the Prevention of Corruption Act 1906 or the Public Bodies Corrupt Practices Act 1889 (for instance in an attempt to seek an account from an officer of NAMA as a constructive trustee of a corrupt gift under the principles established by the Privy Council in *Attorney General for Hong Kong v Reid* [1994] 1 A.C. 324).

Finally, it should be noted that in order for the presumption to arise, subs.(2) requires that the prosecution *show*: (a) receipt of a gift, consideration or advantage, or (b) that the same was given by a debtor in relation to an eligible bank asset or an associated person. In comparable legislation such as s.4 of the Prevention of Corruption (Amendment) Act 2001 the prosecution is required to *prove* points (a) and (b). The significance of the difference is unclear. If it imports a lowering of the standard of proof required in a criminal prosecution then it is submitted that s.16(2) is constitutionally suspect per *Murphy v GM* [2001] 4 I.R. 113 at 136.

Liability of NAMA, etc.

17.—Without prejudice to any defence otherwise available to, or immunity otherwise enjoyed at law by NAMA, a NAMA group entity or a person specified in *section 34(1)*, no action for damages shall lie against NAMA, a NAMA group entity or such a person in respect of or arising out of the performance or non-performance in good faith of any of the functions provided for in *Parts 4, 5* and *6*, or in respect of any decision made in good faith to perform or not to perform any of the functions provided for in *Parts 8* and *9*.

NOTES AND COMMENTARY

This is one of several sections which provide NAMA with immunity from suit in the carrying out of its functions. It should be noted that unlike earlier drafts of this section, the immunity is not limited to non-feasance but applies to misfeasance also.

In *Dellway Investments v NAMA* [2010] IEHC 364, the High Court emphasised that the immunity conferred by this section, in relation to Pt 9, only extends to the making of NAMA's decision to perform or not perform its function under that Part. The section has no application to a claim against NAMA arising from "the manner in which any of the relevant powers might be exercised." (see [7.38]). In the Supreme Court judgment ([2011] IESC 14), Finnegan J. noted that the effect of the section would be to provide NAMA with a defence to an action for breach of duty when exercising a mortgagee's power of sale and that remedies for such a breach of duty are further restricted by ss.182 and 192 which place restrictions on the availability of injunctive relief.

CHAPTER 2

Membership of Board and Related Matters

Functions of Board

18.—(1) There shall be a Board of NAMA, whose functions are as follows:
- (*a*) to ensure that the functions of NAMA are performed effectively and efficiently;
- (*b*) to set the strategic objectives and targets of NAMA;
- (*c*) to ensure that appropriate systems and procedures are in place to achieve NAMA's strategic objectives and targets and to take all reasonable steps available to it to achieve those targets and objectives.

(2) For the purposes of the Board exercising its functions under *subsection (1)*, and without prejudice to any of its powers at law, the Board may provide for the performance of any such function by an officer of NAMA.

(3) In performing its functions, the Board shall act in utmost good faith with care, skill and diligence.

NOTES AND COMMENTARY

Subsection (1) establishes the Board of NAMA and ascribes it the primary function of managing the performance, by NAMA, of the functions ascribed to the Agency by the Act. These functions are set forth in s.11 of the Act and are in turn governed by the objectives of NAMA established by s.10. NAMA's objectives should be read in light of the purposes of the Act as a whole. set out in s.2 of the Act.

Similar provisions can be found in the legislation establishing many public bodies. Examples include s.12 of the Health Act 2004 (establishing the Board of the Health Services Executive); ss.18B and 18D, Central Bank Act 1942, as amended (establishing the Board of the Central Bank); and ss.11 and 13 of the Courts Service Act 1998 (establishing the Board of the Courts Service).

Subsection (2) provides for the Board to authorise an officer of NAMA to exercise its functions. In company law it is clear that the delegation of functions by a board of directors does not relieve the directors of the responsibility to carry out those functions (*Vehicle Imports, Re,* unreported, High Court, Murphy J., November 23, 2000, adopting *Re Barings Plc (No.5)* [1999] 1 BCLC 433).

Subsection (3) imposes a duty of utmost good faith and skill care and diligence on the members of the Board. There are no provisions for the imposition of personal liability on members of the Board for breaches of this duty. The tort of breach of statutory duty (see B. McMahon and W. Binchy, *Law of Torts* 3rd edn (London: Butterworths, 2000), Ch. 21) is unlikely to be available to a private plaintiff to enforce the section.

Subsection (3) imports a two part duty—first to act in the utmost good faith. At the very least this would seem to import the fiduciary duties of a company director to avoid conflicts of interests etc. (see T. Courtney, *Law of Private Companies* 2nd edn (Bloomsbury Professional, 2002), pp.534–542). In addition the obligation may impose an implied duty to disclose information. The second aspect of the board-members' duty is to do with care, skill and diligence. The meaning of such provisions in relation to the boards of public bodies has not been examined by the courts. There may be an analogy with the duty of care owed by company directors set out in *Re City Equitable Fire Insurance Co Ltd* [1925] Ch 407. Recent case law suggests that this duty may have become more demanding in recent years (see *Re Mitek Holdings Ltd* [2010] IESC 31 [73]).

Membership of Board

19.—(1) The Board consists of—

    (*a*) 7 members appointed by the Minister (in this Act referred to as "appointed members"), and

    (*b*) the Chief Executive Officer of NAMA and the Chief Executive of the NTMA as *ex-officio* members.

(2) Subject to *subsections (3), (4)* and *(6)*, the Minister shall appoint a person to be an appointed member only if, in the opinion of the Minister, the person has expertise and experience at a senior level in one or more of the following:

    (*a*) finance and economics;

    (*b*) law;

    (*c*) social housing and community development;

    (*d*) accountancy and auditing;

    (*e*) public administration;

    (*f*) credit management;

    (*g*) project finance;

    (*h*) construction and land development;

(*i*)   property management and sale;

(*j*)   valuation;

(*k*)   urban and land planning;

(*l*)   banking and investment;

(*m*) insolvency and restructuring;

(*n*)   risk management.

(3) A person who is for the time being entitled under the Standing Orders of either House of the Oireachtas to sit in that House or who is a member of the European Parliament is disqualified from appointment as an appointed member of the Board while he or she is so entitled or is such a member.

(4) A person who is a member of a local authority is disqualified from appointment as a member.

(5) A member of the Board shall, not later than 3 months after appointment, furnish to the Minister a tax clearance certificate.

(6) The Minister shall, so far as is practicable and having regard to relevant experience, ensure an equitable balance between men and women in the composition of the Board.

NOTES AND COMMENTARY

This section provides for the appointment of the members of the Board of NAMA. NAMA board members are appointed by the Minister who must be satisfied as to the appointees' expertise in one or more of the areas listed in s.(2)(c). It is a matter for the Minister to determine the precise qualifications necessary to fall within the listed areas.

Members of the Houses of the Oireachtas, the European Parliament and the local authorities are disqualified from membership of the board. There is no restriction on the Minister in seeking candidates who have previously been employed by the banking sector or by participating institutions.

Similar examples are to be found in many statutes establishing public bodies. See, for example, s.14 of the National Oil Reserves Agency Act 2007; National Sports Campus Development Authority Act 2006, and s.153 of the Residential Tenancies Act 2004.

The requirement to furnish a tax clearance certificate under subs.(5) is enforced through s.22(1)(d) which states that a board member who fails to furnish the certificate within three months ceases to be a board member. The provision of a tax certificate is required only on appointment and there is no continuous obligation to furnish additional certificates.

The initial appointments to the Board of NAMA were announced by the Minister for Finance on December 22, 2010. The individuals involved are Frank Daly (Chairperson), Eilish Finan, Michael Connolly, Peter Stewart, Brian McEnery and Willie Soffe. An additional appointment, Dr Steven Seelig was announced May 26, 2010. John Corrigan, Chief Executive of the National Treasury Management Agency and Brendan McDonagh, Chief Executive of NAMA were appointed as *ex officio* members.

Term of office of appointed members

20.—(1) Subject to *subsection (2)*, the term of office of an appointed member is 5 years.

(2) Of the first appointed members, the Minister shall appoint 2 members for a term of office of 3 years and 3 members for a term of office of 4 years.

(3) Subject to *subsection (4)*, an appointed member whose period of office expires by the passage of time is eligible for re-appointment as such a member.

(4) An appointed member is not eligible to serve for more than 2 consecutive terms of office.

The members of the Board serve for a five year term unless they cease to be a member of the Board under s.22. Subsection (2) provides for a staged replacement of the initial board members in order to ensure that departures from office are staggered over a period of time. It is possible for a member of the board to be re-appointed by the Minister for a second five year term though more than two consecutive terms are not permitted.

Under subs.(3) it appears that re-appointment for a second term is only available to a member whose term of appointment expires through passage of time. Given the wording of subs.(3) it is suggested that the maxim *inclusio unius est exclusio alterius* would preclude the re-appointment of a former member who had departed from the Board under s.22(1) or 22(2).

It appears that under subs.(4) a member might serve more than two terms in total provided that there was a gap between the second and third terms. This view seems to be strengthened by comparing the wording of subs.(4) with that of s.25(3) dealing with the term of office of the Chairperson of the Board of NAMA.

Remuneration, etc., of appointed members

21.—(1) An appointed member shall be paid such remuneration and such allowances in reimbursement of expenses incurred as the Minister from time to time determines.

(2) An appointed member holds office on such terms (other than the payment of remuneration and allowances for expenses incurred) as the Minister determines at the time of the member's appointment.

The Minister for Finance is responsible for setting the terms of remuneration and appointment. The legislation does not specify a method of payment of remuneration. The Quarterly Report for the period ended June 30, 2010 published in October 2010 under s.55 recorded a sum of €269,000 as having been paid as "board fees" to Board members (excluding the *ex officio* members) in the period between inception and June 30, 2010.

How appointed members cease to hold office

22.—(1) An appointed member ceases to be such a member if he or she—
  (a) is adjudicated bankrupt,
  (b) makes a composition or arrangement with creditors,
  (c) is convicted of an indictable offence in relation to a company,
  (d) does not furnish a tax clearance certificate as required by *section 19(5)*,
  (e) is convicted of an offence involving fraud or dishonesty, or
  (f) is disqualified or restricted from being a director of a company.
(2) If an appointed member—
  (a) is nominated as a member of Seanad Éireann,
  (b) is elected as a member of either House of the Oireachtas or as a member of the European Parliament,
  (c) is regarded, pursuant to Part XIII of the Second Schedule to the European Parliament Elections Act 1997, as having been elected to the European Parliament to fill a vacancy, or
  (d) becomes a member of a local authority,
he or she thereupon ceases to be an appointed member.

(3) An appointed member may at any time resign his or her membership by letter addressed to the Minister. The resignation takes effect on the date specified in the letter or when the Minister receives the letter, whichever is the later.

(4) The Minister may remove an appointed member on reasonable notice in writing at any time from membership of the Board (or, if the appointed member concerned is the Chairperson, either from the Board or only from being Chairperson) if—

    (*a*) in the Minister's opinion, the member—

        (i) is not adequately performing his or her functions, whether because of incapacity through illness or injury or otherwise,

        (ii) has contravened *section 30* or *31*, or

        (iii) has committed misconduct specified in the written notice,

    (*b*) in the Minister's opinion, a material conflict of interest has arisen in relation to the member, or

    (*c*) his or her removal appears to the Minister to be necessary or expedient for the effective performance by NAMA of its functions.

(5) An appointed member of the Board, upon the expiry or other termination of his or her term of office, shall also be taken to have resigned from any directorship of a NAMA group entity.

NOTES AND COMMENTARY

Subsections (1) and (2) deals with situations in which a member of the board is automatically removed. Both sections are closely related to the qualifications for membership which are set out in s.19. Section 22(1)(d) concerns a situation in which an appointed member fails to produce a tax clearance certificate within three months of their appointment as is required by s.19(5). Members of the Houses of the Oireachtas, the European Parliament or local authorities are disqualified from board membership by ss.19(3) and (4) and accordingly members of the Board who are elected or appointed to such provisions are automatically removed.

Subsection (3) facilitates board members who wish to resign their positions.

Subsection (4) allows the Minister for Finance to remove a member of the board from his or her position by notice in writing at any time. There is no definition of reasonable notice. If an individual board member has a contract of employment with NAMA the Minimum Notice and Terms of Employment Act 1973 would appear to apply.

Subsection (4) allows the Minister to remove a member on a number of grounds, namely:

(a) The member is not adequately performing his functions whether by reasons of incapacity owing to illness or injury or otherwise.

(b) The member has failed to make a disclosure of interest when required to do so under s.30 or has failed to give notice of registerable interests under s.31.

(c) A material conflict of interest has arisen with regard to the member

(d) The Minister forms the view that the member's removal is necessary or expedient for the performance of NAMA's functions.

It should be noted that the initiative rests with the Minister and that neither the Board itself nor the Chief Executive Officer of NAMA have a role in the removal of board members. While the text of the section indicates that the Minister has a discretion in taking a decision to remove a board member, it is clear that this discretion is neither unfettered nor unreviewable. In *Garvey v Ireland* [1981] 1 I.R. 75, the Supreme Court held that the Government was required to observe the requirements of natural and constitutional justice when removing an office holder (in that case the Garda Commissioner) from office.

Subsection (5) establishes that a once a member of the board is removed he or she is deemed to be removed from related positions without need for additional action.

It would seem to follow from s.20(3) of the Act, that a member who ceases to be a member under this section is not eligible for reappointment to the NAMA Board. See the notes accompanying that section.

How *ex-officio* members cease to be Board members

23.—(1) An *ex-officio* member of the Board ceases to be a member if he or she—

> (*a*) ceases to be the Chief Executive Officer of NAMA or the Chief Executive of the NTMA, as the case may be,
>
> (*b*) is adjudicated bankrupt,
>
> (*c*) makes a composition or arrangement with creditors,
>
> (*d*) is convicted of an indictable offence in relation to a company,
>
> (*e*) is convicted of an offence involving fraud or dishonesty, or
>
> (*f*) is disqualified or restricted from being a director of a company.

(2) If an *ex-officio* member of the Board—

> (*a*) is nominated as a member of Seanad Éireann,
>
> (*b*) is elected as a member of either House of the Oireachtas or as a member of the European Parliament,
>
> (*c*) is regarded, pursuant to Part XIII of the Second Schedule to the European Parliament Elections Act 1997, as having been elected to the European Parliament to fill a vacancy, or
>
> (*d*) becomes a member of a local authority,

he or she thereupon ceases to be an *ex-officio* member.

(3) An *ex-officio* member of the Board, upon the expiry or other termination of his or her term of office, shall also be taken to have resigned from any directorship of a NAMA group entity.

NOTES AND COMMENTARY

This section is very similar to the previous section dealing with full members of the Board. Under s.19 the Chief Executive Officers of NAMA and the NTMA are *ex officio* members of the Board. Under subss.(1) and (2) the *ex offico* members are automatically removed if they cease to occupy their positions as Chief Executive Officers of NAMA or the NTMA, or cease to qualify for membership. It should be noted that the *ex officio* members are not required to furnish a tax certificate within three months of their appointment under s.19(5). The section does not empower the Minister to remove the *ex officio* members in an analogous manner to that provided by s.22(4).

Subsection (3) is identical in effect to s.22(5).

Filling of casual vacancies, etc.

24.—(1) If an appointed member dies, resigns, retires, becomes disqualified or is removed from office, the Minister may appoint a person to fill the vacancy so occasioned. The person so appointed shall be appointed in the same manner as, and for the remainder of the term of office of, the member whose death, resignation, retirement, disqualification or removal occasioned the vacancy.

(2) In the circumstances mentioned in *subsection (1)*, and without prejudicing the Minister's powers under that subsection, the Minister may appoint a person to act temporarily as a member of the Board. The duration of such an appointment, and the terms under which the person appointed holds office, shall be as the Minister determines at the time of appointment.

(3) Subject to this Act, NAMA may act notwithstanding one or more vacancies

among the members of the Board.

This is a standard section in legislation providing for the appointment of persons to public bodies. For similar examples see s.10(15) of the Consumer Protection Act 2007; s.18(10) of the National Social and Economic Development Office Act 2008; and s.31(9) of the Food Safety Authority of Ireland Act 1998. Unlike some other examples, there is no obligation on the Minister to appoint a replacement member within a specified period of time. Subsection 3 seems to envisage a situation where the NAMA Board needs to act without having a full complement of members. This may be to allow for time for the Minister to locate and recruit a person with suitable qualifications who is prepared to accept appointment. Since a replacement Board member is to be appointed in the same manner as the Board member who is being replaced, the requirements as to qualifications and the submission of a tax certificate within three months of appointment apply.

Another curious aspect of this section is the reference to retirement. There is no provision within the legislation permitting board members to retire, though the practical effect could easily be achieved by resignation under s.22(3). This would appear to be a drafting error.

Subsection (2) permits the Minister to appoint a temporary member to the Board pending an appointment under subs.(1). The terms of this appointment are at the Minister's discretion and it is not expressly stated that the appointee would have to satisfy the requirements of ss.19(2) and (5) in order to be so appointed. The strictures of s.19 apply only to appointed members while subs.(2) appears to create a different category of temporary member.

Nomination and remuneration, etc., of Chairperson

25.—(1) The Minister shall nominate one of the appointed members as Chairperson.

(2) The Chairperson holds that office for 5 years or until the end (whether by the passage of time, resignation or removal under *section 22*) of his or her term of office as an appointed member, whichever is the earlier.

(3) A person may hold the office of Chairperson for 2 terms only, whether or not the terms are consecutive.

(4) The Chairperson may at any time resign that office (with or without also resigning as an appointed member) by letter addressed to the Minister. The resignation takes effect on the date specified in the letter or when the Minister receives the letter, whichever is the later.

(5) If the Chairperson dies, resigns, retires, becomes disqualified or is removed from office, the Minister shall nominate another person to fill the vacancy so occasioned. The person nominated may be an appointed member.

(6) In the circumstances mentioned in *subsection (5)*, and without prejudicing the Minister's powers under that subsection, the Minister may appoint a person to act temporarily as Chairperson. The duration of such an appointment, and the terms under which the person appointed holds that office, shall be as the Minister determines at the time of appointment.

(7) An appointment pursuant to *subsection (5)* may be for all or a specified part of the term of office of the person replaced.

(8) If the Minister proposes to nominate a person under *subsection (5)* who is not already an appointed member, the Minister may—

    (*a*) appoint that person to the Board as an appointed member, even though doing so will cause the number of appointed members specified in *section 19* to be exceeded, and (*b*) nominate the person as Chairperson.

(9) The Minister may determine that the Chairperson shall be paid additional remuneration or allowances on account of his or her responsibilities as Chairperson.

NOTES AND COMMENTARY

This section permits the Minister to designate one of the members of the Board to act as Chairperson for a 5 year term. Under subs.(3) the Chairperson may only serve for two terms as Chairperson regardless of whether those two terms are consecutive or not. This would seem to indicate that it is possible to serve more than two terms as a member of the Board provided that no more than two consecutive terms are served. See the notes to s.20.

Although the section does not provide a power to remove the Chairperson of the board, the Minister has a power of removal under s.22(4). The Minister may opt to remove the Chairperson on any of the grounds set out in that section. Removal as Chairperson does not automatically result in the removal as a member of the Board. See the notes on s.22 for details of the constraints on the Minister's power of removal.

Subsection (4) provides of the resignation of the Chairperson.

Subsections (5)–(8) set out the procedure for filling a vacancy which results from the death, resignation, retirement, disqualification or removal of the Chairperson. As with s.24, the reference to retirement appears misplaced and is likely a drafting error. Subsections (5) and (6) provide that the Minister may appoint another person to the position of Chairperson in like manner to the provisions for filling a vacancy left by the departure of a member of the Board. Unlike s.24 however, the Minister has an option under subs.(7) to appoint a replacement Chairperson to serve only a portion of the outgoing Chairperson's remaining term.

Section 19(1) fixes the size of the Board at seven appointed members and two *ex officio* members. Subsection (8) permits the Minister to fill a vacancy arising under subs.(5) by making an appointment from outside the Board. The Minister is authorised to exceed the limit of the size of the Board for this purpose.

Subsection (9) makes provision for additional remuneration to be paid to the Chairperson, in addition to the remuneration provided for in s.21.

Meetings of Board

26.—(1) The Board shall hold such meetings as are necessary for the performance of its functions.

(2) The Board shall hold its first meeting on the establishment day or as soon as is practicable after that day.

(3) The quorum for a meeting of the Board is 5, or, if there is a vacancy in the Board, 4 while the vacancy exists.

(4) A meeting held while there is a vacancy in the Board is validly held notwithstanding the vacancy, so long as there is a quorum.

(5) At a meeting of the Board—

    (*a*) if the Chairperson is present, he or she shall preside over the meeting, and

    (*b*) if the Chairperson is not present or the office of Chairperson is vacant, the appointed members present shall choose one of themselves to preside over the meeting.

(6) At a meeting of the Board each member present has a vote and any question on which a vote is required in order to establish the Board's view on the matter shall be determined by a majority of votes of members present and voting on the question. In the case of an equal division of votes, the Chairperson or other member presiding over the meeting has an additional casting vote.

(7) Subject to this Act, the Board shall regulate, by standing orders or otherwise, its procedure and business.

NOTES AND COMMENTARY

This section requires the Board to meet to discharge its functions. The functions of the Board are set out in s.18 and include overseeing the performance of NAMA's functions under s.11, setting strategic objectives and targets for the Agency and ensuring that appropriate systems are in place to enable the objectives to be achieved.

The establishment day was December 21, 2009 under the National Asset Management Agency Act 2009 (Establishment Day) Order 2009 (S.I. No. 547 of 2009).

The quorum for a board meeting is five members. There is no necessity for the members to be physically present (see s.27). The quorum drops to four members where there is a vacancy on the Board through the operation of s.22 or s.23. This would seem to place a practical limit of the operation of s.24(3) which provides that the Board can continue to act through periods of a vacancy, though the written resolution procedure might enable continued operations even in the unlikely event that the Board's membership was allowed to fall below four.

There is no distinction made for the purposes of voting or quorum purposes between appointed members and *ex officio* members. The Board could validly meet in times of a vacancy with just two appointed members together with the two *ex officio* members.

Subsection (7) requires the Board to regulate its proceedings and business, though the use of standing orders is not mandatory. It would appear however that the Board must keep minutes of its meetings since s.30 requires certain matters to be recorded in them.

Electronic meetings

27.—(1) In addition to meeting with all participants physically present, the Board may hold or continue a meeting by the use of any means of communication by which all the participants can hear and be heard at the same time. Such a meeting is referred to in this section as an "electronic meeting".

(2) A member of the Board who participates in an electronic meeting is taken for all purposes to have been present at the meeting.

(3) The Board may establish procedures for electronic meetings (including recording the minutes of such meetings) in its standing orders.

NOTES AND COMMENTARY

This section provides that the Board may conduct its meetings using telecommunications technology.

Subsection (3) allows for the inclusion of rules pertaining to such a meeting within the Board's standing orders, though the adoption of such rules is at the Board's discretion. The Board may validly conduct an electronic meeting under subs.(1) notwithstanding the fact that its standing orders do not make provision for such meetings. The quorum requirements of s.26(4) are not expressly applied to an electronic meeting.

This appears to be the first time that an Irish statute has made express provision for the use of electronic meetings. It should be noted that as a matter of company law, the validity of such meetings has long been recognised in England. In *Byng v London Life Assurance Company* [1990] 1 Ch 170, the Court of Appeal held that a general meeting of a company held via a video conferencing link between two different buildings was a validly constituted meeting. The Irish courts have not yet ruled on the point.

Resolutions by circulation of copies

28.—(1) The Board may pass a resolution without a meeting being held if—

    (*a*) all of the members entitled to vote on the resolution are given notice of the resolution, and

    (*b*) a majority of them sign a document containing a statement that they are in favour of the resolution in the document.

(2) A resolution referred to in *subsection (1)* may be passed by the members or some of them signing separate copies of the document referred to in *paragraph (1)(b)* if the date and time of each signature is indicated on the document.

(3) A resolution passed in accordance with this section is taken to have been passed at the time when a majority of members entitled to vote on the resolution have signed, or have signed copies of, the document referred to in *paragraph (1)(b)*.

<small>NOTES AND COMMENTARY</small>

This section provides the Board with the ability to adopt written resolutions without need for a meeting either physical or electronic. The section seems to be modelled on s.141(8) of the Companies Act 1963 which provides that the members of a company may adopt a resolution by signature in writing by all the members entitled to attend and vote at a general meeting of the company. There are a number of differences between the two provisions. First, s.28 permits resolutions to be adopted by a majority of the members. Secondly, s.28(1) requires the members to sign copies of a document indicating their assent rather than a copy of the resolution itself. Thirdly, members may sign different copies of the assent document provided that the time and date of signature is recorded. The necessity for such records is explained by subs.(3) which provides for the resolution to become valid when the last member required for a majority signs the resolution.

There is no requirement for the Board to regulate the use of the written resolution procedure in its standing orders. It should also be noted that the section does not contain a quorum requirement for the use of the procedure. This would appear to allow the Board to continue to function by means of written resolution even where its membership dropped below the four member quorum needed to hold a meeting under s.26(4).

It is unclear whether the Board of NAMA may take decisions by oral agreement or other assent of the members outside of a meeting in line with the principle in *Re Duomatic Ltd* [1969] 2 Ch 365. There it was held that when all the members of a company have assented to a particular course of action on a matter which a general meeting had a power to decide on, their assent was binding by estoppel in the same way as a resolution of a general meeting.

Seal of NAMA, etc.

29.—(1) The Board shall, as soon as possible after the establishment day, provide NAMA with a seal.

(2) The seal of NAMA shall be authenticated by the signature of any 2 members of the Board or in any other way that the Board resolves.

(3) Judicial notice shall be taken of the seal of NAMA. A document purporting to be an instrument made by, and sealed with the seal of, NAMA, and purporting to be authenticated in accordance with *subsection (2)*, shall be received in evidence and be taken to be such an instrument unless the contrary is shown.

(4) The Board may, as the Board thinks fit, delegate the authority to enter into a contract or instrument that, if entered into by an individual, would not be required to be under seal.

<small>NOTES AND COMMENTARY</small>

The section requires NAMA to have a seal. The requirement to have a seal is a standard feature of legislation regarding bodies corporate. See for example s.114(1)(b) of the Companies

Act 1963. Unlike a company's common seal there is no requirement to have the name of NAMA inscribed on its seal. The establishment day was set at December 21, 2009 by the National Asset Management Agency Act 2009 (Establishment Day) Order 2009 (S.I. No. 547 of 2009).

Subsection (2) governs the formalities to be observed when affixing the seal of NAMA. The subsection creates a default rule requiring the signatures of two members of the Board. No distinction is drawn between appointed members and *ex officio* members for this purpose. The Board may choose to depart from this requirement and substitute any other method of authentication it sees fit. It is unclear how the Board is to exercise this right to substitute another method of authentication but presumably a resolution of the Board is required. The scope of the Board's powers to regulate the authentication of the seal appears to be very broad. Section 18(2) authorises the Board to delegate its functions to an officer of NAMA; however, since the authentication of the seal is not strictly a function of the Board there appears to be nothing to stop the Board from delegating authentication to someone who is not an officer of NAMA.

Subsection (3) provides that a document authenticated with the seal of NAMA is presumed to be authenticated in accordance with s.(2) until the contrary is proven. It is unclear whether an outsider would be affected by a procedural irregularity in the authentication of the seal where the outsider had no notice of the irregularity, see *Royal British Bank v Turquad* (1856) 6 E&B 327.

Subsection (4) permits the Board to delegate authority to enter into contracts or instruments not required to be under seal in the manner that the Board sees fit. The Board seems to have a complete discretion to choose the identity of the delegatee. There seems to be a tension between subs.(4) and s.18(2) which only authorises delegation of the functions of the Board to officers of NAMA. It is notable that s.18(3) as originally drafted in the public consultation document contained a general power of delegation but this was amended by the time the bill was initiated to restrict powers of delegation to officers of NAMA.

Disclosure of interests

30.—(1) If a member of the Board has a pecuniary interest or other beneficial interest in, and material to, a matter that falls to be considered by the Board—

    (*a*) he or she shall disclose to the other members of the Board the nature of his or her interest in advance of any consideration of the matter,

    (*b*) he or she shall not influence nor seek to influence a decision to be made in relation to the matter,

    (*c*) he or she shall take no part in any consideration of the matter,

    (*d*) he or she shall absent himself or herself from the meeting or that part of the meeting during which the matter is discussed, and

    (*e*) he or she shall not vote or otherwise act on a decision relating to the matter.

(2) If a member discloses an interest pursuant to *subsection (1)*, the disclosure shall be recorded in the minutes of the meeting of the Board or otherwise duly recorded. The Board may, at its discretion, refer to the disclosure in NAMA's quarterly report.

(3) If a member of the Board fails to disclose an interest pursuant to *subsection (1)*, and with that member present the Board makes a decision on the matter, a contract entered into by NAMA in consequence of the decision is not, by reason only of that fact, invalid or unenforceable.

(4) If a member of the Board fails to disclose an interest pursuant to *subsection (1)*, and with that member present the Board makes a decision on the matter, the decision is not invalid if the Board subsequently reconsiders the matter without that member present and confirms the decision. If the Board does so, the decision shall be taken to have always been valid.

(5) If at a meeting of the Board a question arises as to whether or not a course of conduct, if pursued by a Board member, would constitute a failure by him or her to comply with *subsection (1)*, the Chairperson or member of the Board presiding over the meeting may determine the question. The Chairperson's or presiding member's decision is final. If such a question arises in relation to the Chairperson or person presiding over a meeting, he or she shall retire from the chair and the question shall be determined by majority vote of the remaining Board members. In either case particulars of the determination shall be recorded in the minutes of the meeting.

(6) If the Minister is satisfied that a member of the Board has contravened *subsection (1)*, the Minister may, if he or she thinks fit, remove that member from office.

(7) The Board shall issue guidelines as to what constitutes an interest for the purposes of this section having regard to the definitions in the Ethics in Public Office Act 1995.

Notes and Commentary

This section deals with the disclosure requirements for members of the Board who have a pecuniary or beneficial interest in a matter which comes before the Board for decision. Subsection (1) sets out the steps which a member must take in the event that he or she has such a conflict of interest. The member must disclose the conflict to other members of the board, may not vote on, or partake in any consideration of the matter, may not seek to influence the decision of other board members and must absent themselves from the meeting or part of the meeting at which the board members consider the decision. Disclosure must be made in advance of the decision being considered and, under subs.(2), must be recorded in the minutes of the meeting.

Subsection (5) provides for a situation where a member is in doubt about whether a disclosure from him or her is required. Under the section the Chairperson, or in his or her absence, the presiding member, is entitled to take a decision on the matter and such a decision is declared to be final. Since the minutes of the meeting are required to record decisions taken under s.(5) it would appear that the circumstances giving rise to the doubt would have to be disclosed to the meeting. Subsection (5) also provides that where doubt arises in relation to the Chairperson or presiding member, that person must withdraw from the chair and the matter is to be determined by a majority of the remaining members. This determination is also to be recorded in the minutes. No distinction is drawn between appointed and *ex officio* members in this section.

Subsection (2) also provides for the Board to publish the fact of a decision under s.30(1) in NAMA's quarterly reports under s.55. Publication is not mandatory and it seems that the Board is not necessarily obliged to disclose the details of the conflict of interest.

Subsections (3) and (4) and (6) detail the consequences should a member of the Board fail to take the steps required by subs.(1) when required to do so. Under subs.(3) a contract entered into by NAMA is not invalid solely by reason of its being the result of a decision made without compliance with subs.(1). The state of knowledge of the contractual counterparty appears to be irrelevant. Subsection (4) allows for the Board to reconsider a decision taken without compliance with subs.(1). If the Board decides to confirm its decision, the initial decision is to be treated as having been validly taken.

Subsection (4) does not provide a clear consequence in the event that the Board, on reconsideration, does not confirm, or confirms its initial decision with modifications. Byrne and McEntagart suggest that in such circumstances a contract entered into by NAMA on foot of the first decision would be invalid (see H. Byrne and L. McEntagart, *The National Asset Management Agency Act 2009: Annotations and Commentary* (Bloomsbury Professional, 2010), p.36).While there is no clear answer in the text of the Act, it is submitted that this may not be correct. Subsection (3) states that contracts are not invalid solely by reason of the fact that the decision to enter them involved a breach of subs.(1). Subsection (3) does not distinguish between an attempt to set such a contract aside by NAMA and an attack on the contract by a counterparty. It is suggested that there is no basis for implying such a distinction. Furthermore, the reasoning from rule in *Turquand's Case* (*Royal British Bank v Turquad* (1856) 6 E&B 327) might well be held applicable and dictate a different result, especially if dealing with a counterparty who had no notice of the non-compliance with subs.(1). In *Motor Racing Circuits Ltd, Re,* unreported, Supreme Court, Blayney J., January 31, 1997, writing for the court, summarised the rule by saying that an outsider dealing with a company was "entitled to assume that what is called the internal management of the company had been complied with." While the rule in *Turquand's* Case developed in relation to companies, there is no reason to believe that it would not apply to a statutory corporation such as NAMA.

Under subs.(6) and s.22(4)(a)(ii) the Minister for Finance may remove a member of the Board who has acted in breach of his or her obligations under subs.(1). The Minister has a discretion in the matter and removal is not automatic once a breach has been established. Section 23 does not create a comparable right for the Minister to remove an *ex officio* member; however *ex officio* members cease to be members of the Board on removal from their respective positions under s.23(1)(a). The Chief Executive Officer of NAMA can be removed by the Minister for a breach of s.30 under s.40(2)(a)(ii). The Minister can remove the Chief Executive of the NTMA from office for stated reasons under s.6(7)(d) of the National Treasury Management Agency Act 1990.

The terms "pecuniary interest or other beneficial interest" are not defined in the Act. Section (7) provides that the Board must issue guidelines on their meaning and that such guidelines must have regard to the definitions set out in the Ethics in Public Office Act 1995. Somewhat surprisingly neither term is expressly defined in that Act. The Second Schedule of the 1995 Act contains a lengthy list of interests including remunerative trades, professions or employments, ownership of shares and debentures and the receipt of gifts. The Schedule covers gifts to a spouse or child of the person concerned. Section 2(1) of the 1995 Act defines a benefit as referring to:

(a) a right, privilege, office or dignity and any forbearance to demand money or money's worth or a valuable thing;

(b) any aid, vote, consent or influence or pretended aid, vote, consent or influence;

(c) any promise or procurement of or agreement or endeavour to procure, or the holding out of any expectation of, any gift, loan, fee, reward or other thing aforesaid;

(d) any other advantage and the avoidance of a loss, liability, penalty, forfeiture, punishment or other disadvantage.

No guidelines made under this section have been published (though the Code of Practice— Conduct of NAMA Officers, published under s.35 does deal with the matter). The lack of a publication requirement can be contrasted with the codes of practice under s.35. The section does not make any provision (beyond that which maybe incorporated into the guidelines under subs.(7)) for conflicts of interest arising by virtue of the activities of family members and other persons connected to Board members.

Register of Board members' interests

31.—(1) As soon as practicable after the establishment day, NAMA shall prepare a Register of Members' Interests.

(2) By 31 January in each year—

(*a*) each member of the Board, each officer of NAMA who has been directed by the Board to do so and each director of each NAMA group entity shall give notice to NAMA of all of his or her registrable interests (within the meaning given by the Ethics in Public Office Act 1995), and

(*b*) NAMA shall ensure that each registrable interest so notified is entered in the Register of Members' Interests.

(3) Part VI of the Ethics In Public Office Act 1995 applies in relation to a contravention of *subsection (2)* as that Part does in relation to a contravention

of Part IV of that Act.

NOTES AND COMMENTARY

This section requires NAMA to prepare a Register of Members' Interests as soon as possible after its establishment. Subsection (2) requires the register to be updated annually with disclosures of interest to NAMA being due from Board members and directors of NAMA Group entities on January 31 each year. The Board may also require that individual officers of NAMA disclose their interests. Unlike the Registers of Members' Interests of the Dáil and Seanad Éireann, there is no requirement for the publication of the register, either in *Iris Oifigiúil* or elsewhere.

Subsection (3) provides for the application of Pt VI of the Ethics in Public Office Act 1995 to a contravention of the requirements of subs.(2).

Audit committee, credit committee, finance committee and riskmanagement committee.

32.—(1) As soon as practicable after the establishment day, the Board shall establish 4 committees, and shall (subject to *subsection (2)*, in the case of the audit committee) appoint members to them, as follows:

(*a*) an audit committee;

(*b*) a credit committee;

(*c*) a finance committee;

(*d*) a risk-management committee.

(2) There shall be 6 members of the audit committee. The Minister shall appoint 2 members from among qualified persons who are not members of the Board, and shall determine the terms of their service on the Committee, including removal and resignation. The Board shall appoint the other 4 members from among the members of the Board.

(3) The Board shall not appoint the Chairperson or an *ex-officio* member of the Board as a member of the audit committee.

(4) The members of the credit committee, the finance committee and the risk-management committee shall be members of the Board or officers of NAMA. At least 2 members of each of those committees shall be members of the Board.

(5) A member of a committee (other than a member of the audit committee appointed by the Minister) established under *subsection (1)* serves on the committee concerned on such terms (including term of office, removal and resignation) as the Board determines.

(6) The Board shall determine the terms of reference and procedures of each committee established under *subsection (1)*.

(7) With the approval of the Minister, NAMA, from its own resources, may remunerate a member of the audit committee who is not a member of the Board.

(8) The Board may dissolve a committee established under *subsection (1)*. If the Board dissolves such a committee, the Board shall re-establish that committee as soon as practicable.

(9) *Sections 27* and *28* apply in relation to a committee established under *subsection (1)*.

(10) *Section 30* applies in relation to a member of a committee established under *subsection (1)* who is not a member of the Board. For the purposes of that application—

(a) references to members of the Board shall be construed as references to members of the committee,

(b) references to the Board shall be construed as references to the committee, and

(c) guidelines made for the purposes of *section 30(7)* apply with the modifications set out in *paragraphs (a)* and *(b)*.

NOTES AND COMMENTARY

This section requires the Board to establish the four committees listed in subs.(1) as soon as possible after the establishment day. The terms of reference and procedures of the committees must be determined by the Board under subs.(6).

The audit committee is to be composed of four members of the Board and two members appointed by the Minister. The Minister is required to choose the two members from among "qualified persons". The term "qualified person" is not defined in the Act. Section 19 sets out a series of qualifications required for membership of the Board itself but these do not seem to extend to persons appointed to the audit committee. Presumably, a person who satisfied the requirements for appointment as auditor to a company under s.187 of the Companies Act 1990 (as amended) would fall within the term "qualified person". The Minister sets the terms of the two members appointed to the audit committee including making provision for their resignation and removal. Unlike appointed members of the Board the Minister is not restricted in the grounds on which he may seek to remove a member of the audit committee. Under subs.(7) the NAMA may provide remuneration for a member of the audit committee who is not a member of the Board. Such arrangements must be sanctioned by the Minister and the payments are to be made from NAMA's resources.

The membership of the audit committee is further constrained by subs.(3) which prohibits the Board from appointing the Chairperson or either of the *ex-officio* officers of NAMA to the committee. Since the Board has only seven appointed members, one of whom is debarred from membership as Chairperson, the Board must choose its four nominees from a restricted pool of four members. Unlike the other committees created by this section the Board may not seek to appoint an external candidate.

In addition to the audit committee, subs.(1) requires the Board to form three other committees dealing with credit, finance and risk-management. The size of these committees is not specified by the Act, though under subs.(2) there must be at least two members of the Board on each committee. The Board's power of selection is limited. Only persons who are officers of NAMA or members of the Board may be appointed. The Board can set the terms of appointment (including provisions of resignation and removal).

Under subs.(8) the Board has a power to dissolve any of the committees formed under subs.(1) provided that a replacement committee is re-established as soon as practicable. The power applies to the audit committee as well as the other committees listed in subs.(1). This leads to the anomalous situation where the Board can in effect remove a Ministerial appointment from office by dissolving the audit committee notwithstanding that subs.(2) reserves the power of removing an appointed member of the audit committee to the Minister. The Minister could of course effect a reversal of the Board's decision by re-appointing the same candidates.

Subsection (9) applies the rules for electronic meetings and the written resolution procedure to meetings of the committees. This would appear to derogate from the provision in subs.(6) permitting the Board to determine the procedures of the committees. The rules in s.26 concerning physical meetings of the Board are not applied to the committees. Thus any quorum requirement would be for the Board to establish under subs.(6).

Subsection (10) applies the requirements relating to disclosure of conflicts of interests set out in s.30 to members of the committee. Interestingly there is no parallel requirement for committee members who are not Board members to be included on the members' register of interests, though the Board could require appointed committee members to make a disclosure under s.31(2)(a). There is no analogous power for the Board (or the Minister in the case of the audit Committee) to remove a member for breach of the requirements of s.30 as there is for Board members under s.22(4). Such a power could easily be taken by the Committee or the Minister by drafting appropriate terms of engagement.

The role of the Risk Management Committee is discussed in "Code of Practice—Risk Management including with Regard to Debtors" issued by NAMA under s.35 of the Act. According to para.3.5 of the Code the Committee is responsible for defining an appropriate risk management framework. The key features of this framework which are listed by the document are as follows:

(a) Enterprise wide, covering all material risks to which NAMA is exposed.

(b) Defined risk tolerances and associated limits and delegated authorities.

(c) Governance arrangements which include segregation of duties and independence.

(d) Segregation of duties; including two committees of the Board to oversee risk and credit decisions.

(e) Portfolio-based with focus on both transaction level and portfolio level risk performance.

(f) Supported by rigorous quantitative analysis—decisions at all times taken with specific regard to those risks and justified accordingly in terms of maximising expected (i.e. risk-adjusted) recovery on a discounted (i.e. Net Present Value) basis.

Other committees

33.—(1) The Board may establish—

(*a*) such advisory committees as it considers necessary or desirable to advise it in the performance of its functions, and

(*b*) such other committees and sub-committees as it considers necessary or expedient,

and may appoint members to such a committee as it considers necessary.

(2) A committee established under *subsection (1)* may include persons who are not members of the Board, but a majority of the members of such a committee shall be members of the Board.

(3) A member of a committee established under *subsection (1)* shall serve on the committee on such terms (including term of office, removal and resignation) as the Board determines.

(4) The Board shall determine the terms of reference and procedures of a committee established under *subsection (1)*.

(5) With the approval of the Minister, NAMA, from its own resources, may remunerate a member of a committee established under *subsection (1)* who is not a member of the Board.

(6) *Sections 27* and *28* apply in relation to a committee established under *subsection (1)*.

(7) *Section 30* applies in relation to a member of a committee established under *subsection (1)* who is not a member of the Board. For the purposes of that application—

(*a*) references to members of the Board are to be construed as references to members of the committee,

(*b*) references to the Board are to be construed as references to the committee, and

(*c*) guidelines made for the purposes of *section 30(7)* apply with the modifications set out in *paragraphs (a)* and *(b)*.

Notes and Commentary

This section allows the Board to establish additional committees where this is necessary or desirable to obtain advice on the performance of its functions or where it is otherwise expedient to do so. Unlike the committees established by s.32, the Board has discretion on whether to establish additional committees or not. Subsection (2) authorises the Board to determine the membership of additional committees. Unlike the committees established by s.32 membership is not restricted to Board members and officers of NAMA. Subsection (5) permits the committee to agree arrangements for remuneration of committee members who are not members of the Board subject to the approval of the Minister. As with remunerated members of the audit committee under s.32 any remuneration is payable from the funds of NAMA itself.

Subsection (3) permits the Board to establish the terms of service for committee members including making provision for a power of removal. Subsection (6) makes provision for electronic meetings and the written resolution procedure. The Board does not have an express power to dissolve a committee established under s.33 as in s.32(8).

Indemnification of members of Board and officers of NAMA, etc.

34.—(1) This section applies to the following persons:

(*a*) each member of the Board;

(*b*) each member of a committee established under *section 32* or *33*;

(*c*) each officer of NAMA;

(*d*) a director of a NAMA group entity;

(*e*) a member of the staff of the NTMA.

(2) Where the Board is satisfied that a person to whom this section applies has discharged the functions appropriate to that person in relation to the functions of NAMA in good faith, NAMA shall indemnify that person against all actions or claims however they arise in relation to the discharge by that person of those functions.

(3) The Board shall not be prevented from revoking an indemnity granted to, or recovering any payment made pursuant to such an indemnity from, a person who is subsequently found to have carried out his or her duties in bad faith.

NOTES AND COMMENTARY

This is one of a number of sections which allow for the relieving of certain persons of liability for certain acts carried out in good faith (see s.17). The section is curious since it gives the Board a very broad discretion to relieve a wide range of people from an unspecified range of liabilities which might arise by reason of their association with NAMA. Power under the section rests with the Board alone and the Minister has no supervisory role. The only limit on the Board's discretion is that the actions or claim arise from the performance of the indemnified party's functions "in relation to the functions of NAMA". The functions of NAMA are set out in s.11 of the Act.

The section is silent on what is meant by good faith. It is worth noting that under s.18(3) Board members are required to exercise the utmost good faith in the performance of their duties. There seems to be tension between this provision and subs.(2) which contemplates providing an immunity from all actions (including presumably actions by the Minister or NAMA in relation to a breach of s.18(3)) provided that a Board member's behaviour has reached the lower standard of "good faith".

The section does not provide for any procedures regarding how the Board is to decide whether a specific person has acted in good faith or not. The concept of "bad faith" can presumably be equated to the opposite of good faith. In exercising its discretion under this section the Board would have to have regard to the financial interests of the taxpayer in line with ss. 2 and 10.

Codes of practice

35.—(1) Within 3 months after the establishment day, NAMA shall prepare codes of practice for approval by the Minister in relation to the following matters:

    (*a*) the conduct of officers of NAMA;

    (*b*) servicing standards for acquired bank assets;

    (*c*) risk management, including with regard to debtors;

    (*d*) disposal of bank assets;

    (*e*) the manner in which NAMA is to take account of the commercial interests of credit institutions that are not participating institutions;

    (*f*) any other matter in relation to which the Minister directs NAMA to prepare a code of practice.

(2) A code of practice referred to in *subsection (1)(a)* shall set out—

    (*a*) what constitutes misconduct in office for the purposes of *section 43*,

    (*b*) the procedures for the investigation of an officer of NAMA suspected of misconduct, and

    (*c*) the procedures for the suspension of such an officer from his or her duties for misconduct in office.

(3) After a code of practice is approved by the Minister, every person to whom it applies shall have regard to and be guided by that code in the performance of his or her functions and in relation to any other matters to which the code relates.

(4) If in the opinion of the Minister adequate provision has not been made in a code of practice drawn up by NAMA under *subsection (1)*, the Minister may—

    (*a*) direct NAMA to modify the code of practice, or

    (*b*) substitute his or her own code of practice.

(5) NAMA shall publish a code of practice, issued under this section as approved by the Minister, on the NAMA website.

NOTES AND COMMENTARY

Subsection (1) requires that NAMA submit proposed codes of conduct to the Minister for approval within three months of the establishment date. There is no timeframe imposed for the Minister to make a decision to approve it. No timescales are provided in the event that the Minister utilises his powers to direct a modification of the submitted codes or decides to substitute his own code.

Five codes of practice were approved by the Minister on July 5, 2010. A letter from the Minister to the Chief Executive Officer of NAMA, which was published along with the code, indicates that the Minister consulted various "interested parties" including the European Commission before approving the codes. The letter also indicates that the Minister asked for certain unspecified amendments to the draft codes. The Minister does not appear to have invoked his powers under subs.(4) to direct a change to the codes, rather the amendments (which are not specified in the published letter) were a condition precedent to the Minster's approval under subs.(1).

Code of Practice—Conduct of NAMA Officers

This code is expressed to apply to all employees of the NTMA who are assigned to NAMA from time to time and thus become officers of NAMA under s.42 of the Act. The code has four substantive sections which are designed to give practical guidance to officers of NAMA in respect of confidentiality, dealing with conflicts of interest, market abuse and the regulations governing misconduct by officers of NAMA.

Code of Practice—Risk Management including with Regard to Debtors

This code sets out NAMA's approach to managing risk. The document begins by listing the various kinds of risks which NAMA is exposed to in the course of managing its assets. It then details some of the internal arrangements which NAMA has put in place to manage those risks. These are organised around a number of key principles:

(a) Debtors will be treated in a reasonable manner. Under this heading the document lays out NAMA's general approach to dealing with its debtors including the review of debtor's business plans, and the decision making process for making credit advancement decisions and decisions regarding recovery plans.

(b) Mutual Obligations. This section contains an acknowledgement of NAMA's contractual obligations to debtors and declares that NAMA requires the provision of full and accurate information to be delivered by debtors on a timely basis.

(c) Decision Making and Risk Management. These sections commit NAMA to operating a strong corporate governance framework and sets out the key features of the NAMA's risk management framework.

(d) No proprietary trading or transacting with financial instruments not related to the management of loans. This section commits NAMA to the development of policies to manage foreign exchange and interest rate risks. Responsibility falls primarily on the Chief Executive Officer subject to review by the Board.

(e) Powers and Rights of NAMA. This section details NAMA's approach to the exercise of its statutory powers. The details will be considered in the various sections which confer special statutory powers on NAMA in respect of acquired bank assets and related sections.

Code of Practice on the Commercial Interests of Non-Participating Institutions

This code of practice regulates NAMA's approach to non-participating credit institutions that have a relationship with a debtor whose obligations are acquired by NAMA. The code sets out a framework for reciprocal consultation between NAMA and non-participating institutions where a common approach to the management of a particular debtor has already been, or can be agreed. The code establishes the NAMA Head of Portfolio Management as the key point of contact for non-participating institutions and provides that non-participating institutions should designate a senior contact point for NAMA.

The code also addresses NAMA's role when it acquires a credit facility which forms a part of a syndicate. Here, NAMA is committed to operate the legal arrangements agreed in the establishment of the syndicate and NAMA is committed to consultation with other syndicate members in the management of the syndicate. Where NAMA acquires a right to instruct the person holding the security on behalf of a syndicate, para.3.7 sets out the approach which NAMA will in adopt deciding whether and when to exercise that right. As with the risk management code, the document concludes with a discussion of the circumstances in which NAMA will exercise its various statutory powers. See the notes to Pt 9 for details.

Code of Practice—Disposal of Bank Assets

This code commits the Board to establishing a strategy for the disposal of bank assets in line with best international practice and the Code of Practice for Governance of State Bodies (2009). The Board is required to establish procedures for disposals which must include an independent appraisal of each asset, with two such appraisals to be obtained where an asset is above €100 million in value. Timing of disposals is to be determined by the Board.

Application of certain provisions of this Chapter to directors of NAMA group entities

36.—(1) With the modifications set out in *subsection (2)*, the following provisions of this Chapter apply in relation to directors of NAMA group entities:

   (*a*) *subsections (1), (2), (3)* and *(4)* of *section 22*;

   (*b*) *section 30.*

  (2) The modifications referred to in *subsection (1)* are—

   (*a*) references to an appointed member shall be read as references to the director concerned,

   (*b*) references to the Board of NAMA, or to members of that Board, shall be read as references to the directors of the NAMA group entity concerned, and

   (*c*) the reference to NAMA in *section 30(3)* shall be read as a reference to the NAMA group entity concerned.

NOTES AND COMMENTARY

    This section applies some of the rules relating to the members of the Board to the directors of a NAMA group entity. The provisions of subs.(1)(a) would allow the Minister to remove a Board member who was also a director of a NAMA group entity to remove that person from a directorship without simultaneously removing him from the Board. Under s.22(5) a directorship of a NAMA group entity ceases automatically if the director ceases to be a member of the Board.

CHAPTER 3

Chief Executive Officer

Appointment of first Chief Executive Officer

   37.—(1) The Minister, after consultation with the Chief Executive of the NTMA and the Chairperson of NAMA, shall appoint as the first Chief Executive Officer of NAMA a person who is, in the Minister's opinion, suitably qualified.

   (2) A person shall not be appointed under *subsection (1)* if he or she is disqualified from being appointed to the Board.

   (3) Upon appointment as Chief Executive Officer, the person so appointed shall be appointed as a member of the staff of the NTMA if he or she is not already such a member. The term of office, remuneration, allowances and other terms and conditions (including the provision of superannuation benefits) of appointment of the Chief Executive Officer shall be determined in accordance with sections 7(2) and 8 of the National Treasury Management Agency Act 1990.

   (4) The Chief Executive Officer is not a civil servant within the meaning of the Civil Service Regulation Act 1956.

NOTES AND COMMENTARY

    This section allows for the appointment of a Chief Executive Officer for NAMA. The Minister is required to consult the Chairperson of NAMA and the Chief Executive Officer of the NTMA prior to making the appointment. It is unclear whether the Minister must have regard to the list of qualifying areas of knowledge in s.19(2) when making an appointment. Subsection (2) prevents the Minister from appointing a person who is disqualified from membership of the Board as Chief Executive Officer. Under s.19(3)–(4) members of the Houses of the Oireachtas are disqualified from appointment to the Board of NAMA. It would seem therefore that the Minister need only be satisfied as to a candidate's suitability.

    Section (3) provides that the Chief Executive Officer is a member of staff of the NTMA. Under s.7(2) of the National Treasury Management Agency Act 1990 the employment conditions of NTMA staff are settled by the NTMA. Section 8 of the National Treasury

Management Agency Act 1990 gives the NTMA a power to make superannuation arrangements available for its staff.

A civil servant is defined by s.1(1) of the Civil Service Regulation Act 1956 as "a person holding a position in the Civil Service and includes a member of the staff of the Houses of the Oireachtas".

Mr Brendan McDonagh was formally appointed under this section on December 22, 2009, the same day as the rest of the Board of NAMA.

Chief Executive Officer's functions

38.—(1) The Chief Executive Officer shall manage and control generally the administration and business of NAMA and the staff assigned to it, and shall perform any other functions conferred on him or her by or under this Act or by the Board.

(2) The Chief Executive Officer is responsible to the Board for the performance of his or her functions and the implementation of NAMA's strategic targets and objectives.

(3) Such of the functions of the Chief Executive Officer as he or she may from time to time specify, with the consent of the Board, may be performed by an officer or officers of NAMA authorised by the Chief Executive Officer for that purpose. A reference in a provision of this Act to the Chief Executive Officer includes any officer so authorised.

(4) The functions of the Chief Executive Officer may be performed during his or her absence or when the position of Chief Executive Officer is vacant by an officer of NAMA designated for that purpose by the Board. A reference in a provision of this Act to the Chief Executive Officer includes any officer so designated.

(5) The Chief Executive Officer is the person who is accountable for the purposes of the Comptroller and Auditor General (Amendment) Act 1993.

NOTES AND COMMENTARY

The Chief Executive Officer is appointed by the Minister under s.37 and is responsible for the implementation of the targets and objectives assigned to NAMA by the Board under s.18(2). Subsection (3) establishes that the Chief Executive Officer may delegate his functions with the consent of the Board. Notwithstanding that the Chief Executive Officer of NAMA is a member of staff of the NTMA under s.37(3), he or she reports to the Board of NAMA.

Unlike the Chairman and members of the Board there is no fixed term of office for the Chief Executive of NAMA, accordingly there is no need for provisions governing re-appointment. Unlike members of the Board of NAMA there is no obligation on the Chief Executive to produce a tax clearance certificate under s.19(4) within three months of appointment. For the circumstances in which the office of Chief Executive Officer becomes vacant, see s.40 and the notes thereto.

There was a lengthy discussion at Committee Stage in the Dáil debate as to whether the Chief Executive Officer should be an accounting officer for the purposes of appearing before the Public Accounts Committee (see the note to s.58), the Minister for Finance explained that an accounting officer under the Comptroller and Auditor General (Amendment) Act 1993 must have a vote of monies from the Oireachtas and as such the formulation "person who is accountable" was appropriate. (22 *Dáil Debates: Special Committee on Finance and the Public Service* Col. 859 (October 28, 2009))

Resignation of Chief Executive Officer

39.—The Chief Executive Officer may resign his or her office by letter addressed to the Minister. The resignation takes effect on the date specified in the letter or when the Minister receives the letter, whichever is the later.

NOTES AND COMMENTARY

This section is identical to s.22(3) (resignation of an appointed member of the Board) and s.25(4) (Resignation of the Chairperson of NAMA).

Removal of Chief Executive Officer from office

40.—(1) The Chief Executive Officer ceases to hold that office if he or she—

    (*a*) is adjudicated bankrupt,

    (*b*) makes a composition or arrangement with creditors,

    (*c*) is convicted of an indictable offence in relation to a company,

    (*d*) is convicted of an offence involving fraud or dishonesty, or

    (*e*) is disqualified or restricted from being a director of a company.

(2) The Minister may remove the Chief Executive Officer from office by reasonable notice in writing if—

    (*a*) in the Minister's opinion, the Chief Executive Officer—

        (i) is not adequately performing his or her functions, whether because of incapacity through illness or injury or otherwise,

        (ii) has contravened *section 30* or *31*, or

        (iii) has committed misconduct specified in the written notice,

    (*b*) in the Minister's opinion, a material conflict of interest has arisen in relation to the Chief Executive Officer, or

    (*c*) his or her removal appears to the Minister to be necessary or expedient for the effective performance by NAMA of its functions.

(3) If the Chief Executive Officer dies, resigns, retires, becomes disqualified or is removed from office, the Board, after consulting the Minister and the Chief Executive of the NTMA, shall appoint another person to fill the vacancy so occasioned.

(4) An appointment pursuant to *subsection (3)* may be for all or a specified part of the term of office of the person replaced.

(5) In the circumstances mentioned in *subsection (3)*, and without prejudicing the Board's powers under that subsection, the Board may appoint a person to perform the duties of the Chief Executive Officer temporarily. The duration of such an appointment, and the terms under which the person appointed holds that office, shall be as the Board determines at the time of appointment.

NOTES AND COMMENTARY

This section provides that the Chief Executive of NAMA automatically ceases to hold office on the occurrence of any of the events listed in subs.(1). This list is identical to that which applies to members of the Board of NAMA under s.22(1) with the exception that there is no obligation on the Chief Executive Officer to produce a tax clearance certificate to the Minister after his appointment.

Subsection (2) permits the Minister to remove the Chief Executive by notice in writing on any of the grounds set out in the subsection. An identical provision is to be found in s.22(4) relating to members of the Board. Notwithstanding that the Chief Executive is responsible to the Board for the performance of his functions under s.38(2), it is the Minister who has the power of removing the Chief Executive from office. As with s.22(4), while the text of the section indicates that the Minister has a discretion in taking a decision to remove a Board member, it is clear that this discretion is neither unfettered nor unreviewable. In *Garvey v Ireland* [1981] 1 I.R. 75, the Supreme Court held that the Government was required to observe the requirements of natural and constitutional justice when removing an office holder (in that case the Garda Commissioner) from office.

CHAPTER 4

NAMA's Relationship with NTMA

NTMA to provide resources to NAMA

41.—(1) The NTMA shall provide NAMA with such business and support services and systems as the Board determines, acting upon the recommendation of the Chief Executive Officer of NAMA and after consultation with the Chief Executive of the NTMA, to be necessary or expedient for NAMA to perform its functions under this Act.

(2) Where the NTMA is unable for any reason to provide business and support services or systems referred to in *subsection (1)*, the NTMA, as agent of NAMA, may procure such services or systems as are necessary.

NOTES AND COMMENTARY

When the Minister for Finance announced the establishment of NAMA on April 5, 2009, it was announced the Agency would be "under the aegis of the National Treasury Management Agency" (679 *Dáil Debates* Col. 678). This section continues that relationship. Subsection (1) requires the NTMA to provide services requested by the Board of NAMA. While the Board is required to consult with the Chief Executive of the NTMA (who is an *ex officio* member of the Board in any event) it is clear that it is the Board of NAMA who are entitled to take decisions on what services and systems are necessary for NAMA to perform its functions. Where the NTMA is unable to provide necessary services or systems it may procure them as agent of NAMA. Unlike s.42(4) in respect of NTMA staff assigned to NAMA, there is no provision in this section for the NTMA to be reimbursed by NAMA for the cost of providing such services.

NTMA to provide staff to NAMA

42.—(1) The NTMA shall assign so many of its staff to NAMA as the Board determines, upon the recommendation of the Chief Executive Officer of NAMA, after consultation with the Chief Executive of the NTMA, to be necessary for the performance by NAMA of its functions under this Act.

(2) Before employing or otherwise engaging a person to be assigned to NAMA under *subsection (1)*, the NTMA shall ascertain to its satisfaction that the person—

    (*a*) is of good character and has not been convicted of any offence likely to render him or her unfit or unsuitable to perform the duties that the person is required to undertake or is likely to be required to undertake,

    (*b*) has not been disqualified or restricted from acting as a director under the Companies Acts, and

    (*c*) has no material conflict of interest, whether actual or potential.

(3) Before the NTMA assigns a member of its staff to NAMA under *subsection*

(1), the NTMA shall ensure that he or she provides a statement of his or her interests, assets and liabilities to the Chief Executive Officer of NAMA and the Chief Executive of the NTMA in a form that the NTMA specifies.

(4) NAMA shall reimburse the NTMA for the costs incurred by the NTMA in consequence of its assigning staff to NAMA under this section.

NOTES AND COMMENTARY

This section permits the Board of NAMA to determine how many staff it requires for the performance of its functions. This decision is to be taken on the recommendation of the Chief Executive Officer of NAMA following consultation with the Chief Executive of the NTMA. The NTMA is required to meet such a request and there is no requirement on the Board of NAMA to have regard to the impact of its requests on the functions of the NTMA beyond consultation with its Chief Executive.

Subsection (2) permits the NTMA to employ or engage additional staff for the purposes of assigning them to NAMA. This provision extends the NTMA's existing power to employ staff under s.7 of the National Treasury Management Agency Act 1990. The NTMA is required to satisfy itself of the matters lists in subss.(2)(a)–(c) before engaging a person to be assigned to NAMA. There are no equivalent requirements governing the recruitment of ordinary NTMA staff recruited under s.7 of the 1990 Act. In addition it appears that the NTMA need not be satisfied of the matters listed in subss.(2)(a)–(c) in respect of members of its existing staff who are assigned to NAMA.

While the legislation does not expressly specify consequences for a person who makes an incorrect declaration, it is clear from para.4.2.3(g) of the Code of Practice—Conduct of Officers of NAMA that an incorrect declaration would amount to misconduct on the part of the officer.

Subsection (3) requires all members of staff of the NTMA who are assigned to NAMA to disclose their interests, assets and liabilities to the Chief Executive of the NTMA and the Chief Executive Officer of NAMA. Since a person employed by the NTMA under subs.(2) would then be assigned to NAMA under subs.(1) it seems clear that persons falling into subs.(2) will have to make a disclosure.

Subsection (4) requires NAMA to reimburse the NTMA for the costs of assigning staff under this section. As noted in the notes to s.41 there is no equivalent provision for NAMA to reimburse the costs of the provision of services and systems to NAMA.

Suspension of officers of NAMA

43.—The Chief Executive Officer of NAMA, after consultation with the Chief Executive of the NTMA, may suspend, on such terms and conditions as he or she thinks fit, an officer of NAMA from his or her duties as such an officer if—

(*a*) the officer has been convicted at any time of—

(i) an offence of theft, fraud or dishonesty, or

(ii) any other offence that the Chief Executive Officer considers likely to render him or her unfit or unsuitable to perform his or her duties,

(*b*) the officer is restricted or disqualified from acting as a director under the Companies Acts,

(*c*) the officer—

(i) is not adequately performing his or her functions, whether because of incapacity through illness or injury or otherwise, or

(ii) has committed misconduct in relation to his or her duties as an officer of NAMA,

(*d*) in the Chief Executive Officer's opinion, a material conflict of interest in relation to his or her duties as an officer of NAMA has arisen in relation to the officer, or

(*e*) the officer's suspension appears to the Chief Executive Officer to be necessary or expedient for the effective performance by NAMA of its functions.

This section permits the Chief Executive Officer of NAMA to suspend an officer of NAMA on specified grounds. The grounds set out are similar to those which justify the removal of a member of the Board under s.22(4) or of the Chief Executive Officer under s.40(2).

It should be noted that although it is the NTMA which assigns staff to NAMA, the suspension of staff is carried out by the Chief Executive Officer of NAMA, with the Chief Executive of the NTMA having only a consultative role. The section does not result in the suspension of the officer concerned from employment with the NTMA. It seems that the NTMA would have to undertake subsequent disciplinary proceedings, though the Code of Conduct referred to below does make provisions for the carrying out of a single investigation for both the NAMA and NTMA disciplinary processes.

Misconduct is not defined in the Act; however guidance can be found in the Code of Practice—Conduct of Officers of NAMA, issued under s.35. The code provides general guidance on the conduct of officer of NAMA in para.4.2.1 which states:

"Officers of NAMA must at all times act in the best interests of NAMA, act in good faith in the performance of their duties and responsibilities, conduct themselves in a professional manner and with propriety, be competent in their work, perform their job duties to the standards reasonably required by NAMA, be faithful to NAMA in the course of their work and discharge their duties and responsibilities with the highest standards of integrity. Without prejudice to the generality of the foregoing, Officers must not at any time permit themselves to be lobbied or engage in lobbying on behalf of any organisation, association, person, firm, company or other legal entity with respect to any matter that NAMA has or may have an interest in or conduct themselves in a manner that is or may be inimical to the interests of NAMA."

Paragraph 4.2 gives an extended definition for the concept of misconduct for the purposes of the code. The Code of Practice also sets out the procedures for investigating suspected misconduct by officers of NAMA.

CHAPTER 5

Contracted Service Providers

Power to engage service providers, etc.

44.—(1) Without prejudice to the powers of NAMA under *section 12* or otherwise, NAMA may engage the services of any expert adviser or other service provider where NAMA considers it necessary or expedient to do so in connection with the performance of its functions.

(2) Without prejudice to the generality of *subsection (1)*, NAMA may engage a person (including a credit institution that is not a participating institution) to manage or dispose of acquired bank assets as it thinks fit on such terms and conditions as it thinks fit.

(3) The services that NAMA may engage an expert adviser or service provider to provide include relevant services (within the meaning given by *section 128*).

(4) In performing its functions under this Act, in particular in relation to the

development of land, NAMA may take account of the resources available to it from the National Building Agency or any other appropriate State agency.

This section provides NAMA with an option to directly engage the services of an expert or other service provider from outside the NTMA. Unlike s.41(2) there is no need for the NTMA to act as an agent of NAMA in procuring business services and systems. Subsections (2) and (3) confirm that NAMA may engage service providers to arrange for the disposal of bank assets as well as the management administration and restructuring of bank assets.

Professional standards and audit

45.—In contracts for the provision of services to NAMA by expert advisers and service providers, NAMA shall seek to ensure that each expert adviser or service provider—

(*a*) operates to the highest standards of honesty and fairness and with due skill, care, prudence and diligence in conducting its business activities under the mandate given to it so as to promote the best interests of NAMA,

(*b*) effectively employs the resources and procedures that are necessary for the proper performance of such business activities,

(*c*) makes every effort to avoid or manage conflicts of interest and to declare any such conflict (actual or potential) to NAMA,

(*d*) complies with any regulatory regime to which it is subject,

(*e*) permits NAMA to engage auditors to carry out an audit of the books, accounts and other financial statements of the expert adviser or service provider so far as they relate to the services performed for NAMA, and

(*f*) is obliged to co-operate fully in such audits.

Sections 18 and 37 impose qualification requirements which candidates for appointment to the Board of NAMA or Chief Executive Officer of NAMA must meet in order to be appointed. Similarly officers of NAMA are subject to ongoing obligations in how they conduct themselves in the course of their actions as officers of NAMA. This section requires NAMA to seek to ensure that similar standards are observed by service providers and experts engaged under s.44.

PART 3

FINANCE, PLANNING, ACCOUNTABILITY AND REPORTING

Financing arrangements, expenses and advances from Central Fund

46.—(1) The expenses incurred by NAMA or a NAMA group entity in the performance of NAMA's functions under this Act shall be charged on and paid out of funds at the disposal of NAMA and the NAMA group entities.

(2) The Minister may advance to NAMA or a NAMA group entity such sums of money as are necessary for the performance of its functions from the Central Fund or the growing produce of that Fund on such terms and conditions (including

as to repayment of principal and interest) as he or she determines.

(3) *Subsection (2)* does not affect NAMA's borrowing powers.

NOTES AND COMMENTARY

Various provisions of the Act provide for the payment or reimbursement of the expenses of NAMA in the course of its operations. Examples include s.42(4) which requires NAMA to reimburse the NTMA for the expenses associated with the provision of NTMA staff to NAMA and s.21(1) which permits the payment of remuneration and allowances to Board members as directed by the Minister. This section, together with subsequent sections, explains how NAMA is to finance the payment of these and other expenses. The section does not define the term "expenses". Under s.10(2) achieving the best available financial return for the State is among the purposes of NAMA. Section 11 requires NAMA to perform its functions "in order to achieve its objective" so the reference to expenses must be interpreted in light of s.10(2).

Subsection (1) permits NAMA and NAMA group entities to pay such expenses as are necessary out of their own funds. Subsection (2) allows for the Minister to provide necessary sums from the Central Fund for the payment of expenses by NAMA or NAMA group entities. The Minister is permitted to impose conditions on the provision of Exchequer funding. Requests for Exchequer funding are also limited to requests for sums which are necessary for the performance of NAMA's functions. This may suggest that NAMA should first have regard to its own resources when paying expenses. Should those resources be inadequate it can then apply for an advance from the Central Fund. The consent of the Minister for this latter course of action is required. Presumably the choice between which of the two powers should be used in a given situation is made by the Board in light of NAMA's overall purposes under s.10(2).

Section 12(2)(b) provides NAMA with a power to borrow on such terms as it sees fit. Subsection (3) confirms that the option of obtaining sums necessary for the performance of its functions from the Exchequer does not impact on the power to borrow.

Financing arrangements — Minister may issue debt securities

47.—(1) The Minister may, whenever and so often as he or she thinks fit, create and issue such debt securities that he or she specifies by order, charged on the Central Fund or the growing produce of that Fund and ranking *pari passu* with debt securities issued by the Minister under section 54 of the Finance Act 1970—

(*a*) bearing interest at such rate as he or she thinks fit, or no interest,

(*b*) for such cash or non-cash consideration or deferred consideration as he or she thinks fit, and

(*c*) subject to such terms and conditions as to repayment, repurchase, cancellation and redemption or any other matter as he or she thinks fit.

(2) When the Minister issues securities under this section he or she shall specify which of the following is the purpose of the issue:

(*a*) the financing of the general operations of NAMA and NAMA group entities;

(*b*) the providing of consideration for the acquisition of bank assets.

(3) Securities issued under this section shall be used only for the purpose specified under *subsection (2)*.

NOTES AND COMMENTARY

At Committee Stage in the Dáil the Minister for Finance explained that the words "bearing interest at such rate as he or she thinks fit, or no interest" were intended to afford the Minister the broadest possible discretion in setting interest rates and were included to cover the possibility of central banks setting a negative interest rate. See (22 *Dáil Debates: Special Committee on Finance and the Public Service* Col. 874 (October 28, 2009)).

Financing arrangements — NAMA, etc., may issue debt securities

48.—(1) NAMA or a NAMA group entity may, whenever and so often as it thinks fit, create and issue debt securities—

    (*a*) bearing interest at such rate as it thinks fit, or no interest,

    (*b*) for such cash or non-cash consideration or deferred consideration as it thinks fit, and

    (*c*) subject to such terms and conditions as to repayment, repurchase, cancellation and redemption or any other matter as it thinks fit.

(2) When NAMA or a NAMA group entity issues debt securities under this section NAMA or the NAMA group entity shall specify which of the following is the purpose of the issue:

    (*a*) the financing of the general operations of NAMA or the NAMA group entity, as the case may be;

    (*b*) the providing of consideration for the acquisition of bank assets.

(3) The Minister may guarantee debt securities issued by NAMA or a NAMA group entity under this section.

(4) Securities issued under this section shall be used only for the purpose specified under *subsection (2)*.

    The Minister has made a direction under s.13 in relation to the pricing of government guaranteed debt by NAMA under this section.

    The Minister has exercised his power under subs.(3) to guarantee senior debt securities issued National Asset Management Limited to a maximum sum of €51,300,000,000.

Financing arrangements — NAMA, etc., may issue subordinated debt securities

49.—(1) NAMA or a NAMA group entity may, whenever and so often as it thinks fit, create and issue subordinated debt securities of such class or type as it specifies—

    (*a*) bearing interest at such rate as it thinks fit, or no interest,

    (*b*) for such cash or non-cash consideration or deferred consideration as it thinks fit, and

    (*c*) subject to such terms and conditions as to repayment, subordination, repurchase, cancellation or redemption or any other matter as it thinks fit.

(2) Subordinated debt securities issued under this section shall be used only for the purpose of providing part of the consideration for the acquisition of bank assets in accordance with *section 92*.

(3) To the extent that the terms and conditions of the subordinated debt securities (including the terms of subordination) are referenced to or based on a measure of financial performance, the measure shall be the financial performance of NAMA in totality and not any part or parts of the acquired portfolio.

(4) Subordinated debt securities may be subject to different terms and

conditions for different classes or types of those securities.

(5) The total amount of subordinated debt securities issued under this section shall not exceed 5 per cent of the aggregate total portfolio acquisition value. Such securities will be issued to the participating institutions *pro rata*.

NOTES AND COMMENTARY

As it originally appeared when the Bill was initiated in the Dáil, this section gave the Minister a power to vary by order the total amount of securities issued under the section. Any orders made were to be laid before Dáil Éireann in draft form and a resolution of the Dáil was required before the order could be made. The section was amended and the ceiling of five per cent was inserted at Committee Stage in the Dáil. The Minister for Finance explained that the purpose of utilising subordinated debt instruments was to introduce an element of risk sharing between the State and the participating institutions. The cap of five per cent was chosen to limit the interest bill payable by NAMA while also ensuring that the bonds amounted to adequate compensation for the assets acquired. (See 22 *Dáil Debates: Special Committee on Finance and the Public Service* Cols 888–893).

This section permits NAMA and its group entities to issue subordinated debt securities. The power to issue subordinated debt securities is limited in three ways. First, the power is confined to raising finance as a part of consideration for the acquisition of eligible bank assets. NAMA may not issue subordinated debt for any other purpose. This should be contrasted with the power to issue senior debt under s.48(2)(b). Second, the total issue of subordinated debt securities may not exceed 95 per cent of the overall value of the bank assets acquired. Third, under subs.(5) subordinated debt securities are to be issued to the participating institutions on a pro rata basis.

Financing arrangements — limits on borrowings

50.—(1) NAMA may, from time to time, exercise its power to borrow, with or without the guarantee of the Minister, such sums of money as are required for the performance of its functions under this Act.

(2) The Minister may guarantee the repayment by NAMA or a NAMA group entity of the principal of any sum borrowed by NAMA or the NAMA group entity or the payment of interest on that sum or the repayment of both principal and interest.

(3) The aggregate of the principal of all sums outstanding for purposes other than the provision of consideration for the acquisition of bank assets shall not exceed €5,000,000,000 or such other amount that the Minister specifies by order for the purposes of this subsection.

(4) The aggregate of the principal of all debt securities issued to enable the provision of consideration for the acquisition of bank assets shall not exceed €54,000,000,000 or such other amount as the Minister may specify by order for the purposes of this subsection.

(5) Where the Minister proposes to make an order under *subsection (3)* or *(4)*—

    (*a*) he or she shall cause a draft of the proposed order to be laid before Dáil Éireann, and

    (*b*) he or she shall not make the order unless and until a resolution approving of the draft has been passed by Dáil Éireann.

(6) Within 30 working days after any issue of debt securities under *section 47, 48* or *49*, the Minister shall lay before each House of the Oireachtas a statement giving details of the securities.

NOTES AND COMMENTARY

Section 50 establishes an upper limit on the level of borrowing by NAMA and its group entities. Subsection (1) grants NAMA a power to borrow monies for the performance of its functions. Subsections (3) and (4) impose monetary limits on the power to borrow viz a limit of €54,000,000,000 is established for monies to be paid for acquired bank assets while the rest of NAMA's functions attract a borrowing ceiling of €5,000,000,000. Borrowings beyond these limits would be ultra vires. Although the Minister can raise the limits by order with the consent of the Dáil, there is no power to ratify borrowings which breach the ceilings prior to an extension.

Section 12(2)(b) provides NAMA with a power to borrow for the purposes of achieving its purposes and performing its functions. It is not entirely clear whether that power is to be read as being subject to the limits established in subss.(3) and (4), however since subs.(3) refers to "purposes other than the provision of consideration for the acquisition of bank assets", it is suggested that the s.12 power is subject to the limits.

Application of Borrowing Powers of Certain Bodies Act 1996

51.—Section 5 of the Borrowing Powers of Certain Bodies Act 1996 does not apply to the giving of guarantees, letters of credit or other similar instruments by NAMA or a NAMA group entity.

NOTES AND COMMENTARY

Sections 3 and 5 of the Borrowing Powers of Certain Bodies Act 1996 provide that certain public bodies must obtain the consent of the Minister for Finance before engaging in finance leasing, the issue of debt instruments, discounting of bills of exchange, debtor discounting or other forms of factoring, letters of credit, guarantees and other similar instruments and the securitisation of assets.

This section exempts NAMA from the requirement to obtain the Minister's consent before engaging in the provision of letters of credit, guarantees and other similar instruments. The other requirements of ss.3 and 5 of the 1996 Act are unaffected.

Financing arrangements — treasury services

52.—The NTMA shall provide NAMA with treasury services and advice in connection with debt securities, any borrowings of NAMA and debt securities issued by NAMA or a NAMA group entity, and for any other purpose and in connection with the provision of such treasury services, may enter into transactions of a normal banking nature with any person, as agent of NAMA.

NOTES AND COMMENTARY

NAMA was first announced as a statutory agency "under the aegis of the NTMA" in the Minister for Finance's speech to the Dáil on April 5, 2009 (679 *Dáil Debates* Col. 678). This section builds on the relationship established between NAMA and the NTMA by ss.41 and 42 which require the NTMA to provide services and staff to NAMA. When questioned on the purpose of this arrangement during the Committee Stage debate on s.40 in the Dáil the Minister explained that it was hoped that the arrangement would enable NAMA to benefit from the "substantial international reputation of the NTMA" (22 *Dáil Debates: Special Committee on Finance and the Public Service* Col. 863, October 22, 2009).

The section provides the NTMA with a role in the provision of advice to NAMA on treasury matters. It is clear that NAMA is not required to follow this advice. Under s.9(3) NAMA is required to be independent in carrying out its functions, which would suggest that the Board of NAMA must form their own view as to the correctness or otherwise of the NTMA's advice.

Annual statements

53.—(1) NAMA shall—

    (*a*) for the financial year 2010, before 1 July 2010, and

    (*b*) for each subsequent financial year 3 months before the commencement of it,

prepare a statement that complies with *subsection (3)*, and submit the statement to the Minister.

(2) The Minister shall cause copies of each statement to be laid before each House of the Oireachtas not later than—

    (*a*) in the case of 2010, 30 November 2010, and

    (*b*) in the case of a statement for any other financial year, one month after the beginning of the subsequent financial year.

(3) A statement submitted to the Minister under *subsection (1)* shall specify—

    (*a*) the proposed objectives of NAMA's activities and those of each NAMA group entity for the financial year concerned,

    (*b*) the proposed nature and scope of the activities to be undertaken,

    (*c*) the proposed strategies and policies for achieving those objectives, and

    (*d*) the uses to which it is proposed to apply NAMA's resources and those of each NAMA group entity.

(4) The Minister may omit from a copy of a statement laid before the Oireachtas under *subsection (2)* any matter that would disclose confidential information. If the Minister omits such matter from such a copy, he or she shall insert in its place a statement that matter has been omitted and a general description of the omitted matter.

NOTES AND COMMENTARY

This section imposes an annual requirement on NAMA to disclose its strategic objectives to the Minister for Finance. The Minister for Finance is then obliged to lay a copy of the report before the Houses of the Oireachtas for the information of members.

Subsection (3) permits the Minister to redact portions of the report which are confidential, though the Minister must indicate the fact of redaction and give an outline of the information which has been withheld. The language used in subs.(3) is unique to the NAMA Act. At Committee Stage in the Dáil, the Minister for Finance explained that the need for the power arose from the need for NAMA to operate under a commercial mandate and to permit NAMA to communicate freely with the Minister. (23 *Dáil Debates: Special Committee on Finance and the Public Service* Col. 874 (October 28, 2009)). It would seem that it is the Minister alone who determines whether information needs to be withheld under subs.(3).

Annual accounts

54.—(1) NAMA shall keep, in the form that the Minister directs, proper and usual accounts of money received and expended by it and of all financial transactions undertaken in the performance of its functions.

(2) The accounts shall include a separate account of the administration fees and expenses incurred by NAMA and of each NAMA group entity in the performance of its functions.

(3) The accounts shall include—

(*a*) a list of all debt securities issued for the purposes of this Act,

(*b*) a list of debt securities issued to and redeemed by each participating institution,

(*c*) a list of all advances made to NAMA from the Central Fund,

(*d*) a list of all advances made by NAMA and each NAMA group entity,

(*e*) a list of all asset portfolios held by NAMA and each NAMA group entity, and the book valuation placed on each portfolio, and

(*f*) a list of Government support measures, including any guarantees, received by NAMA and each NAMA group entity, and may include any other information that the Minister considers appropriate.

NOTES AND COMMENTARY

This section obliges NAMA to maintain books of account in the manner directed by the Minister. Subsection (1) requires NAMA to keep "proper and usual accounts", though no elaboration is provided on what is to be considered proper and usual. The phrase has been used in several statutes since 2007 which impose accounting requirements on public bodies. Examples include: s.103 of the Medical Practitioners Act 2007 (imposing accounting obligations on the Health Service Executive (HSE) in respect of the Postgraduate Medical and Dental Board); s.23(2) of the Consumer Protection Act 2007 (accounting obligations of the National Consumer Agency); and s.5(1)(a) of the Carbon Fund Act 2007 (accounting obligations of the National Treasury Management Agency in respect of the Carbon Fund). During the Dáil Committee Stage the Minister for Finance acknowledged that the phrase "'proper and usual' seems somewhat relaxed" and committed to addressing the issue at Report Stage following consultation with the Attorney General. No Report Stage amendment was tabled and the matter does not seem to have arisen in the subsequent parliamentary debates. (See 23 *Dáil Debates: Special Committee on Finance and the Public Service* Col. 931 (October 29, 2009))

Section 202 of the Companies Act 1990 requires companies to maintain books of account which "give a true and fair view of the state of affairs of the company and explain its transactions". Section 202(1) and (3) set out several issues which the accounts must address in order for the company's accounts to meet the "true and fair view" standard. For a detailed analysis of the company law accounting requirements see L. McCann, "Duty to Keep Proper Books of Account" (1991) 9 I.L.T. 177. Unlike the equivalent companies legislation there is no requirement that the accounts be open for inspection by the members of the Board of NAMA (see s.202(8) of the Companies Act 1990).

It is also worth noting s.57, which provides for the audit of NAMA's accounts, requires the Comptroller and Auditor General to certify that the accounts represent a "true and fair" view of the state of affairs of NAMA or a NAMA group entity.

Quarterly reports

55.—(1) Every 3 months NAMA shall make a report (referred to in this Act as a "quarterly report") to the Minister of its activities and the activities of each NAMA group entity.

(2) The first quarterly report shall be for the period ending on 31 March 2010 and shall be submitted to the Minister on or before 30 June 2010. Each subsequent quarterly report shall be for the period ending on a 30 June, 30 September, 31 December or 31 March, and shall be submitted to the Minister within 3 months after the end of the relevant quarter.

(3) The Minister shall cause copies of a quarterly report to be laid before each House of the Oireachtas, and shall send a copy of the report to a Committee (or a subcommittee of such a Committee) appointed by either House of the

Oireachtas or jointly by both Houses of the Oireachtas (other than the Committee on Members' Interests of Dáil Éireann or the Committee on Members' Interests of Seanad Éireann) to examine matters relating to NAMA.

(4) A quarterly report shall be in the form, and shall include information regarding the matters, that the Minister directs.

(5) In a quarterly report, NAMA shall report on its compliance with—

    (a) any guideline issued by the Minister under *section 13*, and

    (b) any direction given by the Minister under *section 14*.

(6) A quarterly report shall include the following information for the relevant quarter:

    (a) the number of all loans outstanding and the condition of those loans, categorised as between performing and nonperforming loans;

    (b) non-performing loans categorised as to the degree of default, distinguishing where default has occurred on capital payment as well as interest payments;

    (c) the number of loans being foreclosed or otherwise enforced during the relevant quarter;

    (d) the number of cases where liquidators and receivers have been appointed in the relevant quarter;

    (e) a list of all legal proceedings (except any proceeding in relation to which a rule of law prohibits publication) commenced by NAMA and each NAMA group entity in relation to bank assets during the quarter, setting out for each proceeding—

        (i) its title,

        (ii) the parties to the proceeding, and

        (iii) the reliefs sought by NAMA or the NAMA group entity concerned;

    (f) a schedule of any finance raised by NAMA and each NAMA group entity in the relevant quarter;

    (g) sums recovered from property sales in the relevant quarter;

    (h) other income from interest-bearing loans owned by NAMA and each NAMA group entity;

    (i) an abridged balance sheet of the assets and liabilities of NAMA and each NAMA group entity;

    (j) a complete schedule of income and expenditure of NAMA and each NAMA group entity in the relevant quarter;

    (k) an updated schedule of all information described in *subsections (2) and (3)* of *section 54*;

    (l) any other matter directed by the Minister.

NOTES AND COMMENTARY

This section requires NAMA to present the Minister with a detailed report on its activities and financial position on a quarterly basis. The report must then be laid before the Oireachtas. It should be noted that the Minister has no power to redact portions of the quarterly report analogous to his powers under s.53(4), which permit him to omit any confidential information from the published copy of NAMA's annual statement of objectives. The difference between the sections may be explained by the fact that s.53 statements relate to NAMA's future objectives and conduct and are thus of greater sensitivity than a statement of NAMA's current and previous actions.

It should be noted that much of the information contained in the quarterly report will already be in the public domain. For instance, information regarding legal actions commenced by NAMA at High Court level is available on an ongoing basis through the Courts Service website. Some details of the finances raised by NAMA and the Minister must be laid before the Houses of the Oireachtas under s.50(6).

Other reports to Minister

56.—(1) The Minister may require NAMA to report to him or her, at any time and in any format that the Minister directs, on any matter, including—

    (*a*) the performance of its functions under this Act, and

    (*b*) any information or statistics relating to the performance of its functions.

(2) NAMA shall comply with a requirement of the Minister under *subsection (1)*.

(3) The content of a report provided to the Minister under this section may be taken to be confidential information.

(4) A reference in *subsection (1)* to the performance of the functions of NAMA includes the performance of those functions by a NAMA group entity.

NOTES AND COMMENTARY

This section enables the Minister to request an additional report from NAMA on any matter. There is nothing to prevent the Minister from using this power to request more regular updates on the matters contained in NAMA's quarterly reports under s.55.

Unlike the other reports made to the Minister by NAMA, a report under s.56 need not be laid before the Houses of the Oireachtas at any time. Subsection (3) provides that the content of a report is to be confidential information, with the consequence that unauthorised disclosure is a criminal offence under s.7.

Audit of accounts by Comptroller and Auditor General

57.—(1) NAMA and each NAMA group entity shall submit its accounts to the Comptroller and Auditor General for audit within 2 months after the end of the financial year to which they relate, and the Comptroller and Auditor General shall—

    (*a*) if he or she is satisfied that the accounts represent a true and fair view of the state of the affairs of NAMA or the NAMA group entity concerned, so certify, or

    (*b*) otherwise qualify the accounts.

(2) NAMA shall present a copy of the accounts of NAMA and each NAMA group entity as audited to the Minister as soon as may be and the Minister shall cause a copy of the audited accounts to be laid before each House of the Oireachtas.

NOTES AND COMMENTARY

This section requires that NAMA's accounts, maintained under s.54 be audited on an annual basis by the Comptroller and Auditor General. Similar provisions are contained in s.12 of the National Treasury Management Agency Act 1990. As with other reports, the Minister is required to lay copies of the audited accounts before the Houses of the Oireachtas.

As noted in relation to s.53, NAMA is required to maintain "proper and usual" accounts.

Under subs.(1)(a) the audit is to examine the accounts' compliance with a "true and fair" view standard.

Accountability to Committee of Public Accounts

58.—(1) The Chairperson, and the Chief Executive Officer, shall, whenever required by the Committee of Dáil Éireann established under the Standing Orders of Dáil Éireann to examine and report to Dáil Éireann on the accounts and reports of the Comptroller and Auditor General, give evidence to that Committee on—

(a) the regularity and propriety of the transactions recorded or required to be recorded in any book or other record or account subject to audit by the Comptroller and Auditor General that NAMA or a NAMA group entity is required by or under an enactment to prepare,

(b) the economy and efficiency of NAMA and each NAMA group entity in its use of the resources made available to it under this Act,

(c) the systems, procedures and practices employed by NAMA and each NAMA group entity for evaluating the effectiveness of its operations, and

(d) any matter affecting NAMA or any NAMA group entity referred to in—

    (i) any special report of the Comptroller and Auditor General under section 11(2) of the Comptroller and Auditor General (Amendment) Act 1993, or

    (ii) any other report of the Comptroller and Auditor General (in so far as it relates to a matter specified in any of *paragraphs (a)* to *(c)*) that is laid before Dáil Éireann.

(2) In appearing before a Committee referred to in *subsection (1)*, the Chief Executive Officer appears as an accountable person and not as an accounting officer.

(3) The Chairperson and the Chief Executive Officer, in giving evidence under *subsection (1)*, shall not question or express an opinion on the merits of any policy of the Government or a Minister of the Government or on the merits of the objectives of such a policy.

NOTES AND COMMENTARY

This is a standard section dealing with appearances by senior officials of public bodies before the Public Accounts Committee. Similar provisions are to be found in s.19 of the Broadcasting Act 2009; s.16 of the Legal Services Ombudsman Act 2009; s.41 of the Dublin Transport Authority Act 2008.

Subsection (1) provides that the Public Accounts Committee may summon the Chairperson and Chief Executive of NAMA to give evidence on the various matters listed in paras (a)–(c). Paragraph (d) permits the committee to seek evidence relating to reports by the Comptroller and Auditor General. Subparagraph (i) permits the committee to question the Chairperson and Chief Executive Officer regarding a special report by the Comptroller and Auditor General. The Comptroller and Auditor General (Amendment) Act 1993 permits the Comptroller and Auditor General to issue a special report when he considers it appropriate to do so. Under s.11(3) the Minister to whom a special report is addressed must cause the report to be laid before Dáil Éireann within three months of the date of receiving the report.

Subparagraph (ii) permits the Committee to examine the Chairperson and Chief Executive as regards other reports of the Comptroller and Auditor General in so far as they relate to matters specified in paras (a)–(c). This would include the audit reports on the NAMA accounts produced under s.57.

Subsection (2) provides that the Chief Executive Officer of NAMA appears before the Committee as an accountable person rather than as an accounting officer. The concept of an accounting officer is the creation of s.22 of the Exchequer and Audit Departments Act 1866 which required the Treasury to designate a public officer to account for the expenditure of monies voted by parliament to a specific department. Section 19 of the Comptroller and Auditor General (Amendment) Act 1993 provides the Public Accounts Committee with a right to ask certain questions of accounting officers appearing before them.

The term "accountable person" is not defined by the Act. There were lengthy discussions at Committee Stage regarding whether or not the Chief Executive Officer should appear before the Public Accounts Committee as an accountable person. The Minister for Finance suggested, on advice from the Comptroller and Auditor General that in order for a person to be an accountable officer for the purposes of the Comptroller and Auditor General (Amendment) Act 1993 that person would have to have a vote from the Oireachtas. (22 *Dáil Debates: Special Committee on Finance and the Public Service* Cols 859, 969–971 (October 28 and 29, 2009)); see also the note to s.38(5).

Subsection (3) is a standard provision regulating the conduct of senior officials giving evidence at the Public Accounts Committee. Equivalents are to be found in s.105 of the Adoption Act 2010; s.22(2) of the Charities Act 2009; and s.43(3)(a) of the Garda Síochána Act 2005.

The Comptroller and Auditor General has produced a report on the acquisition of bank assets by NAMA entitled "Special Report Number 76: 'National Asset Management Agency'". This report was discussed by the Chairperson and Chief Executive Officer of NAMA with the Public Accounts Committee on November 18, 2010.

Appearances before another Oireachtas Committee

59.—(1) The Chairperson and the Chief Executive Officer of NAMA shall, if requested to do so by a Committee (or a subcommittee of such a Committee) appointed by either House of the Oireachtas or jointly by both Houses of the Oireachtas (other than the Committee on Members' Interests of Dáil Éireann or the Committee on Members' Interests of Seanad Éireann) to examine matters relating to NAMA—

> (*a*) attend before that Committee, and
>
> (*b*) provide that Committee with such information as it requires.

(2) The Chairperson and the Chief Executive Officer, in giving evidence under *subsection (1)*, shall not question or express an opinion on the merits of any policy of the Government or a Minister of the Government or on the merits of the objectives of such a policy.

NOTES AND COMMENTARY

This section permits Oireachtas Committees with the exception of the Public Account Committee and the Committees on Members' Interests to compel the attendance of the Chairperson and Chief Executive Officer of NAMA to attend and answer questions. The committees are given a wide ranging power to obtain documents. The Chairperson and Chief Executive Officer are under identical restraints when giving evidence as when appearing before the Public Accounts Committee under s.58(3).

Oireachtas Committees have a general power to compel the attendance of witnesses under s.3, Committees of the Houses of the Oireachtas (Compellability, Privileges and Immunities of Witnesses) Act 1997.

Repayment to Central Fund to redeem debt

60.—(1) NAMA or a NAMA group entity shall repay any funds advanced to it by the Minister out of the resources available to NAMA and the NAMA group entities from time to time.

(2) NAMA may, from time to time, after consultation with the Minister—

(*a*) use any surplus funds of NAMA to redeem and cancel debt securities issued under this Act, and

(*b*) transfer any surplus funds remaining after that redemption to the Central Fund.

(3) The assets of NAMA and of any NAMA group entity at the eventual dissolution of NAMA will be transferred to the Minister or paid into the Exchequer as the Minister directs.

NOTES AND COMMENTARY

Sections 46 authorises the Minister to advance sums to NAMA for the purpose of achieving its functions under the Act. Section 47 authorises the issuing of debt securities by the Minister to provide funds to NAMA. This section permits NAMA to repay sums advanced from its own resources. Although the language of subs.(1) is directive, the inclusion of the phrase "from time to time" seems to indicate that NAMA has a discretion as to whether to use funds it has on hand to repay advances or to apply them to another of NAMA's functions. The legislation does not provide for a timeline for repayment of advances made to NAMA.

Subsection (2) requires NAMA to consult the Minister prior to repaying any of the debt securities issued under the Act. Debt securities can be those issued by the Minister under s.47 or those issued by NAMA under ss.48 and 49. The Minister's role here is consultative only and NAMA is not required to follow the Minister's advice and retains its duty to act independently under s.9(3).

PART 4

DESIGNATION OF CREDIT INSTITUTIONS AS PARTICIPATING INSTITUTIONS AND DESIGNATION OF ELIGIBLE BANK ASSETS

CHAPTER 1

Designation of Participating Institutions

Definition (*Chapter 1*)

61.—In this Chapter "group", in relation to a credit institution, means—

(*a*) the credit institution,

(*b*) its subsidiaries, if any, and

(*c*) any entity of which it is a subsidiary.

NOTES AND COMMENTARY

"Credit institution" and "subsidiary" are defined in s.4(1).

Applications for designation as participating institution

62.—(1) A credit institution may apply to the Minister, within 60 days (or such longer period that the Minister prescribes by order under this subsection) after the establishment day, for it and its subsidiaries to be designated as participating institutions. A credit institution that applies under this subsection shall include all of its subsidiaries in the application (including those that it has requested be excluded from designation).

(2) An applicant credit institution may include in its application a request to exclude particular subsidiaries from designation, and shall give reasons for any requested exclusion.

(3) An application under *subsection (1)* shall be in the form that the Minister directs. The Minister may direct that different forms shall be used for that purpose by different credit institutions.

(4) The Minister may direct an applicant credit institution to provide, as part of its application, a certificate, supported by a statutory declaration, in relation to it and all of its subsidiaries collectively, jointly by the chief executive officer and chief financial officer of the applicant credit institution—

> (a) that since 30 July 2009, it and each of its subsidiaries has dealt in the way required by *section 66(1)* with such of its bank assets as the Minister specifies, or if to any extent it has not done so, the extent to which it has not done so, and

> (b) that the information in the application is accurate and complete.

(5) An applicant credit institution that is a subsidiary shall furnish an undertaking by its parent company to provide any information and do anything else required of the parent company or any other member of its group to enable the Minister to consider the application. The Minister is not obliged to consider an application by a subsidiary if no such undertaking is given.

(6) An applicant credit institution shall undertake to obtain all necessary consents, in accordance with any applicable law including the consents of all its subsidiaries (including subsidiaries that it has requested be excluded from designation) and any necessary consent of any other member of its group. The Minister may consider the relevant application whether or not he or she has evidence that any relevant consent has been obtained and is not required to seek evidence of any such consent.

(7) An applicant credit institution may make an application under this section notwithstanding that at the time of the application it has not yet received any or all of the necessary consents.

NOTES AND COMMENTARY

Five institutions applied and were designated as participating institutions under this section, viz Bank of Ireland, Allied Irish Bank, Anglo Irish Bank, Irish Nationwide Building Society and Educational Building Society.

The Minister for Finance published an application form entitled "Application for Designation as a Participating Institution under the National Asset Management Agency Act 2009" on January 8, 2010.

The section contains two unusual features. First, under subs.62(4)(a) the Minister can request that an applicant institution provide a certificate, supported by a statutory declaration, that it has dealt with its assets in the manner specified in s.66(1) since July 1, 2009. Section 66(1) requires that the bank to exercise an appropriate level of care and skill in relation to eligible bank assets and to deal with them in good faith having regard to the purposes of the Act. July 30, 2009 is the date on which the NAMA Bill was published and thus potential participating institutions would have had notice of the intended shape of the Act from that date. It is notable however that the public consultation draft published on July 30, 2009 indicated that applicant institutions were required to comply with the entirety of the equivalent to s.66. In particular, s.66(2) imposes a wide ranging set of restrictions on an applicant institution's freedom to deal with eligible bank assets without consent of NAMA.

The second unusual feature is contained in subs.(7). It provides that a credit institution may apply for inclusion in the scheme notwithstanding that it has not received "and or all of the necessary consents". The term "consents" is not defined. In subs.(6) applicant institutions are required to give an undertaking to obtain all necessary consents, including consents from its subsidiary. Presumably the term is to be taken as meaning resolutions of boards of directors/ members in general meeting which would be required for a given institution to part take in the scheme. Section (7) seems to have the effect of overriding the internal management rules of companies within a participating institution. That in turn might impact on the rights of shareholders which are constitutionally protected by Arts 40.3.2 and 43 of the Constitution (*Private Motorists' Provident Society v Attorney General* [1983] I.R. 339, see in particular 349). It should be noted that the section does not contain a savings clause equivalent to that found in s.65(3) which would preserve the rights of any members of a subsidiary company to seek a remedy against the company in the event of its engaging in ultra vires activities.

Effect of application for designation, etc.

63.—(1) By making an application under this Chapter the applicant credit institution and all of its subsidiaries shall be taken to undertake, subject to any prohibition in any applicable law, to comply with the provisions of this Act (including this Act as amended from time to time) and of any regulations made under it (including any regulations made designating further classes of bank assets as eligible bank assets), so far as those provisions apply to it as an applicant or participating credit institution. As and from the making of the application they shall be bound to comply with that undertaking.

(2) The service of a notice on, or any communication with, an applicant credit institution is for all purposes effective as service of the notice on, or communication with, every subsidiary of the credit institution.

NOTES AND COMMENTARY

Under this section, institutions applying to be included as participating institutions are deemed to give an undertaking to comply with the requirements of the Act and regulations made under it. This undertaking is deemed to be given by the subsidiaries of a credit institution notwithstanding that the application can be made without the consent of the subsidiaries being obtained (see s.62 and the notes thereto). Communications with a credit institution are also deemed to function as a communication with its subsidiaries which has the effect of transferring the burden of communicating with all elements of a participating institution to the internal management of the institution itself.

Information, etc., to be provided in support of application for designation

64.—(1) An applicant credit institution shall provide any information, explanation, books, documents and records that the Minister requires to consider the application, and in particular shall provide any information, explanation, books, documents and records that the Minister considers necessary to enable him or her to make a decision in relation to the matters set out in *section 67(2)*.

(2) The Minister may direct an applicant credit institution to procure that any of its subsidiaries provides the information, explanation, books, documents and records referred to in *subsection (1)* in relation to the subsidiary.

(3) The Minister may direct an applicant credit institution that any information

provided by the credit institution or any of its subsidiaries under *subsection (1)* or *(2)* is to be certified as accurate and complete jointly by the chief executive officer and chief financial officer of the credit institution.

(4) An applicant credit institution shall, in a certificate under *subsection (3)*, disclose in utmost good faith all matters and circumstances in relation to the credit institution or any subsidiary that might materially affect, or might reasonably be expected to materially affect, the Minister's decision in relation to the matters mentioned in *subsection (2)* of *section 67* (except *paragraph (b)(iv)* of that subsection).

NOTES AND COMMENTARY

Under s.62(3) the Minister for Finance is entitled to designate a form in which applicant institutions must supply information relevant to their application. An application form entitled "Application for Designation as a Participating Institution under the National Asset Management Agency Act 2009" was published on January 8, 2010.

This section permits the Minister to request additional information from applicant institutions or their subsidiaries. Under subs.(3) the Minister may direct that the accuracy of the information be certified in writing by the chief executive officer or the chief financial officer of the institution concerned, though there is no provision for such a certificate to be backed by a statutory declaration as in s.62(4). The Minister's power to request information extends to all the subsidiaries of a credit institution notwithstanding that the institution has applied to exclude the relevant subsidiary from participation under s.62(2).

Capacity of applicant credit institutions, etc.

65.—(1) An applicant credit institution and each of its subsidiaries shall be taken to have, and always to have had, as part of its functions and objects, the power and capacity to—

(*a*) apply for designation as, and become, a participating institution pursuant to this Act,

(*b*) warrant the truth, accuracy and completeness of the information supplied to NAMA in relation to bank assets, and

(*c*) indemnify NAMA in relation to—

(i) any breach of such a warranty, or

(ii) any claim or obligation under *section 135*.

(2) An applicant credit institution and each of its subsidiaries shall be taken to have, and always to have had, as part of its functions and objects, the power and capacity to engage in the following activities in so far as they relate to its designated bank assets:

(*a*) the provision of credit facilities;

(*b*) the entering into of joint venture, partnership, co-ownership, shareholder or other similar agreements;

(*c*) the entering into of contracts (including contracts in a currency other than the currency of the State) whose purpose or one of whose purposes is—

(i) to eliminate or reduce the risk of loss arising from changes in interest rates, currency exchange rates or from other factors of a similar nature, or

(ii) to eliminate or reduce the costs of raising funds or borrowing or the cost of other transactions carried out in the ordinary course of business;

  (*d*) the entering into of contracts to increase the return on an investment (including a credit facility);

and shall be taken to have and always to have had, as part of its functions and objects, the power to engage in any other transaction in so far as it relates to the acquisition of designated bank assets by NAMA.

  (3) Nothing in this section limits the liability of an applicant credit institution or subsidiary to any person based on a transaction beyond its powers. However, any claim based on such a transaction—

  (*a*) is enforceable only against the applicant credit institution or subsidiary and not against NAMA or any NAMA group entity, and

  (*b*) gives rise to a remedy in damages only.

NOTES AND COMMENTARY

  This section purports to confer capacity on credit institutions to make an application for designation as a participating institution. Subsection (2) provides applicant credit institutions with necessary powers for the operation of the NAMA scheme. Under s.25 of the Companies Act 1963 the memorandum and articles of association of a company are a contract between the members and the company as well as the members *inter se*. The section would appear to have the effect of altering the terms of the s.25 contract. In *Borland's Trustee Co v Steele* [1901] 1 Ch 279 at 288, Farwell J. suggested that the text of the memorandum and articles is one of the legal incidents of a share. In *PMPS and Moore v Attorney General* [1983] I.R. 339 at 359. O'Higgins C.J. recognised that such rights attract constitutional protection. This section may therefore interfere with the constitutional property rights of shareholders in applicant credit institutions and their subsidiaries.

  Section 8(2) of the Companies Act 1963 permits member of the company to restrain the commission of ultra vires acts by injunctions. There may also be various remedies available against the company or its directors by way of restitution or the imposition of a constructive trust—for details see T. Courtney, *Law of Private Companies,* 2nd edn (Bloomsbury Professional, 2002), pp.369–373. Section (3)(a) confines remedies arising from the commission of an ultra vires act to actions in damages against the credit institution or the subsidiary concerned. Subsection 3(b) prevents the members of the company from having recourse to injunctive relief under s.8(2) of the 1963 Act. The aim of the section seems to be to minimise the interference with vested property rights identified in the previous paragraph.

Dealings by applicant credit institutions, etc., with eligible bank assets after application for designation

  66.—(1) An applicant credit institution and each of its subsidiaries shall, until the Minister makes or is taken to have made a decision on the application—

  (*a*) administer, service and deal with all of its eligible bank assets in the same manner as, and with the same level of professional skill, care and diligence as, a prudent lender acting reasonably would so administer, service and deal, and

  (*b*) so act in relation to those bank assets in good faith having regard to the purposes of this Act.

  (2) An applicant credit institution and each of its subsidiaries shall not without the prior written approval of NAMA—

  (*a*) deal with any of its eligible bank assets otherwise than in the ordinary course of its business,

  (*b*) deal with any of its eligible bank assets in such a way as to prejudice or impair NAMA's prospective interests or priorities in relation to such a bank asset,

(*c*) compromise, release, vary or relinquish any claim or otherwise take or omit to take any action if its doing so could reduce, lessen or impair any security, right, obligation, ranking or priority held or enjoyed, directly or indirectly, in connection with such a bank asset, or

(*d*) amend or vary any contract relating to such a bank asset unless contractually obliged to do so.

(3) NAMA may issue guidelines or policy statements in relation to the kinds of transactions that it is likely to be prepared to approve under *subsection (2)*.

NOTES AND COMMENTARY

This section restricts the capacity of applicant credit institutions to deal with eligible bank assets while the Minister decides on the outcome of their application for designation under s.67. The obligation to manage the assets in good faith and with the same level of care and skill as would be expected from a prudent lender is mandatory for all applicant institutions in all circumstances. Under s.62(4) applicant institutions are required to certify their compliance with subs.(1) since the publication of the consultation draft of the bill on July 30, 2009. This certificate must be supported by a statutory declaration by the chief executive officer and the chief financial officer of each applicant institutions.

Subsection (2) sets out a range of restrictions on applicants institutions' right to deal with eligible bank assets. These restrictions only apply from the date that an application for designation as a participating institution is made. Unlike the obligations in subs.(1), the restrictions contained in subs.(2) may be waived by NAMA in writing. NAMA's powers under the subsection are confined to approval of proposals from applicant institutions. It has no power to direct an applicant institution to carry out any of the operations listed in paras (a)–(d). Under subs.(3) NAMA may issue guidelines or policy statements on the circumstances where it is likely to give consent under subs.(2). Unlike the codes of practice which NAMA must issue under s.35, NAMA is not required to issue guidelines under subs.(3), nor is it obliged to publish any guidelines or policy statements which it issues under the subsection.

Designation of participating institutions

67.—(1) The Minister, after consultation with the Governor and the [...], may designate an applicant credit institution as a participating institution if the credit institution has applied under *section 62* to be so designated.

(2) The Minister shall not designate an applicant credit institution as a participating institution unless he or she is satisfied that—

(*a*) the applicant credit institution is systemically important to the financial system in the State,

(*b*) the acquisition of bank assets from the applicant credit institution or its subsidiaries is necessary to achieve the purposes of this Act, having regard to—

(i) support that—

(I) is available to,

(II) has been received by, or

(III) in normal commercial circumstances might reasonably be expected, or might reasonably have been expected, to be or to have been available to,

the applicant credit institution or its subsidiaries from the State, any other Member State or a member of the group of the applicant credit institution,

(ii) the financial situation and stability of the applicant credit institution and its subsidiaries,

(iii) the financial situation and stability of the applicant credit institution's group in the event that bank assets are not acquired from the applicant credit institution or its subsidiaries, and

(iv) the resources available to NAMA and the Minister,

and

(*c*) the applicant credit institution has complied with all of its applicable obligations under this Act.

(3) The designation of an applicant credit institution as a participating institution operates to designate as participating institutions all of its subsidiaries except any subsidiary excluded under *subsection (6)*.

(4) Designation (including designation of a subsidiary in accordance with *subsection (3)*) has effect notwithstanding the absence of any necessary consent to the relevant application. Designation of a subsidiary does not prejudice any rights that the subsidiary may have against the relevant applicant credit institution.

(5) Before deciding whether to designate an applicant credit institution as a participating institution, the Minister, having consulted the [Central Bank], may direct that specified due diligence and stress testing of the applicant credit institution or any member of its group be carried out.

(6) If the Minister designates an applicant credit institution as a participating institution, he or she may exclude any subsidiary of the applicant credit institution from designation on any condition that he or she specifies, if he or she is satisfied that the subsidiary should not be designated.

(7) Where the Minister has specified a condition under *subsection (6)* in relation to the exclusion of a subsidiary of an applicant credit institution, and there is a failure to comply with the condition, the Minister may, by written notice to the applicant credit institution and the subsidiary, designate the subsidiary as a participating institution as at and from the date of the notice or a later date that the Minister specifies in the notice.

(8) If the Minister has not designated a credit institution as a participating institution within 3 months after its application under *section 62*, the Minister is taken to have refused the application.

NOTES AND COMMENTARY

Amendment History

References to the Regulatory Authority in subss. (1) and (5) were amended to refer to the Central Bank by s.15(11), Sch.2 Pt 11, of the Central Bank Reform Act 2010.

Comments

The National Asset Management Agency Act 2009 (Establishment Day) Order 2009 (S.I. No. 547 of 2009) appoints the December 21, 2009 as the establishment day for NAMA.

Subsection (1) requires the Minister to consult with the Governor of the […] and the Central Bank in deciding on an application for designation as a participating institution.

Subsection (2) sets out the mandatory criteria which must be satisfied in order for the Minister to accept an application. An application cannot succeed unless all of the criteria are satisfied and the Minister has no discretion to waive any of the criteria. Nor is there any suggestion that the Minister can give greater weight to some criteria over others. Subsection

(8) establishes a three month timeframe for the making of the Minister's decision. Time starts to run from the date on which an application is made. Under s.62, applications are to be made within 60 days of the establishment date or within such a period as the Minister provides for by order. Once an application has been rejected, there is no provision in the Act for a fresh application to be made.

Subsections (3), (6) and (7) deal with the position of subsidiaries of applicant institutions. Under subs.(3) the default position is that a decision to designate a credit institution operates so as to include all the subsidiaries of that institution. Under s.(6) the Minister has a power to conditionally exclude certain subsidiaries if he is not satisfied that they should be designated as forming part of a participating institution. Section 64(2) permits an applicant institution to apply to exclude specific subsidiaries from its application. In determining which, if any, subsidiaries are to be excluded, the Minister is not bound by this application. There is nothing to prevent the Minister from excluding a subsidiary for which no application under s.64(2) was made. The section does not specify the criteria on which the Minister should make this decision. Subsection (7) permits the Minister to include a previously excluded subsidiary where a condition for exclusion set down in subs.(6) is not complied with. There is no time frame set down for the Minister to act under subs.(7).

Section (4) permits the Minister to designate a subsidiary notwithstanding that it has not consented to the making of an application by its parent under s.62. This subsection corresponds to s.62(7) and readers should refer to the notes on that section above.

Obligations of participating institutions

68.—(1) A participating institution shall—

  (a) when making a report, or providing information, books, records or an explanation, whether or not in answer to a request from NAMA or the Minister, make full disclosure in utmost good faith of matters relevant to the making of a decision by NAMA whether or not to acquire a bank asset or the determination of its acquisition value,

  (b) co-operate promptly and fully (including by way of supplying information, books, records and explanations to NAMA in response to any request by NAMA) with NAMA in its due diligence processes in relation to bank assets being considered for acquisition,

  (c) provide such services (including relevant services within the meaning given by *section 128*) as NAMA directs in connection with an acquired bank asset, in accordance with any terms and conditions that NAMA specifies,

  (d) comply with any direction given by the Minister or NAMA in relation to the performance of the participating institution's obligations under this Act,

  (e) comply with such monitoring of lending and balance sheet management as the Minister in consultation with the [Central Bank] directs, and

  (f) comply with any other requirement that the Minister specifies to achieve an effective acquisition of bank assets by NAMA.

(2) A participating institution shall provide such information, explanations, books, documents and records as the Minister requires to perform his or her functions under this Act.

(3) A participating institution shall be taken to have consented to any disclosure of information under *section 205*.

NOTES AND COMMENTARY

Amendment History

Section 15(11) and Sch.2 Pt 11 of the Central Bank Reform Act 2010 (No.23 of 2010) amends the reference "Regulatory Authority" to "Central Bank" in subs.(1)(e).

Comments

Subsection (1) imposes various duties on participating institutions to comply with the instructions from NAMA. No consequences are provided for breach of these obligations by the sections. In s.130 there is a provision which would seem to allow a participating institution to be made liable for breaches of their obligations under the Act.

Subsection (2) permits the Minister to demand the disclosure of book, records etc., to enable him to perform his functions under the Act. The Act does not provide an exhaustive description of the Minister's functions but as the Minister has an important role under s.69 in relation to the designation of eligible bank assets for which access to the book and records of participating institutions would be of clear importance.

Section 205 permits the Minister, the Governor of the Central Bank and the Central Bank to share information received from participating institutions. The power is restricted by the EU treaties and the statute of the ESCB. Information disclosed may be used by the recipients in the performance of their functions.

CHAPTER 2

Designation of Eligible Bank Assets

Eligible bank assets

69.—(1) The Minister may, after consultation with [NAMA and the Governor], and considering the purposes of NAMA and the resources available to the Minister, prescribe, by regulation, classes of bank asset as classes of eligible bank asset.

(2) The classes of bank assets prescribed under *subsection (1)* may include—

    (*a*) credit facilities issued, created or otherwise provided by a participating institution—

        (i) for the purpose, whether direct or indirect and whether in whole or in part, of purchasing, exploiting or developing development land,

       (ii) where the security connected with the credit facility is or includes development land,

      (iii) where the security connected with the credit facility is or includes an interest in a company engaged in purchasing, exploiting or developing development land,

      (iv) where the credit facility is directly or indirectly guaranteed by a company referred to in *subparagraph (iii)*,

       (v) directly or indirectly to a debtor who has provided security referred to in *subparagraph (ii) or (iii)*, or

      (vi) directly or indirectly to a person who is an associated debtor of a debtor to whom a credit facility described in any of *subparagraphs (i)* to *(iii)* has been provided,

    (*b*) credit facilities and classes of credit facilities (other than credit facilities referred to in *paragraph (a)*) relating to debtors or associated debtors of participating institutions (or classes of debtors or associated debtors of participating institutions) where the total amount of indebtedness in respect of such facilities is such that, in the opinion of the Minister, acquisition by NAMA is necessary for the purposes of this Act,

(*c*) other rights arising directly or indirectly in connection with a credit facility described in *paragraph (a)* or *(b)* including—

    (i) a contract to which the participating institution is a party or in which it has an interest,

    (ii) a benefit to which the participating institution is entitled, and

    (iii) any other asset in which the participating institution has an interest,

(*d*) bank assets associated with bank assets specified in *paragraphs (a)* and *(b)*, and

(*e*) any other class of bank asset of a participating institution the acquisition of which the Minister is of opinion, after consultation with the Commission of the European Communities, is necessary for the purposes of this Act.

(3) In forming an opinion for the purpose of *subsection (2)(b)*, the Minister may take into account—

(*a*) the total number of credit facilities or classes of credit facilities provided by the participating institution to those debtors and associated debtors or classes of debtors and associated debtors, and

(*b*) the aggregate indebtedness of debtors and associated debtors or classes of debtors or associated debtors referred to in *subsection (2)(b)* owed to any other participating institution.

(4) A bank asset that is in a class prescribed under *subsection (1)* is referred to in this Act as an "eligible bank asset".

(5) A class of bank asset prescribed under *subsection (1)* shall be taken not to include a credit facility that entered a participating institution's balance sheet after 31 December 2008. For the avoidance of doubt, where a credit facility entered a participating institution's balance sheet on or before 31 December 2008, but security was taken for the credit facility after that date, and the credit facility is otherwise an eligible bank asset, the credit facility is an eligible bank asset.

(6) Notwithstanding *subsection (5)*, a bank asset in a prescribed class is an eligible bank asset if, in the opinion of NAMA, the related credit facility entered a participating institution's balance sheet on or before that date even if renegotiated or refinanced after that date. For the purposes of determining whether a credit facility entered a participating institution's balance sheet on or before 31 December 2008, NAMA may take into account the terms of any renegotiation, restructuring or refinancing of a credit facility effected after 31 December 2008.

NOTES AND COMMENTARY

Amendment History

In subs.(1), the reference to "NAMA, the Governor and the Regulatory Authority" was substituted for "NAMA and the Governor" by s.15(11), Sch.2 Pt 11 of the Central Bank Reform Act 2010 (No.23 of 2010).

Comments

The Minister exercised his powers under subs.(1) to issue the National Asset Management Agency (Designation of Eligible Bank Assets) Regulations 2009 (S.I. No. 568 of 2009) on December 23, 2009.

This section permits the Minister to define the scope of an eligible bank asset by regulation. Subsection (2) provides an indicative list of categories which the Minister may include within the definition. There is no time limit on the use of the Minister's powers. Section 97(3) suggests that the Minister may make more than one designation of bank assets under this section.

Subsection (5) provides that assets which fall within a designated class are only to be considered eligible where the assets in question were on an eligible institution's balance sheet before December 31, 2008. Subsection (6) permits NAMA to take account of terms regarding restructuring, reorganisation and refinancing when applying subs.(5) to particular bank assets. Such terms would also have to be considered by the expert reviewer when determining whether a particular bank asset is eligible or not under s.114.

In *Dellway Investments v NAMA* [2010] IEHC 364, the High Court held (at [9.15]) that there was nothing in this section, or in the regulations made under it which "which restricts the classes of bank assets which may be acquired by NAMA to impaired assets or assets associated with impaired borrowers".

In *Dellway Investments v NAMA* [2010] IESC 14, the Supreme Court considered arguments that s.69 was unconstitutional. The appellants had argued that the definition of eligible assets in subs.(2), coupled with NAMA's broad discretion as to which assets should be acquired (see s.84) would make it impossible for a court to properly judicially review decisions about the acquisition of assets since the court would be unable to determine whether the decision was *intra vires* NAMA or not. The Attorney General argued that there is no constitutional impediment to the use of very broad definitions in civil statutes. In the alternative, the Attorney General argued, the provisions of s.69 were not unnecessarily broad having regard to the functions and purposes which NAMA and the NAMA legislation was designed to achieve.

In the unanimous judgment of the Supreme Court, Murray C.J. held that "the Oireachtas was entitled, as a matter of policy, to include in the Act a very broad definition of eligible bank asset". In particular, the court noted that it seemed to the court to be "entirely rational" for the Oireachtas to adopt such a course in order to avoid the risk that bank borrowings which pose a threat to the financial stability of the banking sector would fall outside the scope of the Act. Murray C.J. stated that the court was satisfied that s.69 when read in light of s.84 (which governs the acquisition of eligible bank assets by NAMA) was sufficiently certain to enable judicial review to be carried out in the usual manner. The court noted that the arguments made by the applicant were similar to the sort of arguments which might be made in a challenge to the compatibility of the Minister's power to make regulations under subs.(1) with Art.15 of the Constitution; however, since no separation of powers arguments had been made by the appellants, the point was not decided by the court.

Meaning of "associated debtor" in this Act

70.—(1) For the purposes of this Act, a person is an "associated debtor" of a debtor if the person—

    (*a*) is or was at any time directly or indirectly indebted or otherwise obligated to a participating institution under or in connection with a credit facility, and

    (*b*) is or was at any time—

        (i) a body corporate that was a subsidiary of, or a related company (within the meaning given by section 140(5) of the Companies Act 1990) to, the debtor,

        (ii) a nominee of the debtor, including a person who may or does in fact act at the express or implied direction or instruction of the debtor or another associated debtor of the debtor,

       (iii) acting in the capacity of trustee of a declared or undeclared trust the beneficiaries of which include (directly or indirectly)—

          (I) the debtor,

          (II) a person referred to in *subparagraph (ii)*, or

          (III) a body corporate controlled by the debtor or a person referred to in that subparagraph,

       (iv) in partnership, within the meaning of the laws of any relevant place, with the debtor, in relation to a bank asset which at the time of the partnership was, or subsequently became, of a class of bank assets prescribed under *section 69(1)*,

       (v) a body corporate of which the debtor is the sole member, or

      (vi) a body corporate controlled by the debtor,

      or

    (*c*) a member of any other class of person prescribed by the Minister for the purposes of this subsection.

(2) For the purposes of *subsection (1)(b)(vi)*, a body corporate shall be taken to be controlled by a debtor if the debtor is (whether alone or together with any one or more of the persons mentioned in *subparagraphs (i)* to *(v)* of *subsection (1)(b)*, and whether directly or indirectly)—

    (*a*) interested in one-quarter or more of the equity share capital of the body, or

    (*b*) entitled to exercise or control the exercise of one-quarter or more of the voting powers at any general meeting of the body.

(3) In *subsection (2)*—

    (*a*) "equity share capital" has the same meaning as it has in section 155 of the Companies Act 1963, and

    (*b*) the reference to voting power exercised by a debtor includes voting power exercised by a nominee of the debtor or another body corporate which that debtor controls.

(4) Section 54 of the Companies Act 1990 applies for the purpose of determining, for the purposes of *subsection (2)*, whether a person holds an interest in shares.

Notes and Commentary

    This section sets out the definition of associated debtor. In the Committee Stage debate in the Dáil, the Minister explained that the concept was necessary in order to ensure that the entire exposure of a particular borrower was captured by the legislation and to ensure that NAMA would be able to acquire all loan assets required to fulfil its purposes. (23 *Dáil Debates: Special Committee on Finance and the Public Service* Col. 1032 (October 29, 2009)).

Dealings by participating institutions with eligible bank assets

71.—(1) A participating institution shall, until it has been served with a completion notice or NAMA directs otherwise—

    (*a*) administer, service and deal with all of its eligible bank assets in the same manner as, and with the same level of professional skill, care and diligence as, a prudent lender acting reasonably would so administer, service and deal, and

    (*b*) so act in relation to those bank assets in good faith having regard to the purposes of this Act.

(2) A participating institution shall not without the prior written approval of NAMA—

    (*a*) deal with any of its eligible bank assets otherwise than in the ordinary course of its business,

    (*b*) deal with any of its eligible bank assets in such a way as to prejudice or impair NAMA's prospective interests or priorities in relation to such a bank asset,

    (*c*) compromise any claim or release, vary, relinquish or otherwise take or omit to take any action if its doing so could reduce, lessen or impair any security, right, obligation, ranking or priority held or enjoyed, directly or indirectly, in connection with such a bank asset, or

    (*d*) amend or vary any contract relating to such a bank asset unless contractually obliged to do so.

(3) NAMA may issue guidelines or policy statements in relation to the kinds of transactions that it is likely to be prepared to approve under *subsection (2)*.

NOTES AND COMMENTARY

This section continues the obligations imposed on applicant institutions' capacity to deal with bank assets between the time of their designation by the Minister for Finance as participating institutions under s.67 and the completion of the acquisition process by NAMA.

PART 5

VALUATION METHODOLOGY

Interpretation (*Part 5*)

72.—(1) In this Part "property" means property that is the subject of the security for a credit facility that is a bank asset.

(2) In this Part:

    (*a*) a reference to the market value of property is a reference to the estimated amount that would be paid by a willing buyer to a willing seller in an arm's-length transaction after proper marketing (where appropriate) where both parties act knowledgeably, prudently and without compulsion,

    (*b*) a reference to the market value of a bank asset is a reference to the estimated amount that would be paid by a willing buyer to a willing seller in an arm's-length transaction after proper marketing (where appropriate) where both parties act knowledgeably, prudently and without compulsion,

    (*c*) a reference to the long-term economic value of property is a reference to the value, as determined by NAMA in accordance with this Part, that it can reasonably be expected to attain in a stable financial system when the crisis conditions prevailing at the passing of this Act are ameliorated and in which a future price or yield of the property is consistent with reasonable expectations having regard to the long-term historical average, and (*d*) a reference to the long-term economic value of a bank asset is a reference to the value, as determined by NAMA in accordance with this Part, that it can reasonably be expected to attain in a stable financial system when the crisis conditions prevailing at the passing of this Act are ameliorated.

NOTES AND COMMENTARY

This section defines the various values which are used throughout this Act to determine the price to be paid by NAMA when acquiring bank assets. Subsections (2)(a) and (2)(b) provide for the use of a familiar methodology of valuation by reference to a hypothetical transaction between a willing buyer and a willing seller.

The language used in this section is more elaborate than the standard language used in assessing compensation for compulsorily acquired property. Section 2(3) of the Acquisition of Land (Assessment of Compensation) Act 1919 simply refers to the price which a willing seller would achieve in the open market. Similarly s.548(1) of the Taxes Consolidation Act 1997 refers to the price which assets "might reasonably be expected to fetch on the open market." Thus the references to "proper marketing" as well as the knowledge and prudence of the parties seem to be a unique feature of this section. For this reason it is difficult to state with any certainty how the previous authorities on the valuation of land should be applied to this section.

For details of the assessment rules under the Acquisition of Land (Assessment of Compensation) Act 1919, see S. McDermott and R. Woulfe, *Compulsory Purchase and Compensation: Law and Practice in Ireland* (London: Butterworths, 1992), Ch.10.

Determination of acquisition values — valuation dates, etc.

73.—(1) NAMA may specify a date or event by reference to which the market value of a bank asset or type of bank asset or property or type of property is to be determined.

(2) Under *subsection (1)* NAMA may specify different dates or events for any or any type of bank assets or property.

(3) Under *subsection (1)* NAMA may specify a date before the coming into operation of this Act.

(4) The specification of a date or event under *subsection (1)* has effect for the determination of a market value for any purpose under this Act (including for the purposes of *Chapter 2* of *Part 7*).

NOTES AND COMMENTARY

The date for the purposes of valuation is set by NAMA alone and without consultation with the Minister or the NTMA.

Under subs.(3) NAMA is entitled to set acquisition dates in advance of the commencement of the Act. A number of sections of the Act have elements of retrospective effect (see for instance s.62(1) and s.111(3)(d)); however in most cases the retrospective element is limited to the date on which the consultation draft of the Bill was published. Subs.(3) contains no such limitation.

The date specified under this section plays an important role in the calculation of long-term economic values under the National Asset Management Agency (Determination of Long-Term Economic Values of Property and Bank Assets) Regulations 2010. See notes to s.75 for details.

Determination of acquisition values — guidelines, etc.

74.—NAMA may, for the purpose of determination of values in accordance with this Part, adopt such guidelines or rules as it considers necessary for efficiency or consistency.

NAMA is not required to consult or seek the approval of the Minister for guidelines issued under this section. The power to make guidelines is subject to the Minister's power to make regulations governing the determination of long term economic value under ss.75, 76 and 79. Thus any NAMA guidelines on the issue will have to be compatible with the National Asset Management Agency (Determination of Long-Term Economic Value of Property and Bank Assets) Regulations 2010 (S.I. No. 88 of 2010).

The section seems to regard guidelines issued under it as internal documents of NAMA. Unlike the codes of practice issued under s.35 of the Act, there is no obligation on NAMA to publish these guidelines.

Acquisition values

75.—(1) Subject to *subsection (2)* and any regulations made by the Minister under *subsection (3)*, the acquisition value of a bank asset is its long-term economic value as determined by NAMA.

(2) NAMA may, if it considers it appropriate after consultation with the Minister, and subject to any regulations made by the Minister under *subsection (3)*, having regard to—

(*a*) the purposes of this Act,

(*b*) the expected date of acquisition of the bank asset concerned,

(*c*) the type of bank asset,

(*d*) the laws of the European Communities governing State aid, and

(*e*) any other relevant matter affecting valuation,

determine that the acquisition value of a bank asset shall be—

(i) its market value, or

(ii) a value (between its long-term economic value and its market value) that NAMA considers appropriate in the circumstances, having regard to the matters specified in *paragraphs (a)* to *(e)*.

(3) The Minister may make regulations for the purposes of the application of *subsection (2)*. For that purpose the Minister shall have regard to the factors set out in *paragraphs (a)* and *(c)* to *(e)* of *subsection (2)*.

The National Asset Management Agency (Determination of Long-Term Economic Value of Property and Other Bank Assets) Regulations 2009 (S.I. No. 546 of 2009) were made by the Minister on December 21, 2009. These regulations were repealed by the second set of regulations. The second set of regulations, the National Asset Management Agency (Determination of Long-Term Economic Value of Property and Other Bank Assets) Regulations 2010 (S.I. No. 88 of 2010). The amending regulations entered into force on March 3, 2010.

This section provides for NAMA to establish the price at which it will acquire bank assets. Subsection (1) sets out the general rule that NAMA shall acquire assets at their long term-economic value. The methodology for determining long-term economic value is set out at s.76.

Subsection (2) authorises NAMA to depart from the primary rule set out in subs.(1). The decision to pay a sum other than long-term economic value is to be taken by NAMA and would presumably require a resolution of the Board. NAMA must consult with the Minister in advance of taking such a decision and the Minister has the option of setting limits to NAMA's use of this power by making regulations under subs.(3). NAMA is also required to have regard to the matters listed in paras (a) to (e). This list is not exhaustive of the matters to which NAMA may have regard. Under subs.(2) NAMA can only pay a sum which is between the market value and the long-term economic value. NAMA has no authority to pay more than the long-term economic value for bank assets.

Subsection (3) permits the Minister to make regulations which prescribe the circumstances in which NAMA may utilise its discretion under subs.(2). Unlike NAMA, the Minister is not required to have regard to the likely date of the acquisition or to the European rules on state aid when making regulations under this provision. However if such considerations are relevant the Minister is permitted to have regard to them under subpara.(2)(e).

Determination of long-term economic values

76.—(1) NAMA shall determine the long-term economic value of a bank asset having regard to the following:

(*a*) the market value of the property;

(*b*) the market value of the bank asset;

(*c*) the long-term economic value of the property;

(*d*) the long-term economic value already determined by NAMA, in accordance with the valuation methodology, of any other similar property or bank asset;

(*e*) any report prescribed under *section 78* that is reasonably available to NAMA when it carries out the valuation of the particular property or bank asset,

in accordance with—

(i) any regulations made by the Minister under *section 79*, and

(ii) the laws of the European Communities governing State aid.

(2) Notwithstanding any other provision of this Act or any regulations made under it—

(*a*) the long-term economic value determined by NAMA for a parcel of land shall not exceed the market value of the parcel by more than such fraction as the Minister may determine by regulations for the purposes of this paragraph,

(*b*) the total long-term economic value of all land held as security in an acquired portfolio shall not exceed the total market value of that land by such fraction as the Minister may determine by regulations for the purposes of this paragraph,

(*c*) NAMA may determine that, with regard to any particular class of property, or in the particular circumstances applicable to a parcel of land, its long-term economic value shall not exceed its market value, and

(*d*) the long-term economic value of a bank asset shall be calculated on the basis of net present value methodology.

<small>NOTES AND COMMENTARY</small>

This section sets out the valuation methodology for calculating the long-term economic value of bank assets. Each asset must be valued separately and NAMA must have regard to each of the factors listed in subs.(1).

The National Asset Management Agency (Determination of Long-Term Economic Value of Property and Other Bank Assets) Regulations 2009 (S.I. No. 546 of 2009) were made by the Minister on December 21 2009. These regulations were repealed by the second set of regulations. The second set of Regulations, the National Asset Management Agency

(Determination of Long-Term Economic Value of Property and Other Bank Assets) Regulations 2010 (S.I. No. 88 of 2010). The amending regulations entered into force on March 3, 2010.

In determining the long-term value of land for the purposes of this section, the Regulations require NAMA to apply an "adjustment factor" to the market value. The calculation of the adjustment factor is governed by reg.5. Under reg.5 the adjustment factor is to be set by NAMA "in such manner as it thinks fit" by reference to any of a list of factors set out in the Regulations which it thinks are appropriate.

Where the asset is a bank asset reg.7 details the valuation methodology. Where the bank asset is secured on land, NAMA is required to take account of a sliding scale of discount rates depending on the size of the adjustment factor for the land determined in accordance with regs 5 and 6. NAMA is also required to take account of the long term value of the property and various other aspects of the value of the property on which the asset is secured.

Subsection (2)(a) permits the Minister to establish a ceiling for long term economic value. Under reg.9 of the National Asset Management Agency (Determination of Long-Term Economic Value of Property and Other Bank Assets) Regulations 2010 (S.I. No. 88 of 2010) this is set at one quarter of the market value of the asset.

Subsection 2(b) imposes a further restriction on the valuation of the acquired portfolio of each participating institution. The Minister is required to establish a ceiling for the total long term economic value of a portfolio. Under reg.9(2) of the National Asset Management Agency (Determination of Long-Term Economic Value of Property and Other Bank Assets) Regulations 2010 (S.I. No. 88 of 2010) this is set at one fifth of the aggregate market value of the land in the portfolio.

Subsection 2(c) allows NAMA to set additional limits on the long-term value of certain properties of classes of asset.

Subsection 2(d) requires the use of a net present value methodology in the valuation of bank assets.

Market values

77.—(1) In determining the market value of property, NAMA may take into account—

    (*a*) any value that the participating institution concerned submits as being, in its opinion, the market value of the property,

    (*b*) any report prescribed under *section 78* that is reasonably available to NAMA when it carries out the relevant valuation, and

    (*c*) the market value already determined by NAMA of another similar property.

(2) In determining the market value of a bank asset NAMA may take into account—

    (*a*) any value that the participating institution concerned submits as being, in its opinion, the market value of the bank asset,

    (*b*) the market value already determined by NAMA of any other similar bank asset,

    (*c*) the creditworthiness of the debtor or obligor concerned,

    (*d*) the performance of that asset, and

    (*e*) the market value of property determined by NAMA under *subsection (1)*.

NOTES AND COMMENTARY

The market value of property and of bank assets is defined in s.72 and represents the lowest sum which NAMA is permitted to pay under s.75(2) when acquiring property or bank assets. This section sets out factors to which NAMA may have regard when determining the market value of property. Among the factors are the reports to be specified under s.78 by the

Minister for Finance (see the notes to that section for further detail).

It is not clear whether NAMA is confined to considering the factors listed in the section when determining market values. In particular, the question may arise as to whether NAMA is entitled to have regard to the statutory rules for determining market value in compulsory purchase schemes under s.2 of the Acquisition of Land (Assessment of Compensation) Act 1919. The use of the term "may" would seem to indicate that consideration of these factors is optional and that NAMA may adopt an alternative methodology for reaching a valuation. In *People (Attorney General) v McGlynn* [1967] 1 I.R. 238, Ó'Dálaigh C.J. treated the words "shall" and "may" as being interchangeable. Dodd suggests whether a provision is mandatory or not, is matter of interpretation (See D. Dodd, *Statutory Interpretation* (Tottel, 2007) p.320). In regard to this section it seems likely that the term "may" is used in a permissive sense, since the market value of property and bank assets is prescriptively defined in s.72(b).

Regulations in relation to certain reports

78.—The Minister may make regulations prescribing reports or classes of reports (including reports prepared before the commencement of this Act) concerning factors or matters relevant to the valuation of property or of property of a particular type or in specific locations or with specific features or benefits, including—

(*a*) zoning,

(*b*) availability of utilities,

(*c*) availability of similar property in similar locations,

(*d*) historic value of property in particular locations, and

(*e*) recent valuations of similar property in similar locations.

NOTES AND COMMENTARY

This section permits the Minister to determine by regulation the reports and other matters to which NAMA may refer when determining valuations in this Part. Under s.77 such reports may be taken into account by NAMA when determining the market value of property. The Minister has not used his powers under this section. This is in contrast to the National Asset Management Agency (Determination of Long-Term Economic Value of Property and Other Bank Assets) Regulations 2010 (S.I. No. 88 of 2010). Schedules 1 and 2 to the Regulations list a number of sources of statistical information on land prices in Ireland and elsewhere to which NAMA is required to have regard to when determining the long-term value of land located in the State or in other jurisdictions.

Regulations in relation to determination of values

79.—(1) The Minister may make regulations relating to the determination by NAMA of the long-term economic value, or the market value, of a bank asset or a class of bank asset or a property or a class of property, including the matters that NAMA shall or may derive, use, apply or take into account for those purposes.

(2) In making regulations for the purposes of *subsection (1)*, the Minister shall have regard to the laws of the European Communities governing State aid and any relevant guidance issued by the Commission of the European Communities, and may have regard, and may include such provisions relating, to such of the following as he or she thinks appropriate:

(*a*) with reference to the long-term economic value of property—

(i) the extent to which the price or yield of such property has deviated from the long-term historical average,

      (ii) supply and demand projections by reference to the type of asset and its location,

     (iii) macroeconomic projections for growth in the gross domestic product and for inflation or deflation,

     (iv) demographic projections,

      (v) land and planning considerations (including national, regional or local authority development or spatial plans) that may exert an influence on the future value of the asset concerned,

     (vi) analyses presented by the Minister for the Environment, Heritage and Local Government on the extent to which existing land zoning and planning permissions granted and in force meet or exceed projected growth requirements,

    (vii) analyses presented by the Dublin Transportation Office or any national transport authority of existing and future transport planning and the associated supply and demand projections for land use,

   (viii) any analysis by the Minister for Communications, Energy and Natural Resources in relation to the potential rise in energy and other costs due to the long-term decline in non-renewable resources,

     (ix) the specification, for the purposes of the determination of the long-term economic value of particular parcels of land, of a fraction by which the long-term economic value determined by NAMA shall not exceed the market value of each such parcel,

      (x) the specification, for the purposes of the determination of the long-term economic value of all land held as security in acquired portfolios, of a fraction, by which the long-term economic value of that land shall not exceed its total market value;

  (*b*) with reference to the long-term economic value of bank assets—

      (i) the long-term economic value of property,

     (ii) the net present value of the anticipated income stream associated with bank assets of that kind,

    (iii) in the case of rental property, current and projected vacancy rates,

    (iv) loan margins,

     (v) an appropriate discount rate to reflect NAMA's cost of funds plus a margin that represents an adequate remuneration to the State that takes account of the risk in relation to the bank assets acquired by NAMA,

    (vi) the mark-to-market value of any derivative contracts associated with bank assets of that kind,

   (vii) any ancillary security such as personal guarantees and corporate assets, and

  (viii) fees reflecting the costs of loan operation, maintenance and enforcement;

  (*c*) such other matters that he or she considers relevant to the long-term economic value or market value of property or bank assets including—

(i) matters to be derived, used, applied, taken into account or not taken into account;

(ii) the values to be attributed to any matters or the adjustments to be made in or by virtue of their application;

(iii) the data, criteria, information, rules and methodology that may be used or applied in determining the value or application of any matters or in deriving any matters to be used or applied;

(iv) the use of the net present value methodology in determining the value of any property or bank asset;

(v) the appropriate discount rate to reflect NAMA's cost of funds plus a margin that represents an adequate remuneration to the State that takes account of the risk in relation to the acquired bank assets to be applied in determining the net present value of a cash flow;

(vi) the specification, for the purposes of attribution and application across all bank assets, or all bank assets of a particular class, of a standard discount rate, to be attributed to or applied in the calculation of each bank asset, or each bank asset of the particular class, as the case may be, acquired by NAMA, which in the opinion of the Minister is necessary or appropriate to provide for enforcement costs, due diligence costs and other relevant costs incurred or likely to be incurred by NAMA over its lifetime in the discharge of its functions;

(vii) the extension of the maturity date of any bank asset for such period as NAMA considers appropriate after its actual maturity to allow a reasonable period for its management and enforcement;

(viii) the types or classes of property in respect of which the market value shall be deemed to be the longterm economic value.

(3) Every regulation made under *subsection (1)* shall be laid before each House of the Oireachtas as soon as may be after it is made and, if a resolution annulling the regulation is passed by either such House within the next 21 days on which that House has sat after the regulation is laid before it, the regulation shall be annulled accordingly, but without prejudice to the validity of anything previously done under the regulation.

NOTES AND COMMENTARY

This section confers power on the Minister to make regulations setting out the valuation methodology to be followed by NAMA when determining market and long-term economic values of bank assets and other property. The Minister must exercise this power having regard to the laws of the European Communities and to guidance issued by the European Commission The European Commission published a Communication on the Treatment of Impaired Assets within the Community Banking Sector (*http://ec.europa.eu/competition/state_aid/legislation/ impaired_assets.pdf* [accessed on January 8, 2011]) which would seem to be relevant to the making of such regulations.

The section goes on to provide a detailed list of factors to which the Minister may have regard when making regulations under this section. It would seem to follow from the wording of subs.(2) that the Minister is not required to take all of these factors into consideration, although regard to Community law and any guidance issued by the European Commission is mandatory. Subsection (3) requires that copies of such regulations be laid before the Houses of the Oireachtas with the possibility of annulment by a vote of either House.

The Minister has twice exercised his power under subs.(3) to make regulations. The first set of regulations; the National Asset Management Agency (Determination of Long-Term Economic Value of Property and Other Bank Assets) Regulations 2009 (S.I. No. 546 of 2009) were repealed by the second set of regulations; the National Asset Management Agency (Determination of Long-Term Economic Value of Property and Other Bank Assets) Regulations 2010 (S.I. No. 88 of 2010). For details see the notes to s.76.

PART 6

ACQUISITION OF BANK ASSETS AND RELATED MATTERS

CHAPTER 1

Acquisition of Bank Assets

Applicant credit institutions and participating institutions to provide information about eligible bank assets

80.—(1) NAMA may direct an applicant credit institution or a participating institution to provide NAMA with information, in the form directed by NAMA, about each of its bank assets, and (in the case of an applicant credit institution) each bank asset of each of its subsidiaries, that may be an eligible bank asset. In the case of a participating institution, such a direction has effect as a direction to provide that information about the bank assets of the participating institution and each of its subsidiaries that is also a participating institution.

(2) In particular, NAMA may require the provision of information about the debtors, associated debtors, guarantors and sureties concerned and the enforceability and marketability of the security associated with each such bank asset.

(3) When an applicant credit institution or participating institution provides information about bank assets under *subsection (1)* or *(2)*, it shall, if it is of the opinion that a bank asset is not an eligible bank asset, state that fact, that it objects to the acquisition of the bank asset, and the reason for the opinion. If an applicant credit institution or a participating institution wishes to object to the proposed acquisition of a bank asset, it shall do so in that way and the objection shall be dealt with in accordance with *Chapter 1* of *Part 7*.

(4) In a direction under *subsection (1)*, NAMA may require that the information concerned is to be provided in a particular specified manner or form, including by way of tranches described by reference to debtors, associated debtors, security or in any other way.

(5) NAMA may direct an applicant credit institution or a participating institution that any information provided by the applicant credit institution, any of its subsidiaries or the participating institution under *subsection (1)* or *(2)* is to be certified as accurate and complete jointly by the chief executive officer and chief financial officer of the applicant credit institution or participating institution.

(6) An applicant credit institution or participating institution shall, on request by NAMA, provide NAMA with a report or a certificate or both, in the form directed by NAMA, about—

(*a*) any of its bank assets, or those of a subsidiary, that may be eligible bank assets, or

(*b*) any information relevant to the determination of the terms of acquisition (including the acquisition value) of any such bank asset.

(7) An applicant credit institution or a participating institution shall, in a report or certificate under *subsection (5)* or *(6)*, disclose in utmost good faith all matters and circumstances in relation to each bank asset concerned that might materially affect, or might reasonably be expected to materially affect, NAMA's decision to acquire the bank asset or the determination of its acquisition value.

(8) Notwithstanding any legal or contractual restriction, NAMA and a NAMA group entity may disclose to each other any information, or any report, certificate or other document, that either one obtains in connection with the performance of any of its functions.

NOTES AND COMMENTARY

Subsections (1) and (2) empower NAMA to request information from participating institutions and applicant institutions about any asset which may be an eligible bank asset. Where a direction is given to an applicant institution, the direction applies to all subsidiaries of that institution, whereas in the case of a participating institution the direction does not apply to any subsidiaries which have been excluded from participation by the Minister under s.67(6).

Under subs.(1) and (4) NAMA is entitled to specify the form in which information is to be provided. Under subs.(2) the information requested may extend to information about debtors, associated debtors, guarantees and sureties as well as information about the security associated with bank assets. Under s.201 the obligation to disclose information to NAMA applies to personal information within the meaning of the Data Protection Acts 1988 and 2003.

Subsection (3) makes clear that the obligation to provide information about bank assets which may be eligible applies notwithstanding that the participating institution proposes to object to the acquisition of the asset under Pt 7 of the Act.

Subsection (5) provides for NAMA to require the chief executive and chief financial officers of applicant or participating institutions to certify that information provided under subs.(1) and (2) is accurate and complete.

Subsection (6) enables NAMA to demand a report or certificate from a participating or applicant institution relating to specific bank assets. As with subs.(1) and (2), the scope of this power is limited to assets which may be eligible bank assets. Unlike a request made under subs.(1) there is no power to require the chief executive and chief financial officers of the institutions concerned to certify that the information is accurate; however subs.(7) does impose a duty of disclosure in the utmost good faith on the institutions concerned when responding to a request for information under subs.(6).

Subsection (7) also applies the duty of disclosure in the utmost good faith to the applicant or participating institutions when certifying information as accurate and complete under subs.(5). Somewhat strangely, the section does not apply the duty of utmost good faith to the chief executive and chief financial officers individually when providing such a certificate. In contrast to s.62(4), certificates under subs.(5) are not supported by a statutory declaration by the officers concerned and it seems liability for inaccurate certificates would be confined to the institutions concerned. It should, however, be noted that s.7(2) imposes criminal liability on a person who intentionally, recklessly or through gross negligence provides false information to NAMA.

The power to request information under this section is confined to NAMA itself and does not extend to a NAMA group entity. Subsection (8) authorises the sharing of information between NAMA and its group entities notwithstanding any legal or contractual duty of confidentially which may bind either body. Subsection (8) is not confined to information obtained by NAMA under this section and it would seem that it creates a general exemption from contractual and legal duties of confidence for information obtained by NAMA or a NAMA group entity in the performance of their functions.

Production of documentation, books and records for inspection

81.—(1) An applicant credit institution or a participating institution shall, if NAMA so requests, produce to NAMA for inspection the credit facility documentation, books and records kept in connection with any eligible bank asset. The applicant credit institution or participating institution shall give NAMA such facilities for inspecting and taking copies of the contents of any such documentation, book or record as NAMA requires.

(2) NAMA may direct an applicant credit institution or a participating institution to procure that any of its subsidiaries—

    (*a*) produces to NAMA for inspection the credit facility documentation, books and records kept in connection with any eligible bank asset, and

    (*b*) gives NAMA such facilities for inspecting and taking copies of the contents of any such documentation, book or record as NAMA requires.

(3) If an applicant credit institution, participating institution or subsidiary is required under *subsection (1)* or *(2)*—

    (*a*) to produce documentation or a book or record in connection with a bank asset to NAMA, or

    (*b*) to provide facilities to NAMA to inspect or take copies of the contents of any such documentation, book or record,

and fails to do so, NAMA may apply to the Court, on notice to the credit institution or participating institution for an order directing the credit institution, participating institution or subsidiary to produce the documentation, book or record, or provide the facilities, as the case requires.

(4) The Court may make an order pursuant to the application under *subsection (3)* if the Court is satisfied that the production of the documentation, book or record, or the provision of the facilities sought is reasonably necessary to enable NAMA to perform any of its functions under this Act. The Court may make any interlocutory order (including a mandatory order) that it considers necessary in the circumstances.

(5) If the Court is satisfied that for reasons of commercial confidentiality a hearing under this section should be conducted otherwise than in public, the Court may so order.

(6) Subject to the privilege against self-incrimination, a document, book or record produced by a person in answer to a request or order under this section is admissible in evidence.

NOTES AND COMMENTARY

Subsections (1) and (2) extend NAMA's powers under s.80 to request information from applicant and participating institutions, by permitting NAMA to demand the production of books and records relating to eligible bank assets. Institutions which are the subject of request under subs.(1) have a duty to supply NAMA with facilities for inspection and copying such books and records. The section does not make any provision for the costs of such facilities. Under subs.(2) NAMA may require an applicant or participating institution to procure documents from their subsidiaries. Unlike s.80(1) this power applies to all of a participating institution's subsidiaries and not just those who have been designated as participating by the Minister.

Subsection (3) applies for the enforcement of subs.(1) and (2) by way of an application to the High Court. In contrast to s.80(1), there is no express provision governing disputes between NAMA and the institutions of whether a particular asset is an eligible bank asset or not. Presumably this question would have to be determined by the court in an application under s.81(3) since the obligation to make disclosure applies only to eligible bank assets.

Under subs.(4), the court must make an order following an application under subs.(3) where it is satisfied that the production of documents is reasonably necessary for NAMA to perform any of its functions under the Act.

Subsection (4) provides for the granting of interlocutory relief including a mandatory order where the court considers this to be "necessary in the circumstances". The statute is silent as to the level of necessity required and it is not clear whether an application for interlocutory relief would be decided in accordance with the ordinary principles governing such injunctions (see *Campus Oil v Minister for Energy (No.2)* [1993] I.R. 88). The phrase "necessary in the circumstances" seems to be a new statutory formula and it is not found in other statutory provisions authorising the issue of interlocutory injunctions. It may be that the court might be persuaded to have regard to the public interest elements of NAMA's functions when considering the balance of convenience under *Campus Oil.*

Some guidance may be obtained by comparison with s.160(3)(a) of the Planning and Development Act 2000 which also provides for the issuing of a statutory interlocutory injunction. That section permits the court to make such order "as it considers appropriate". Kirwan suggests that Section 160 injunctions should be decided on the ordinary *Campus Oil* criteria, citing a dictum of O'Sullivan J. in *Martin v An Bord Pleanála,* unreported, High Court, July 24, 2002, in which the learned judge suggested that the *Campus Oil* principles apply to all applications for interlocutory injunctions (see B. Kirwan, *Injunctions: Law & Practice* (Dublin: Round Hall, 2008), p.460).

It is also worth noting that there is Irish authority which suggests that mandatory orders are unusually difficult to attain at an interlocutory stage. In *Boyhan v Tribunal into the Beef Processing Industry* [1993] 1 I.R. 210 at 223, the High Court indicated that the applicant would have to establish "a strong and clear case—so that the court can feel a degree of assurance that at a trial of the action a similar injunction would be granted". The effect of the statutory test of "necessary in the circumstances" in this context is unclear.

Subsection (5) permits the court to hear an application under this section other than in public where it is satisfied that this is appropriate in light of commercial confidentiality. In *Re R Ltd* [1989] 1 I.R. 126, Finlay C.J. held that exceptions to the constitutional principle that justice shall be administered in public must be narrowly construed and availed of only in the interests of justice. Walsh J., at 137, writing for the majority, held that in addition to satisfying the relevant statutory test (in that case s.205(7) of the Companies Act 1963), the applicant would have to show that a public hearing "would fall short of doing justice".

Subsection (6) permits the admission into evidence of any document or book disclosed under this section. This is subject to the privilege against self-incrimination in line with Ireland's obligations under art.6 of the European Convention on Human Rights (see *Saunders v United Kingdom* (1996) 23 E.H.R.R. 313); as to the position in domestic law see *Re National Irish Bank Ltd* [1999] 3 I.R. 134.

Provision of information and explanations, etc.

82.—(1) An applicant credit institution or a participating institution shall provide any information and explanations requested by NAMA in relation to the matters referred to in *sections 80* and *81* or any other matter relevant to the acquisition of a bank asset, and shall also secure that an officer or staff member of the applicant credit institution or participating institution shall provide an explanation of any such information, documentation, book or record, including an explanation of any apparent omission from the information, documentation, book or record.

(2) NAMA may direct an applicant credit institution or participating institution to procure that any of its subsidiaries provides the information or explanations

referred to in *subsection (1)* in relation to the bank assets of the subsidiary.

(3) If an applicant credit institution or participating institution is required to secure that an officer or staff member of the applicant credit institution, subsidiary or participating institution provides an explanation or information under this section, and fails to do so, NAMA may apply to the Court, on notice to the applicant credit institution or participating institution, for an order directing the applicant credit institution, subsidiary or participating institution to secure the provision of the explanation or information.

(4) The Court may make an order referred to in *subsection (3)* if the Court is satisfied that the provision of the explanation or information sought is reasonably necessary to enable NAMA to make a decision whether to acquire the bank asset concerned or determine its acquisition value. The Court may make any interlocutory order (including a mandatory order) that it considers necessary in the circumstances.

(5) If the Court is satisfied that for reasons of commercial confidentiality a hearing under this section should be conducted otherwise than in public, the Court may so order.

(6) Subject to the privilege against self-incrimination, information provided by a person in answer to a request or order under this section is admissible in evidence.

NOTES AND COMMENTARY

This section re-enforces NAMA's powers to obtain information by permitting NAMA to require an applicant or participating institution to provide information and explanations about any materials obtained under ss.80 and 81. In addition applicant and participating institutions may also be required to secure such explanations or information from their officers, employees and subsidiaries.

Subsections (3)–(6) provide for an application to court to compel compliance with a request from information or an explanation under this section. Such an application can be made against an applicant or participating institution as well as its officers, employees and subsidiaries. The substantive provisions governing the application are identical to s.81(3)–(6) and readers should refer to the notes to that section.

Obligations to cooperate and act in good faith, etc.

83.—(1) If a person who is a debtor, associated debtor, guarantor or surety of a credit facility has been notified that the credit facility is an eligible bank asset, the person shall co-operate and shall, in good faith, promptly furnish to the participating institution such information relating to the eligible bank asset concerned as the participating institution requests for the purposes of its compliance with a requirement or direction under *section 80, 81 or 82*.

(2) If a person referred to in *subsection (1)* fails to comply with a requirement of that subsection, the participating institution concerned may apply to the Court, on notice to the person, for an order directing the person to comply with the requirement in any way specified in the order, and shall notify NAMA that it has done so.

(3) The Court may make an order (including a mandatory order) under *subsection (2)* if the Court is satisfied that the compliance sought is reasonably necessary to enable the participating institution concerned to comply with the requirement or direction under *section 80, 81 or 82*. The Court may make any

interlocutory order that it considers necessary in the circumstances.

(4) If the Court is satisfied that for reasons of commercial confidentiality a hearing under this section should be conducted otherwise than in public, the Court may so order.

(5) Subject to the privilege against self-incrimination, a document, book or record produced by a person in answer to a request or order under this section is admissible in evidence.

(6) If a participating institution suffers loss as a result of a debtor, guarantor or surety failing to comply with an obligation under *subsection (1)*, the debtor, guarantor or surety shall be liable in damages to the participating institution.

NOTES AND COMMENTARY

This section creates a duty on debtors under eligible bank assets to supply information to participating institutions which have been made the subject of a request for information from NAMA. The section applies solely to participating institutions unlike ss.80, 81 and 82 under which NAMA has powers to request information and explanations from applicant institutions. Where co-operation is not forthcoming, the participating institution has the ability to apply to the High Court for the same remedies as are provided for NAMA by ss.81 and 82 (for details see the notes to s.81).

Under subs.(5), any document given by a person under this section is admissible in evidence subject to the privilege against self-incrimination. It should be noted that this section is not limited to litigation under the section, or indeed under the NAMA Act and thus documents or other evidence disclosed under this section may be admissible in a wide range of contexts other than criminal proceedings against the debtor.

Subsection (6) permits the participating institution to recover any losses incurred as a result of a breach of good faith or by delay on the part of the debtor in complying with its obligations under subsection (1).

Decision about acquisition of eligible bank assets

84.—(1) NAMA may acquire an eligible bank asset of a participating institution if NAMA considers it necessary or desirable to do so having regard to the purposes of this Act and in particular the resources available to the Minister. NAMA is not obliged to acquire any particular, or any, eligible bank asset of such an institution on any grounds.

(2) For the avoidance of doubt, NAMA may acquire, from a participating institution, performing or non-performing eligible bank assets.

(3) For the avoidance of doubt, NAMA may, subject to *Chapter 1 of Part 7*, take steps to acquire an eligible bank asset even though the participating institution concerned has indicated in information provided to NAMA under *section 80* that it does not consider the bank asset to be an eligible bank asset and that it objects to its acquisition.

(4) Without prejudice to the generality of *subsection (1)*, NAMA may, in deciding whether to acquire a particular eligible bank asset, take into account—

    (*a*) whether any security that is part of the bank asset is adequate,

    (*b*) whether any security that is part of the bank asset has been perfected,

    (*c*) the value of that security,

    (*d*) whether the relevant credit facility documentation is defective or incomplete, (*e*) whether the participating institution concerned or any other person has engaged in conduct concerning the bank asset that is or could be prejudicial to the position of NAMA,

(*f*) whether the participating institution has complied with its contractual and legal obligations and its obligations under this Act in relation to the bank asset, or its eligible bank assets generally,

(*g*) whether in NAMA's opinion the participating institution has advanced a sufficient quantum of the credit facility concerned,

(*h*) the quality of the title to any property held as security that is part of the bank asset,

(*i*) any applicable legal, regulatory or planning requirement that has not been complied with in relation to development land held as security that is part of the bank asset,

(*j*) any association with another bank asset of a participating institution,

(*k*) the performance of the bank asset,

(*l*) any matter disclosed in any due diligence carried out by the participating institution or NAMA,

(*m*) the type of other eligible bank assets (whether of the participating institution or any other participating institution) that NAMA has acquired or proposes to acquire, and whether not acquiring the particular eligible bank asset concerned would contribute to the achievement of the purposes of this Act, and

(*n*) any other matter that NAMA considers relevant.

(5) Where NAMA determines that the long-term economic value of the property comprised in the security for a credit facility that is an eligible bank asset is less than the market value of the property, NAMA shall not acquire the bank asset.

NOTES AND COMMENTARY

This section authorises NAMA to acquire bank assets. Subsections (1)–(3) make clear that the NAMA is to make the decision whether to acquire any particular asset. The decision is to be taken in light of the purposes of the NAMA as set out in s.10 of the Act, and the resources provided to NAMA by the Minister.

This section was considered in detail by the High Court in *Dellway Investments v NAMA* [2010] IEHC 364. There the court held that s.84 invests NAMA with a broad discretion when deciding what bank assets it should acquire. The court held that the only consideration which NAMA is positively obliged to take into account when deciding which assets to acquire is the total level of resources provided to NAMA by the Minister. In particular at [6.14], the court stated that the contents of subs.(4) are "permissive rather than mandatory" and that NAMA is not required to have regard to these factors when making its decisions (see [6.26]). The court also held that NAMA is not required to have regard to whether a loan is performing or non-performing. The High Court's decision on this issue was appealed to the Supreme Court but no decision was made on the appeal since the issue was rendered moot by the Supreme Court's disposal of other aspects of the appeal.

It should be noted that under subs.(5) NAMA may not acquire a bank asset if the long-term economic value of the property on which the asset is secured is less than its market value.

NAMA to identify eligible bank assets for acquisition

85.—(1) NAMA shall identify such of the eligible bank assets of a participating institution as NAMA proposes to acquire.

(2) NAMA may, for the purposes of identifying eligible bank assets that it proposes to acquire, consult with the participating institution concerned, but is not obliged to do so. The participating institution shall co-operate expeditiously with NAMA in any such consultation.

(3) If a participating institution has stated in information provided under *section 80* that it does not consider a particular bank asset that NAMA proposes to acquire to be an eligible bank asset and that it objects to its acquisition, NAMA may—

    (*a*) agree not to acquire the bank asset, or

    (*b*) continue with the proposed acquisition and refer the matter to the expert reviewer.

(4) If NAMA proposes to continue with a proposed acquisition in accordance with *subsection (3)(b)*, NAMA shall notify the participating institution concerned of that fact as soon as may be.

(5) NAMA shall inform the participating institution of its proposed timetable for the acquisition of the eligible bank assets identified for acquisition. The timetable may specify that identified bank assets will be acquired on different dates.

NOTES AND COMMENTARY

This section requires NAMA to identify the individual bank assets it decides to acquire under s.84. Participating institutions are required to co-operate with this process and to enter into such consultations as NAMA requires for this purpose. Such consultations are in addition to NAMA's extensive powers to acquire information from participating and applicant institutions under ss.80, 81 and 82. As with s.81, where there is a dispute between NAMA and a participating institution regarding the eligibility of a particular asset for acquisition, the question is to be determined by the expert reviewer under Pt 7 and there is to be no delay in the acquisitions process pending the outcome of the review.

In *Dellway Investments v NAMA* [2010] IEHC 364 the applicant argued that borrowers were entitled to make representations to NAMA as to whether banks assets involving their loans should be acquired. The basis of this claim was that several of the applicant's rights would be adversely affected if NAMA were to acquire its loans. In particular the borrower argued that it had constitutionally protected contractual and quasi-contractual rights in its relationship with its existing bank and that its reputation would be adversely affected were it to "go into NAMA".

The applicant's main contention under the contractual heading was that it had built up a substantial relationship with its banks over several years. The applicant claimed that its relationship gave rise "implicit understandings" and offered expert evidence that the relationships were an important component of any business project. The applicant argued that such rights constituted valuable property which would be adversely affected if its loans were acquired by NAMA. In rejecting this argument the court noted that the applicant's loans did not contain provisions prohibiting their bank from assigning its interest in the loans. Thus the applicant did not have a contractual right capable of protecting its relationship with its banks. Secondly, the court noted that the applicant's contractual relationship with its banks has to be viewed in the context of the deterioration in the commercial position of the participating institution over recent years. Both of the institutions from which the applicant had borrowed had been the recipients of state supports and the court noted that it was unlikely that either could have continued to trade in the absence of such support. In light of that fact, the court held that even if the applicant had any legally enforceable right to its relationship with its banks, this would have no relevance in a context where the banks' position would have been significantly altered by recent events. (see [7.23]–[7.32])

Under the reputational heading the applicant offered evidence that its commercial reputation would be damaged if it were associated with NAMA. The argument was founded on evidence of a public perception of NAMA as a "bad bank". The court dismissed the argument noting that it is not possible "to legislate for misinformation or for the forming of an ill-informed view" ([7.33]).

The applicant's third major contention was that the powers of NAMA differ substantially from those granted to its banks under the relevant loan agreements. The court noted that while the Act did confer powers on NAMA which were capable of causing some alteration in the applicant's position these were not sufficiently significant to justify granting relief.

Overall the court held that the applicant was not entitled to be heard by NAMA when making decisions under this section since the acquisition process did not pose "any significant or proximate threat with a constitutionally protected right, so as to require fair procedures be adhered to" ([7.54]). The High Court's decision on this issue was appealed to the Supreme Court but no decision was made on the appeal since the issue was rendered moot by the Supreme Court's disposal of other aspects of the appeal.

NAMA may specify general terms and conditions of acquisition

86.—(1) NAMA may, from time to time, specify the terms and conditions that are to apply generally to the acquisition of eligible bank assets.

(2) The terms and conditions specified under *subsection (1)* may include the following warranties:

 (*a*) a warranty (which may be subject to any legal reservation approved by NAMA in a particular case) that the security for the relevant bank asset is enforceable;

 (*b*) a warranty that any land that is the security for the bank asset has good and marketable title;

 (*c*) a warranty that the facts in the participating institution's report in relation to the bank asset are complete and accurate;

 (*d*) a warranty that any certificate provided in relation to the bank asset is accurate and complete;

 (*e*) any other warranty customarily included in transactions for the purchase of bank assets.

(3) In relation to any particular acquisition NAMA may amend or vary the terms and conditions specified under *subsection (1)* as it thinks fit, but if it does so, it shall set out the amendment or variation in the relevant acquisition schedule.

NOTES AND COMMENTARY

This section permits NAMA to set and amend the terms on which it acquires bank assets. The section seems to envisage NAMA developing a standard set of terms and conditions which will apply generally to a number of acquisitions. The section does not contain anything preventing NAMA from altering its terms with each transaction. The warranties in subs.(2) are clearly examples of potential uses of this power and do not bind NAMA in the context of any specific transaction. The general terms and conditions of acquisition do not include the determination of the acquisition value. The date on which the acquisition value will be paid to the participating institution is set by s.92(3).

NAMA to prepare acquisition schedule

87.—(1) When NAMA has identified an eligible bank asset of a participating institution that NAMA proposes to acquire, and has determined the acquisition value of that asset, NAMA shall serve on the institution a schedule (referred to in this Act as an "acquisition schedule").

(2) NAMA may nominate a NAMA group entity as the entity that is to acquire a bank asset identified for acquisition.

(3) An acquisition schedule shall set out for each eligible bank asset to be acquired—

    (*a*) a statement of the eligible bank asset and the interest to be acquired,

    (*b*) a statement of any obligations or liabilities excluded from the acquisition,

    (*c*) the acquisition value,

    (*d*) details of how the acquisition value was calculated,

    (*e*) any obligations, additional to those imposed by this Act, to be imposed on the participating institution after the acquisition that are to take effect after the acquisition,

    (*f*) the date of acquisition, and

    (*g*) if the eligible bank asset is not to be acquired by NAMA itself, the NAMA group entity that will acquire it.

(4) In addition to the matters required by *subsection (3)*, NAMA may set out in an acquisition schedule any other matter (including any terms and conditions) that it considers necessary in the particular case.

(5) For the avoidance of doubt, an acquisition schedule may specify any number of particular eligible bank assets.

(6) For the avoidance of doubt, NAMA may serve more than one acquisition schedule on a participating institution.

(7) The date of acquisition of a designated bank asset shall be at least 28 days after the relevant acquisition schedule is served on the participating institution concerned unless NAMA specifies a shorter period in the acquisition schedule.

Notes and Commentary

This section provides for NAMA to set out the details of the assets which it proposes to acquire from a particular participating institution in one or more acquisition schedules. The format of an acquisition schedule is dictated by subs.(3) which sets out a list of information which must be included in a schedule.

Once an acquisition schedule is served, the date of acquisition will be determined in accordance with the terms of the schedule. Subsection (7) provides a default 28-day-period between the service of the acquisition schedule and the date of the acquisition of the asset. There is no timescale governing the preparation of acquisition schedules; however the Minister has issued a direction to NAMA under s.14 requiring it to complete the acquisition process as soon as possible.

In *Dellway Investments v NAMA* [2010] IEHC 364, the High Court noted (at [7.46]) that where an obligation is excluded from acquisition schedule under subs.(3)(b) it remains fully enforceable against the participating institution.

Subsections (3)(e) and (4) continues the approach of s.86 in affording NAMA a broad discretion to set the terms of the acquisitions. It would seem that NAMA has the ability to insert specific terms and conditions into an acquisition schedule which relate to the acquisition of individual bank assets. Other than NAMA's powers and functions as set out in ss.11 and 12 there appears to be no limit to the content of the terms and conditions which NAMA might impose under this section.

Errors or omissions in proposed acquisition schedules

88.—A participating institution may apply to NAMA in writing for the correction of an obvious error or omission in an acquisition schedule. An application under this section is not an objection for the purposes of *section 80* and *section 114*.

NOTES AND COMMENTS

Section 80 provides that a participating institution may object to the acquisition of a bank asset on the basis that it is not an eligible asset. Section 114 provides that objections to the acquisition of bank assets are confined to the grounds specified in s.80. There is no timeframe specified for the making of an application under s.88, however s.89 confines NAMA's ability to amend an acquisition schedule to the period between the date of service and the date of the earliest acquisition date therein.

Amendment of acquisition schedule

89.—(1) After service of an acquisition schedule on a participating institution, but before the earliest acquisition date specified in the acquisition schedule, NAMA may—

(*a*) revoke the acquisition schedule, or

(*b*) amend the acquisition schedule in relation to the bank asset in any way.

(2) Without prejudice to the generality of *subsection (1)(b)*, NAMA may amend an acquisition schedule in any of the following ways:

(*a*) to omit or add a bank asset;

(*b*) to alter the description of such an asset;

(*c*) to alter the acquisition date of such an asset;

(*d*) to alter the acquisition value of such an asset;

(*e*) to alter any of the terms and conditions of the acquisition schedule;

(*f*) to correct an obvious error or omission.

(3) When NAMA has amended an acquisition schedule (in this subsection called the "original acquisition schedule"), NAMA shall serve an amended acquisition schedule on the participating institution. Where NAMA does so, the amended acquisition schedule has effect in place of the original acquisition schedule.

(4) When NAMA has revoked an acquisition schedule, NAMA shall serve on the participating institution a notice of the revocation. The revoked acquisition schedule is of no effect from the date of that service.

(5) References in this Act to an acquisition schedule include an acquisition schedule that has been amended in accordance with this section.

NOTES AND COMMENTARY

This section permits NAMA to amend an acquisition schedule between the date of service and the earliest date on which a bank asset is acquired under the schedule. Subsection (2) appears to be illustrative in nature rather than providing an exhaustive list of NAMA's powers of amendment, though it seems likely that an amended acquisition schedule would have to be in compliance with s.87(3). Subsection (2)(e) contains an express power for NAMA to rectify an acquisition schedule in response to a request under s.88. There appears to be no limit on the number of times which NAMA may amend an acquisition schedule and the time period for amendment can be extended by amending the acquisition date under subs.(2)(e). Under s.121(2)(b) NAMA may also revoke an acquisition schedule where the participating institution objects to the valuation placed on a bank asset.

Effect of service of acquisition schedule

90.—(1) Subject to *subsection (7)*, the service of an acquisition schedule on a participating institution in accordance with *section 87 or 89* operates by virtue of this Act to effect the acquisition of each bank asset specified in the acquisition schedule by NAMA or the specified NAMA group entity, on the date of acquisition specified in the acquisition schedule as the date of acquisition of the bank asset, notwithstanding that the consideration for the acquisition has not been paid.

(2) The acquisition of a bank asset pursuant to *subsection (1)* is subject to the terms and conditions set out in the acquisition schedule and any general terms and conditions specified by NAMA under *section 86(1)* except to any extent that the acquisition schedule excludes or modifies such specified terms and conditions.

(3) Unless otherwise provided in an acquisition schedule, where an eligible bank asset is acquired, every relevant contract is deemed to be assigned to NAMA or the specified NAMA group entity, as the case may be.

(4) In *subsection (3)* "relevant contract" means a contract—

    (*a*) relating to the bank asset,

    (*b*) to which the participating institution is a party or in which it has an interest, and

    (*c*) the existence of which has been disclosed to NAMA in writing.

(5) Unless otherwise provided in an acquisition schedule, where an eligible bank asset is acquired, NAMA or the specified NAMA group entity, as the case may be, becomes entitled to the benefit of—

    (*a*) any certificate of title, solicitor's undertaking, warranty, valuation, report, certificate or document issued to the participating institution or upon which the participating institution is entitled to rely in connection with the asset,

    (*b*) an instruction, order, direction, bond, opinion, search, enquiry, declaration, consent, notice, power of attorney, authority or right given to, held by or issued for the benefit of, directly or indirectly, the participating institution in connection with the asset, and

    (*c*) any other benefit arising under or in connection with any insurance or assurance policy or payment direction relating to the asset.

(6) Subject to *section 91*, *subsections (1)*, *(3)* and *(5)* have effect in relation to a bank asset notwithstanding—

    (*a*) any legal (including contractual) or equitable restrictions on the acquisition of the bank asset or any part of it,

    (*b*) any legal or equitable restriction, inability or incapacity relating to or affecting any matter referred to in the acquisition schedule (whether generally or in particular) or any requirement for a consent, notification, authorisation, licence or document to similar effect (by whatever name and however described), in each case,

    (*c*) any insignificant or immaterial error or any obvious error, or

    (*d*) any provision of any enactment to the contrary.

(7) The service of an acquisition schedule on a participating institution in accordance with *sections 87* and *89* does not have the effects mentioned in *subsections (1)*, *(3)* and *(5)* in relation to a bank asset if—

(*a*) notwithstanding that the participating institution stated in information provided under *section 80* that it did not consider the bank asset to be an eligible bank asset, and that it objected to its aquisition NAMA decided under *section 85(3)* to take steps to acquire the bank asset, and

(*b*) on the acquisition date—

    (i) the Minister has not confirmed the inclusion of the bank asset in the acquisition schedule in accordance with *section 117*, or

    (ii) NAMA—

        (I) has amended the acquisition schedule to remove the bank asset from the acquisition schedule, or

        (II) has revoked the acquisition schedule in accordance with *section 89* or *121*.

Notes and Commentary

This section provides for the transfer of rights of the participating institution in bank assets identified in an acquisition schedule. Under subss.(1) and (2) property in the bank asset is transferred to NAMA on the acquisition date specified in the acquisition schedule prepared in accordance with s.87. The acquisition is subject to the general terms and conditions imposed by NAMA under s.86 as well as any specific terms specified in the acquisition schedule.

Under the section the acquisition schedule is a self-executing document which comes into force on the acquisition date specified on its face. No action is required on the part of the participating institutions. The only exceptions to this principle are set out in subs.(7) which provide for a situation where the participating institution has disputed the eligibility of the bank asset or where NAMA itself has reconsidered its decision to acquire a particular bank asset.

Subsection (6) has the effect of overriding any legal or equitable restrictions on the transfer of any bank assets. Subsection (6) purports to remove such restrictions so that debtors would be unable to rely on the principles established in *Linden Garden Securities Ltd v Lenesta Sludge Disposals Ltd* [1994] 1 A.C. 85. The section also overrides the requirements for, inter alia, notification of the debtor in the legal assignment of a chose in action under s.28(6) of the Supreme Court of Judicature (Ireland) Act 1877.

In *Dellway Investments v NAMA* [2010] IEHC 364, the High Court held that the applicant debtor had no right to fair procedures because in part because it had no contractual right to object to an assignment of its loans by its banks. It is not clear how the court would respond to the attempted acquisition of a loan which contained a non-assignment clause. Such clauses may create constitutionally protected property rights in the debtor. Whether NAMA would be permitted to rely on subs.(6) to override an objection from the debtor is not clear.

Effect of service of acquisition schedule in relation to foreign bank assets

91.—(1) In this Part—

"foreign bank asset" means a bank asset in which the transfer or assignment of any right, title or interest that NAMA proposes to acquire is governed in whole or in part by the law of a state (including the law of a territorial unit of a state) other than the State;

"foreign law", in relation to a foreign bank asset or a transaction in relation to a foreign bank asset means the law of a state other than the State.

(2) In this section, where a bank asset is to be acquired by a NAMA group entity, a reference to NAMA in this section (but not in *sections 92* and *93* as applied by *subsection (10)*) shall be construed as a reference to the NAMA group entity.

(3) To the extent that a bank asset proposed to be acquired by NAMA is or

includes a foreign bank asset—

> (*a*) if the law governing the transfer or assignment of the foreign bank asset permits the transfer or assignment of that asset, the participating institution shall if NAMA so directs do everything required by law to give effect to the acquisition, or
>
> (*b*) if the relevant foreign law does not permit the transfer or assignment of the foreign bank asset, the participating institution shall if NAMA so directs do all that the participating institution is permitted to do under that law to assign to NAMA the greatest interest possible in the foreign bank asset.

(4) A participating institution, to the extent that a foreign bank asset is one to which *subsection (3)(b)* applies—

> (*a*) is subject to duties, obligations and liabilities as nearly as possible corresponding to those of a trustee in relation to that bank asset, and
>
> (*b*) shall hold the bank asset for the benefit and to the direction of NAMA,

in each case subject to the nature of, and the terms and conditions of the acquisition of, the foreign bank asset.

(5) *Subsection (3)* applies in so far as the service of an acquisition schedule would not, of itself, as a matter of foreign law, operate to give effect to the acquisition of a foreign bank asset or otherwise effect or achieve the result referred to in that subsection in relation to such a bank asset.

(6) Without prejudice to *subsection (4)*, a participating institution shall, immediately upon being so directed by NAMA to do so, execute and deliver to NAMA any contract, document, agreements, deed or other instrument that NAMA considers necessary or desirable to ensure that there is effected a binding acquisition by NAMA or the NAMA group entity concerned, under the applicable law, of the interest specified in the relevant acquisition schedule. NAMA may issue more than one direction under this subsection in connection with a foreign bank asset.

(7) A trust, duty, obligation or liability created or constituted by this section shall not be taken to constitute a security.

(8) A participating institution shall comply with any direction of NAMA in relation to any duty, obligation or liability under this section.

(9) A participating institution shall obtain, make, maintain and comply with any authorisation, consent, approval, resolution, licence, exemption, filing, notarisation or registration that is necessary in the State and in any other place in connection with ensuring the legality and enforceability of any act, matter or thing referred to in this section.

(10) *Sections 92* and *93* apply with any necessary modifications in relation to a foreign bank asset.

NOTES AND COMMENTARY

This section requires participating institutions to take all steps directed by NAMA to assign bank assets governed by foreign law. Section 4 establishes participating institutions as trustees of foreign bank assets for the benefit of NAMA to the extent that the governing law of the asset does not permit the asset to be assigned to NAMA.

Participating institutions are required to comply with NAMA's direction under this section.

Under s.92(7) payment for the acquisition of foreign bank assets may be withheld until full compliance has been achieved.

Payment for bank assets

92.—(1) As soon as may be after the service on a participating institution of an acquisition schedule (or after service of an amended acquisition schedule or a decision under *section 117* or *121* to confirm or continue with an acquisition schedule, as the case may be), NAMA shall notify the Minister and the NTMA of the amount payable to the participating institution as the acquisition value of the bank assets to be acquired.

(2) The Minister shall ensure that debt securities to an amount sufficient to allow the payment of the consideration payable under the acquisition schedule (other than any part of the consideration provided by an issue of subordinated debt securities under *section 49*) are issued.

(3) On the date of acquisition of a bank asset, NAMA or the NAMA group entity that acquired the bank asset shall transfer or issue to the participating institution concerned debt securities, or debt securities and subordinated debt securities, equal to the acquisition value of the bank asset.

(4) *Subsections (1), (2)* and *(3)* have effect in relation to a bank asset even if at the relevant time the total portfolio acquisition value is the subject of an objection.

(5) Subject to *subsection (6)*, in the case of the acquisition of a foreign bank asset (within the meaning given by *section 91*), on the date of acquisition, NAMA or the NAMA group entity concerned shall transfer or issue to the participating institution concerned debt securities, or debt securities and subordinated debt securities, equal in value to the acquisition value of the bank asset.

(6) In the case of the acquisition of a foreign bank asset (within the meaning given by *section 91*), NAMA or the NAMA group entity concerned may withhold all or part of the acquisition value of a foreign bank asset until satisfied that the participating institution concerned has met its obligations under *section 91*.

NOTES AND COMMENTARY

Section 47 permits the Minister for Finance to issue debt securities in order to provide consideration for the acquisition of bank assets. Section 48 confers a similar power to issue debt securities on NAMA itself. Section 49 permits the issuing of subordinated securities by NAMA to provide the consideration for the acquisition of bank assets to a maximum of five per cent of the total acquisition value.

This section provides for the payment of participating institutions for the bank assets which are transferred to NAMA under ss.90 and 91. Payment is to be made by NAMA or by the NAMA group entity to which the assets were transferred. The role of the Minister is not entirely clear. Under subs.(1) NAMA must inform both the Minister and the NTMA of amounts payable. Under subs.(2) the Minister is responsible for the issuing of debt securities to allow payment of the necessary consideration. If payment is to be made using securities issued by the Minister then it is not clear why NAMA requires a power to issue such securities under s.48. If on the other hand payment is to be made using NAMA issued securities, then the obligation of ensuring the issue of a suitable volume of securities is logically a question for the Board of NAMA.

During the Committee Stage Debate in the Dáil, the Minister for Finance confirmed that individual acquisition schedules may be acquired using a mix of subordinated and senior securities subject to each participating institution receiving an overall balance of 95 per cent senior and five per cent subordinated securities. (23 *Dáil Debates: Special Committee on Finance and the Public Service* Col. 1096 (October 29, 2009)).

Clawback of overpayments

93.—(1) If a participating institution receives from NAMA or a NAMA group entity an amount in exchange for acquired bank assets that is more than is due to the participating institution under this Act, or receives any other amount from NAMA or a NAMA group entity to which it is not entitled, the institution shall repay to NAMA—

   (*a*) in the case of overpayment of an amount due for the acquisition of bank assets, an amount equal to the overpayment and any accrued interest on it within the period that NAMA determines, or

   (*b*) in any other case, an amount equal to the overpayment and any accrued interest on it within the period that NAMA determines.

(2) A certificate issued by NAMA under its seal as to the amount of an overpayment referred to in *subsection (1)* is admissible as evidence of the amount of that overpayment.

Section 93 is not limited to overpayments in respect of the acquisition of bank assets and appears to apply equally to any other overpayment made by NAMA or a NAMA group entity to a participating institution. Amounts overpaid are to be certified by NAMA and under subs.(1) may include interest. It is unclear how the rate of interest is to be established or the date from which interest is repayable. In the Committee Stage debate in the Dáil the Minister indicated that NAMA would "deal with" questions of accrued interest on overpayments under this section (23 *Dáil Debates: Special Committee on Finance and the Public Service* Col. 1097 (October 29, 2009)).

There is no time limit imposed on the operation of the clawback provision. It also appears that NAMA may issue its certificate at any time in contrast to the similar certificate issued under s.190.

Subsection (2) allows NAMA to certify the amount an overpayment. Such a certificate is evidence of the amount but is not conclusive evidence and thus NAMA's calculation of overpayments can be challenged.

Dealings with bank assets after service of acquisition schedule until date of acquisition

94.—After the service of an acquisition schedule on a participating institution, until the date of acquisition for each bank asset specified in the acquisition schedule, the participating institution—

   (*a*) shall continue to hold and manage each bank asset concerned in accordance with *section 71*,

   (*b*) shall not make nor permit the making of any change to the bank asset concerned without NAMA's written consent, and

   (*c*) shall notify NAMA in writing of any change in the bank asset concerned of which the participating institution is aware.

Section 71 imposes restrictions on applicant participating institutions dealing with eligible bank assets before a completion notice has been served by NAMA. As such, s.71 continues to apply in the period between the service of an acquisition schedule and the date of acquisition in any event. The participating institution is required to act in good faith and to administer and service eligible assets with the same care and skill as might be expected from a prudent lender. There are also additional restrictions on dealing with eligible assets without the written consent of NAMA.

This section imposes two additional restrictions on participating institutions' capacity to deal with bank assets listed in an acquisition schedule prior to the date of acquisition. The meaning of the words "any change to the bank asset" is not quite clear. The restrictions imposed on participating institutions in s.71 include a prohibition on dealing with the assets other than in the ordinary course of business, dealings which would compromise NAMA's prospective interest or priority position, compromising, releasing or otherwise varying any contract or security relating to any asset. It is difficult to see what changes could be made to a bank asset which would not be caught by the s.71 restrictions. This section therefore appears to have been inserted purely as a precautionary measure.

Books, records and title documents of participating institutions

95.—(1) Where NAMA has acquired a bank asset, NAMA may direct the participating institution from which the bank asset was acquired—

    (*a*) to deliver to NAMA all its books and records in relation to the bank asset concerned and any documents of title that it holds for any property that is subject to a security that is part of the bank asset, and

    (*b*) to provide any information or explanation that NAMA requires in relation to those books, records and documents.

(2) A participating institution shall comply with a direction under *subsection (1)*.

(3) Where NAMA directs a participating institution under *subsection (1)* to deliver to NAMA books, records or documents in relation to a bank asset, the participating institution shall also secure that any officer, employee or agent of the participating institution who is able to do so provides an explanation of any such book, record or document, including an explanation of any apparent omission from such a book, record or document.

(4) If a participating institution is subject to a direction under *subsection (1)* and does not comply with the direction, NAMA may apply to the Court, on notice to the participating institution, for an order directing the institution to comply with the direction.

(5) The Court may make an order (including a mandatory or interlocutory order) under *subsection (4)* if the Court is satisfied that the production of the book, record, document or explanation, the provision of the facilities sought is reasonably necessary to enable NAMA to perform any of its functions under this Act.

(6) Where NAMA so directs, a participating institution shall retain custody, on behalf of NAMA, of any book, record, document or document of title referred to in this section subject to the giving of an accountable trust receipt or on other terms that NAMA directs.

NOTES AND COMMENTARY

This section provides NAMA with a power to demand delivery of books, records and documents of title in relation to bank assets which are acquired by NAMA. The power compliments NAMA's powers to inspect and copy these documents prior to acquisition under ss.80–82. The power does not extend to NAMA group entities, though NAMA may exercise its power for the benefit of a group entity under s.12(6). As with the previous section NAMA has the option of enforcing its rights under this section by means of an application to the High Court; however unlike the corresponding applications under ss.81(4) and 82(3), the High Court has no power to order that the hearing of such an application be held other than in public. This is a curious omission and it is worth noting that the courts have no inherent power, beyond that conferred by statute, to restrict public access to the courts (see *Roe v Blood Transfusion Service Board* [1996] 3 I.R. 67).

Notice to debtors, etc., of acquisition of bank assets

96.—(1) Within 60 days after the acquisition of a bank asset from a participating institution, the participating institution shall make reasonable efforts to notify each debtor, associated debtor, guarantor or surety in relation to the credit facility concerned of the acquisition of the bank asset by NAMA or the relevant NAMA group entity.

(2) Where there has been failure or delay in notifying a person in accordance with *subsection (1)*—

(*a*) neither NAMA nor the relevant NAMA group entity is liable for any such failure or delay,

(*b*) the acquisition is valid notwithstanding any such failure or delay, and

(*c*) no objection may be raised by any debtor, associated debtor, guarantor or surety to NAMA's or the relevant NAMA group entity's acquisition of the bank asset concerned based on any such failure or delay.

NOTES AND COMMENTARY

The assignment of debts at law is ordinarily accompanied by an obligation to notify the debtor of the assignment (see s.28(6) of the Supreme Court of Judicature (Ireland) Act 1877). Failure to supply such notice renders the assignment effective in equity only (see *Gorringe v Irwell India Rubber Works* (1887) LR 34 Ch D 128). Serving of notice of an assignment on the debtor also has an important priority consequence for both legal and equitable assignments—under the rule in *Dearle v Hall* (1828) 3 Russ 1, priority between conflicting assignments normally follows the order in which notice to the debtor was given.

This section limits the obligation to notify the debtor of the acquisition of bank assets by NAMA in a number of ways. First, the obligation to notify rests with the participating institution and not with NAMA. Secondly, the obligation is confined to making reasonable efforts to effect notification within 60 days. The obligation to notify does not appear to extend beyond 60 days in the event that the participating institution's efforts are unsuccessful. Thirdly, the validity of the acquisition is not affected by a failure to notify. It is not clear whether the section has the effect of removing the priority consequences of a failure to notify under the rule in *Dearle v Hall*. It may be that the acquisitions process can be distinguished from a normal assignment of debts such that the rule does not apply to it at all.

NAMA to notify participating institutions of completion of acquisition process

97.—(1) When NAMA has served on a participating institution one or more acquisition schedules that specify all the bank assets that NAMA has acquired or at the time proposes to acquire from the participating institution, NAMA shall serve on the participating institution a notice in writing of that fact (in this Act referred to as a "completion notice").

(2) A completion notice shall specify—

    (*a*) all the bank assets (being bank assets that are eligible bank assets at the time of service of the completion notice) that NAMA has acquired or proposes to acquire from the participating institution concerned,

    (*b*) the acquisition value determined by NAMA for each such bank asset, and

    (*c*) the total value for those assets.

(3) NAMA shall not serve any further acquisition schedules on a participating institution after service of a completion notice on the institution unless the Minister prescribes further classes of eligible bank assets.

NOTES AND COMMENTARY

This section provides for the termination of the acquisition process through the service of a completion notice. Once the notice has been served NAMA cannot acquire additional assets unless the Minister extends the classes of eligible assets by statutory instrument under s.69. The completion notice must contain the total acquisition value of all the assets which NAMA has acquired from the participating institution. That figure is required in order to determine appeals to the valuation panel under s.122.

NAMA seems to have some limited discretion in deciding when to serve a completion notice. The obligation to serve the notice is triggered when NAMA has served one or more acquisition schedules which list the entire bank assets which NAMA proposes to acquire from a participating institution. NAMA is not required by the Act to provide a list of the assets which it proposes to acquire and as such the serving of a completion notice could be delayed to allow NAMA additional time to make acquisition decisions. This may be less likely in light of the Minister's direction of October 22, 2010, issued under s.14 of the Act, to complete the acquisition process as expeditiously as possible.

Dispute over acquisition value

98.—(1) If a participating institution wishes to dispute an acquisition value, it shall do so solely in accordance with this section and *sections 121* and *122*.

(2) A participating institution may apply to NAMA in writing for the correction of an obvious error in relation to the value of a bank asset in an acquisition schedule. An application under this subsection is not an objection or dispute for the purposes of *sections 121* and *122*.

NOTES AND COMMENTARY

Sections 121 and 122 provide for the referral of disputes over the total acquisition value to the valuation panel established by Ch.2 of Pt 7. Under s.122 a participating institution may only challenge the acquisition value if it has served notices of objection in respect of 12.5 per cent in value of the bank assets acquired by NAMA. Section 121 provides for the service of notices of objection. Subsection (1) of this section makes clear that the process outlined in ss.121 and 122 is the only method by which NAMA's decisions as to acquisition value may be reviewed or objected to.

Subsection (2) permits the participating institution to request rectification of an obvious error in the completion notice without resort to the formal procedures under s.122. Subsection (2) mirrors the provision in s.88 whereby a participating institution can apply to have an obvious error in an acquisition schedule corrected by NAMA.

CHAPTER 2

Effects of Acquisition of Bank Assets

NAMA to have rights of creditors after acquisition of bank assets

99.—(1) After NAMA or a NAMA group entity acquires a bank asset, and subject to *section 101* and any exclusion of obligations and liabilities from the acquisition set out in the acquisition schedule—

> (*a*) NAMA and the NAMA group entity each have and may exercise all the rights and powers, and subject to this Act is bound by all of the obligations, of the participating institution from which the bank asset was acquired in relation to—
>> (i) the bank asset,
>> (ii) the debtor concerned and any guarantor, surety or other person concerned,
>> (iii) any receiver, liquidator, or examiner concerned, and
>> (iv) the Official Assignee in Bankruptcy,
>> and
> (*b*) the participating institution ceases to have those rights and obligations except to any extent to which this Act provides otherwise.

(2) The reference in *subsection (1)* to the rights, powers or obligations of a participating institution in relation to a bank asset is a reference to the rights, powers or obligations, as the case may be—

> (*a*) derived from the bank asset, and
> (*b*) arising under any law or in equity or by way of contract.

(3) In particular, NAMA and the NAMA group entity may each—

> (*a*) take any action, including court action, that the participating institution could have taken to protect, perfect or enforce any security, right, interest, obligation or liability,
> (*b*) realise any security that the participating institution could have realised,
> (*c*) call up any guarantee that the participating institution could have called up,
> (*d*) participate to the same extent as the participating institution could have participated in any resolution, workout, restructuring, arrangement, reorganisation, scheme or insolvency proceeding in relation to the bank asset, and
> (*e*) exercise any powers conferred by any document that forms part of the bank asset of reviewing or amending any term or condition of any part of the bank asset.

NOTES AND COMMENTARY

This section clarifies the effect of an acquisition by NAMA and a NAMA group entity of a bank asset. NAMA and the acquiring entity, takes over the position of the participating institution and has all the rights in respect of the asset which were formerly enjoyed by the participating institution from which the asset was acquired. This basic principle is qualified by a number of subsequent sections in this part including ss.101 and 102.

It appears from the wording of the section that both NAMA and a NAMA group entity can exercise the transferred rights separately notwithstanding that NAMA has nominated a specific NAMA group entity as the transferee under s.87(2).

This section affects bank assets as they are acquired by NAMA. The date on which this occurs may vary between domestic and foreign bank assets. Under s.90, bank assets which are governed by the law of the State are deemed to be acquired by NAMA or a NAMA group entity on the acquisition date specified in the acquisition schedule. Under s.91 NAMA may direct a participating institution to transfer a bank asset governed by foreign law to NAMA to the greatest extent possible under the relevant law. The acquisition date for a foreign asset will therefore be later than for a domestic asset.

Exercise of certain rights of set-off

100.—(1) If a participating institution has a right to set off a claim owing by it to a debtor against a claim owing by the debtor to it in relation to a bank asset, and NAMA or a NAMA group entity acquires the bank asset, the right is taken to continue in existence as between the participating institution and the debtor as if the bank asset had not been acquired and—

(*a*) the participating institution shall inform NAMA in writing of the existence of the right,

(*b*) if NAMA so directs—

(i) the claims shall be set off as if they were mutual claims when and to the extent that the right of setoff would have become exercisable or would have arisen if there had been no acquisition, and

(ii) the claims shall be taken to have been discharged to the extent of that set-off,

and

(*c*) if the claims are so discharged, the participating institution shall, as soon as may be, pay an amount equal to the amount of the set-off to NAMA or the NAMA group entity concerned.

(2) If a debtor exercises, or is taken to have exercised, a set-off of a claim made by a participating institution against an acquired bank asset, the participating institution shall, as soon as may be, pay an amount equal to the amount of the set-off to NAMA or to the NAMA group entity concerned.

(3) In this section—

(*a*) a reference to a right of set-off includes a right of combination of accounts and any similar right, and

(*b*) a reference to a claim includes a direct or contingent obligation.

(4) Upon and following the acquisition of a bank asset from a participating institution by NAMA or a NAMA group entity, for the purposes only of the set-off pursuant to *subsection (1)* the claims shall be taken to be mutual for the purposes of paragraph 17(1) of the First Schedule to the Bankruptcy Act 1988.

NOTES AND COMMENTARY

This section concerns the effect of the acquisition process on rights of set off. Subsection (1) provides that such rights are to be treated as though the acquisition process had not taken place. Subsections (2) and (3) provide for the payment by a participating institution which obtains a benefit by exercise of a right of set off of a sum of money to NAMA which is equal to the benefit obtained through exercise of the right.

Enforcement of certain representations, etc.

101.—(1) If in relation to a bank asset that NAMA or a NAMA group entity has acquired—

    (*a*) it is alleged that a representation was made to, a consent was given to, an undertaking was given to, or any other obligation was undertaken (by agreement or otherwise) in favour of, the debtor or another person by the participating institution from which the bank asset was acquired or by some person acting or claiming to act on its behalf,

    (*b*) no such representation, consent, undertaking or obligation was disclosed to NAMA in writing, before the service on the participating institution of the relevant acquisition schedule,

    (*c*) the records of the participating institution do not contain a note or memorandum in writing of the terms of any such representation, consent, undertaking or obligation or do not contain a record of any consideration paid in relation to any such representation, undertaking or obligation, and

    (*d*) the representation, consent, undertaking or obligation, if made, given or undertaken, would affect the creditor's rights in relation to the bank asset,

then that representation, consent, undertaking or obligation—

    (i) is not enforceable, and cannot be relied on, by the debtor or any other person against NAMA or the NAMA group entity,

    (ii) is enforceable, and can be relied on, by the debtor or any other person, if at all, only against a person other than NAMA or a NAMA group entity, and

    (iii) is not enforceable, and cannot be relied on, by NAMA or the NAMA group entity against the debtor.

(2) A claim based on a representation, consent, undertaking or obligation referred to in *subsection (1)* gives rise only to a remedy in damages or other relief that does not in any way affect the bank asset, its acquisition, or the interest of NAMA or the NAMA group entity or (for the avoidance of doubt) any property the subject of any security that is part of such a bank asset.

(3) The Court shall not make an order under *section 182* in relation to a claim to enforce a representation, undertaking or obligation referred to in *subsection (1)*.

Notes and Commentary

    This section attempts to insulate NAMA from undisclosed representations or undertakings which would have adversely affected the participating institution's ability to enforce its rights against the debtor. For the section to operate four conditions must be satisfied:

    (a) There must be an allegation that a representation, undertaking or consent was given to debtor or another person by the participating institution or someone purporting to act on its behalf.

    (b) NAMA must not have been notified in writing of the representation, undertaking or consent prior to serving the relevant acquisition schedule.

    (c) The representation, undertaking or consent was not recorded in the books of the participating institution or books do not record the receipt of consideration for the representation, undertaking or consent.

    (d) The representation, undertaking or consent would adversely affect the ability of the participating institution to enforce its rights.

It should be noted that the section only affects representations, undertakings or consents which were not either directly disclosed to NAMA or indirectly disclosed in the books and records of the participating institution. It is not necessary to interfere with disclosed representations and undertakings since these will be taken account of by NAMA when setting the acquisition value for each asset.

The section has the potential to impact representations and undertakings given by agents of participating institutions during the course of negotiations with guarantors and persons providing indemnities as well as debtors directly.

The section is a derogation from the principle established in s.99 that NAMA takes over the position of a participating institution in respect of acquired loans. Where the section is operative, the debtor or any other person affected loses the right to enforce a representation made to them against NAMA. In *Dellway Investments v NAMA* ([2011] IESC 14), Finnegan J. noted that this section alters the position of a mortgagee significantly. Citing JM Paterson, *Kerr on Injunctions* 6th edn (London: Sweet & Maxwell, 1927), pp.523–532 and *Adderley v Dixon* (1824) 1 Sim & St 607; 57 Eng Rep 329, the learned judge noted that this section strips mortgagors of their right to a decree of specific performance to prevent NAMA from improperly exercising the mortgagees' rights of participating institutions.

The section does not entirely eliminate the rights of the recipient of an undisclosed representation but instead limits the available remedies to an action in damages against a person other than NAMA or a NAMA group entity. As originally drafted the section provided for an action in damages specifically against the participating institution. The wording was altered at Committee Stage in the Dáil on the initiative of the Minister for Finance, presumably to permit an action to be taken against the person who gave the representation, undertaking or consent concerned without the authority of the participating institution.

Acquisition of bank assets not to affect conditions, etc.

102.—(1) Subject to the provisions of this Act, after a bank asset is acquired by NAMA or a NAMA group entity, the terms and conditions of the bank asset are unchanged.

(2) Where the documentation for a credit facility forming part of a bank asset that has been acquired by NAMA or a NAMA group entity refers to a reference rate of interest that is set by the participating institution concerned but is no longer available, the documentation shall continue to be construed as though it referred to—

> (*a*) that participating institution's reference rate for credit facilities of that type, or

> (*b*) at NAMA's discretion, another reference rate specified by NAMA.

(3) Where by reason of the acquisition by NAMA or a NAMA group entity of a bank asset, compliance with, or the operation of, a term or condition of the bank asset is no longer, in the opinion of NAMA, reasonably practicable, NAMA may, by notice in writing, change that term or condition. The new term or condition shall be as nearly as possible equivalent to the original term or condition.

(4) For the avoidance of doubt, the acquisition by NAMA or a NAMA group entity of a bank asset under this Act does not affect any relief or remedy to which the participating institution would otherwise be entitled.

NOTES AND COMMENTARY

Subsection (1) restates the principle established in s.99 that the acquisition of an asset by NAMA or a NAMA group entity places NAMA and the relevant entity in the same position as the participating institution. Subsections (2) and (3) permit NAMA to derogate from this principle where loan covenants are not operable as a result of the acquisition process.

Subsection (2) permits NAMA to substitute a reference rate which is no longer available. The substitution can be performed by reference to the participating institution's rates or to another rate set by NAMA. The section and does not list any factors to which NAMA must or may not have regard when deciding whether or not to substitute its own interest rate. The section is also silent on how NAMA is to set an alternative interest rate.

Subsection (3) permits NAMA to alter certain conditions, which, in NAMA's opinion, are no longer operable. The section does not require NAMA to have reasonable grounds for its opinion, however NAMA is not given *carte blanche* to rewrite the terms of the contract and in *Dellway Investments v NAMA* [2010] IEHC 364, the High Court (at [7.43]) described the power conferred by this section as "a very limited power arising only in very limited circumstances… the change must be of the most limited fashion sufficient to solve the problem."

The Code of Practice on the Commercial Interests of Non-Participating Institutions, issued under s.35, states that NAMA will not utilise its powers under subs.(3) without prior consultation with the European Commission (see [3.11(c)]). This is in line with a commitment given by the Irish authorities to the European Commission when obtaining state aid approval for the NAMA scheme (see European Commission, Communication regarding State Aid N725/2009 Ireland of February 26, 2010, C(2010)1155 final, 18).

The debtor does not appear to have any means of appealing a decision taken by NAMA under this section other than resort to judicial review.

Acquisition of bank assets not to give rise to cause of action, etc.

103.—No cause of action lies or is maintainable against NAMA or any NAMA group entity by reason solely of the acquisition of a bank asset by NAMA or a NAMA group entity.

NOTES AND COMMENTARY

This section confers immunity from suit on NAMA and its group entities from suit regarding the acquisition process. It is one of a number of sections of the Act which purports to limit the liability of NAMA and should be read in conjunction with s.17 in particular. The effect of the section was described in *Dellway Investments v NAMA* [2010] IEHC 364 in the following terms at [7.39] of the judgment:

"[A] bank (or, indeed, a borrower) cannot maintain proceedings based simply on the fact that a relevant bank asset in respect of which the bank is the lender and the customer is a borrower has been acquired. What NAMA does thereafter with that asset is not subject to any statutory exclusion of liability."

In the Supreme Court decision in *Dellway* ([2011] IESC 14), Hardiman J. (at p.11 of his judgment) suggested that this section could be read in two ways. It could be read as meaning that no challenge whatsoever can be brought before the courts to any aspect of the acquisition of eligible assets by NAMA. Alternatively, it could mean that though the acquisition itself cannot be challenged, the process by which the decision to acquire the loans was taken can be challenged.

Hardiman J. did not decide the point but it is respectfully submitted that the second alternative is the more likely interpretation. Chapter 3 of Part 10 of the Act makes various provisions for litigation regarding NAMA. Amongst these provisions are ss.192 and 193 which impose limitations in the power to grant injunctive relief and on the right to seek judicial review. Had the Oireachtas intended that these provisions were not to apply to decisions to acquire loans under Pt 6 it could easily have made provision to that effect. Indeed, examples of such provisions are to be found in ss.114 and 121 in respect of challenges by participating institutions to aspects of the acquisition process.

NAMA to be notified of certain matters

104.—If within one year after NAMA or a NAMA group entity acquires a bank asset, the participating institution from which the bank asset was acquired is notified or becomes aware of any significant dealing, event or circumstance or significant proposed or potential dealing, event or circumstance in relation to the bank asset that would adversely affect the bank asset or the rights (including priority), obligations or liabilities of NAMA or the NAMA group entity in relation to it, the participating institution shall notify NAMA of the dealing, event or circumstance without delay.

NOTES AND COMMENTARY

This section creates an on-going obligation of disclosure for participating institutions for a period of one year from the date of acquisition of bank assets. The duty imposed is a passive one—participating institutions are not required to actively seek out information but are instead obliged to pass on that which comes to their attention. Under s.130, a participating institution which is in breach of its obligations under the Act is liable in damages to NAMA and to any NAMA group entity.

Acquisition of bank assets not to render NAMA liable for wrongs by participating institutions

105.—(1) Nothing in this Act renders NAMA or a NAMA group entity liable for any breach of contract, misrepresentation, breach of duty, breach of trust or other legal or equitable wrong committed by a participating institution.

(2) No legal proceedings shall be brought against NAMA or a NAMA group entity in relation to any legal or equitable wrong referred to in *subsection (1)*.

(3) Nothing in this Act deprives any person of a remedy in damages against a participating institution in relation to a legal or equitable wrong referred to in *subsection (1)*.

NOTES AND COMMENTARY

This section grants NAMA and its group entities a sweeping immunity from suit for wrongs committed by participating institutions. Despite the text of the marginal note, the immunity is not limited to acts committed before the acquisition process and would appear to render the participating institution liable for breaches of contract etc., arising from compliance with directions from NAMA under Pt 8.

Rights of others not affected by acquisition of bank assets, etc.

106.—Nothing in this Act relieves NAMA or a NAMA group entity of any obligation, at law or in equity, except to any extent to which this Act specifically provides otherwise.

NOTES AND COMMENTARY

This section preserves any residual liabilities from which NAMA or its group entities are not specifically covered by the Act . The marginal note seems to indicate that this section is intended to affect the liabilities of NAMA in respect of the acquisition of bank assets; however under s.18(g), Interpretation Act 2005 the marginal notes are not a part of the text of the Act and are not to be judicially noticed in interpreting the Act. For examples of liabilities from which NAMA is relieved by the Act, see ss.17, 101, 103, 105 and the notes thereto.

NAMA not required to register certain instruments, etc.

107.—(1) Where a bank asset has been acquired by NAMA or a NAMA group entity—

    (*a*) notwithstanding anything in any Act listed in *subsection (2)* or any other Act that provides for the registration of assets, security or details of them, NAMA or the NAMA group entity is not required to become registered as owner of any security that is part of the bank asset,

    (*b*) notwithstanding sections 62 and 64 of the Registration of Title Act 1964, NAMA or the NAMA group entity has, in relation to any such charge, the powers of a mortgagee under a mortgage by deed, even though NAMA or the NAMA group entity is not registered as owner of any such charge,

    (*c*) NAMA or the NAMA group entity has the powers and rights conferred on the registered owner of a charge by the Registration of Title Act 1964.

(2) The Acts referred to *subsection (1)(a)* are the following:

    (*a*) the Bills of Sale (Ireland) Acts 1879 and 1883;

    (*b*) the Industrial and Commercial Property (Protection) Act 1927;

    (*c*) the Companies Act 1963;

    (*d*) the Registration of Deeds and Title Acts 1964 and 2006;

    (*e*) the Agricultural Credit Act 1978;

    (*f*) the Patents Act 1992;

    (*g*) the Trade Marks Act 1996;

    (*h*) the Taxes Consolidation Act 1997.

(3) For the purposes of an Act referred to in *subsection (1)(a)*, an acquisition schedule has effect in relation to a bank asset as a deed registered on the date of acquisition of the bank asset concerned.

(4) For the purposes of an Act referred to in *subsection (1)(a)*, the registration in relation to an acquired bank asset of a participating institution has effect for all purposes as a registration of NAMA or the NAMA group entity concerned.

(5) Nothing in this section prevents NAMA or a NAMA group entity from registering any interest capable of registration.

(6) Nothing in this section has the effect of relieving NAMA or a NAMA group entity from any obligation under a relevant foreign law.

(7) Sections 23 and 25 of the Registration of Title Act 1964 do not apply to NAMA or a NAMA group entity.

(8) Where a NAMA group entity acquires a bank asset from NAMA or another NAMA group entity, the provisions of this section also apply to the first-mentioned NAMA group entity.

Notes and Commentary

This section purports to exempt NAMA and its group entities from a range of statutory requirements to register the creation of property and security interests. The drafting of the section seems to have been primarily conducted with security interests over land in mind and the section has a number of features which merit comment.

Subsection (3) provides that an acquisition schedule has effect as if it were a deed registered on the date of acquisition. This provision appears to sit poorly with the statutory provisions governing the registration of deeds. Under s.37 of the Registration of Deeds and Title Act 2006 registered deeds are assigned a serial number and under s.38 of the same Act, priority between deeds is ordered in accordance with the serial numbers allocated to them. Since acquisition schedules do not in fact have to be registered by NAMA and its group entities and thus will not have serial numbers assigned by the Registry of Deeds, it is unclear how the priority of an acquisition schedule is to be determined under the 2006 Act.

There also seems to be a tension between subss.(3) and (4) in so far as they relate to the registration of deeds. Under subs.(4) registration performed by the participating institution has effect for all purposes as though it were a registration by NAMA or a NAMA group entity. Thus, NAMA or its group entities would be entitled to the benefit of any deeds registered by the participating institution prior to acquisition. If this is the case, then subs.(3) seems to be an unnecessary complication in determining NAMA's priority position in respect of unregistered land, since NAMA would simply take over the participating institution's position regardless of the acquisition. Furthermore, if the subs.(3) priority position were applied in preference to the subs.(4) rule, NAMA or a NAMA group entity might lose priority to a deed registered between the registration by the participating institution and the date of acquisition. For a detailed consideration of the registration of deeds see J.C.W. Wylie, *Irish Land Law* 4th edn (Dublin: Bloomsbury Professional, 2010), Ch.22.

The second potential difficulty with this section relates to the company charge register. Section (1)(a) refers to NAMA or its group entities as being exempt from the obligation "to become registered as owner of any security". Sections 99(1) and 100 of the Companies Act 1963 as amended require companies to register the particulars of certain charges created by them over company property. Charge-holders are not obliged to "register as owner" and these words do not seem to have any application to the provisions of the Companies Act. The obligation to register lies with the debtor company and not with the creditor. Thus a charge created in favour of NAMA remains registrable by the company concerned. Even if the wording of s.1(a) is capable of preventing an unregistered charge in NAMA's favour from being void against the liquidator and any creditor of the company under s.99 of the 1963 Act, it is worth noting that a failure to register a registrable charge is a criminal offence for the debtor company and any officer thereof who is found to be in default. For the overwhelming majority of company charges which transfer to NAMA, the problem will be resolved through reliance on subs.(4) which will allow NAMA to rely on a previous registration of a charge in favour of the participating institution. Care will be needed however if NAMA or a group entity require debtor companies to create fresh registrable charges in its favour.

The third cause for comment in relation to this section is the list of statutes contain in subs.(2). The list focuses on statutes creating a registration requirement for security interests. In this respect there are two omissions—s.50 of the Mercantile Marine Act 1955 which imposes a registration requirement in respect of ship mortgages over all vessels not propelled by oars; and the International Interests in Mobile Equipment (Cape Town Convention) Act 2005 which imposes a registration requirement for security interests over aircraft. The latter omission may be deliberate in order to ensure that the State continues to be fully compliant with the Convention on International Interests in Mobile Equipment.

Subsection (7) exempts NAMA from the obligation to register title to land in circumstances where the Registration of Title Act would require title to be registered. During the Dáil Committee Stage, the Minister for Finance stated that it was intended that NAMA and its group entities would register title on a voluntary basis and noted that there had been discussions between the Property Registration Authority and the NTMA on the issue (23 *Dáil Debates: Special Committee on Finance and the Public Service* Col. 1107 (October 29, 2009)).

NAMA, etc., may give certificates in relation to bank assets held

108.—(1) NAMA or a NAMA group entity may certify under its seal or common seal, as the case requires, that NAMA or the NAMA group entity holds a bank asset specified in the certificate.

(2) A document purporting to be a certificate issued in accordance with *subsection (1)*—

(*a*) shall be taken to be such a certificate, and to have been certified under the seal of NAMA or the NAMA group entity, as the case may be, unless the contrary is proved, and

(*b*) is conclusive as to the matters set out in it.

NOTES AND COMMENTARY

This section permits NAMA to conclusively certify that it holds bank assets. While the certificate acts as conclusive evidence of matters set out in it, it may be possible to quash the issuing of the certificate itself in the event that NAMA were to issue an inaccurate certificate. The provision of certificates under this section will facilitate NAMA's exercise of many of its powers in relation to bank assets under Pt 9.

NAMA, etc., may give certain directions in relation to bank assets

109.—(1) This section applies, without prejudice to any other provision of this Act or any right arising at law, to a bank asset that NAMA or a NAMA group entity has acquired, the terms and conditions of which entitle the participating institution from which NAMA or the NAMA group entity acquired it to give directions to a third party that holds an interest in the bank asset on behalf of others.

(2) In relation to a bank asset to which or in relation to which this section applies—

    (*a*) NAMA or a NAMA group entity may give directions to the third party concerned to realise any security, enforce any guarantee or surety or do any other act or thing in relation to the bank asset, or

    (*b*) if the third party is not incorporated in the State, but is a subsidiary of an entity that is incorporated in the State, NAMA or a NAMA group entity may direct the entity concerned to secure compliance by the subsidiary with a direction to do any of the things mentioned in *paragraph (a)*.

(3) Where a direction is given under *subsection (2)(a)*, then the third party shall be under an equivalent obligation to comply with the direction as if the direction had been given by the participating institution from which the bank asset concerned was acquired.

(4) Where a direction is given under *subsection (2)(b)*, then the entity shall be under an obligation to secure the compliance of the subsidiary but only to the extent that the subsidiary would be bound to comply with a direction given under *paragraph (a)* of *subsection (2)* if the subsidiary were incorporated in the State.

NOTES AND COMMENTARY

This section continues the policy established in s.99 of placing NAMA and its group entities into the same position as the participating institution from which relevant bank assets were acquired. This section enables NAMA to give instructions to a third party (presumably a security trustee or other similar entity) holding an interest in the bank asset. The power extends to requiring an Irish parent company to procure compliance by a subsidiary incorporated outside the State.

Effect of acquisition of bank assets on certain other rights

110.—(1) In this section "relevant instrument" means an agreement, licence, document, security, obligation or other instrument (other than the Credit Institutions (Financial Support) Scheme 2008 (S.I. No. 411 of 2008)) (or an instrument entered into under that Scheme) to which any of the following is a party or by which any of the following is bound or in which any of the following has an interest:

    (*a*) a participating institution;

    (*b*) a subsidiary of such an institution;

    (*c*) any body corporate in which a participating institution or any of its subsidiaries has any interest.

(2) Any provision in a relevant instrument that would (apart from this subsection) cause any of the consequences specified in *subsection (3)* to follow by virtue of—

    (*a*) the enactment of this Act,

    (*b*) any entity becoming a participating institution,

    (*c*) the provision of any information to NAMA by an applicant credit institution or a participating institution pursuant to this Act,

    (*d*) the acquisition of a bank asset by NAMA or a NAMA group entity under this Act,

    (*e*) any disposition by NAMA or a NAMA group entity of any acquired bank asset, or

    (*f*) any other thing done or authorised to be done under, pursuant to or resulting from any provision of this Act,

is of no effect, without the express consent of NAMA, except to any extent to which the Minister provides otherwise by order under *section 111*.

(3) The consequences referred to in *subsection (2)* are the following:

    (*a*) the creation of an obligation;

    (*b*) the suspension or extinction (however described, and whether in whole or in part) of a right or an obligation or the becoming subject to a right or an obligation;

    (*c*) the termination of the relevant instrument concerned or a right or obligation under it;

    (*d*) a right becoming exercisable to terminate or modify the relevant instrument or a right or obligation under it;

    (*e*) an amount becoming due and payable or capable of being declared due and payable;

    (*f*) any other change in the amount or timing of any payment falling to be made or due to be received by any person;

    (*g*) a right becoming exercisable to withhold, net or set off any payment;

    (*h*) the occurrence of an event giving rise to a default or breach of a right or obligation;

    (*i*) a right becoming exercisable not to advance any amount;

    (*j*) an obligation arising to provide or transfer a deposit or collateral;

    (*k*) a right of transfer or assignment of the asset that is stated to be exercisable only once or for a limited number of times;

    (*l*) a right to enforce a guarantee, indemnity or security interest (however described);

    (*m*) the triggering of any mandatory prepayment;

    (*n*) any obligation to return collateral or its equivalent;

    (*o*) the cancellation of any obligation to advance any amount or to provide credit or a contingent instrument;

    (*p*) legal proceedings becoming maintainable to enforce the relevant instrument, to any extent that such proceedings would not have been maintainable had the bank asset not been acquired or had any other thing done or matter arising by virtue of or in connection with this Act not been done or not arisen, as the case may be;

    (*q*) any other right or remedy (whether or not similar in kind to those referred to in *paragraphs (a)* to *(o)*) arising or becoming exercisable;

    (*r*) the termination or modification of an obligation to provide a service or product.

(4) In making an order referred to in *subsection (2)*, the Minister shall have regard to—

    (*a*) the consequences specified in *subsection (3)* so far as they are relevant,

    (*b*) the matters set out in *subsection (2)*, and

    (*c*) the likely impact of the proposed order on any of the matters specified in *section 2*, and on NAMA's ability to perform its functions under this Act.

NOTES AND COMMENTARY

The purpose of this section is to prevent the operation of the Act from triggering contractual provisions which might have any of the results listed in subs.(3). This is achieved by rendering any such contractual provisions void unless NAMA expressly consents to their operation. The power only applies to obligations which are binding on a participating institution, its subsidiaries or a body corporate in which a participating institution or its subsidiaries have an interest. At Committee Stage of the Dáil debate the Minister for Finance explained the purpose of the section as follows:

"Often, commercial instruments include a termination clause or another clause that may be triggered where ownership of an asset is transferred from one party to another. Some contracts may provide that, in the event of the transfer of the asset from the creditor bank to another creditor, the obligations of the debtor cease. It is essential that a clause be inserted in the legislation to keep all of those obligations owed by the debtor to the creditor bank alive." See (23 *Dáil Debates: Special Committee on Finance and the Public Service* Col. 1100 (October 29, 2009)).

Minister's power to modify application of *section 110*

111.—(1) In this section "relevant instrument" has the same meaning as in *section 110*.

(2) If the Minister is satisfied that in the special circumstances of—

    (*a*) a particular case, or

    (*b*) a particular class of cases,

the effect of *section 110* would be unduly onerous or would cause undue unfairness or undue hardship, and that it is appropriate in all the circumstances to do so, he or she may by order provide that, notwithstanding anything in that section, a provision in a relevant instrument that provides for a consequence mentioned or referred to in that section has effect to the extent specified in the order.

(3) An order under *subsection (2)*—

    (*a*) may make provision in relation to the effect of a provision—

        (i) in a particular relevant instrument,

        (ii) in relevant instruments of a particular class,

        (iii) on rights held under a relevant instrument by—

(I) a particular person, or

(II) a particular class of person,

or

(iv) on rights held under relevant instruments of a particular class by—

(I) a particular person, or

(II) a particular class of person,

(b) in the case of an order that makes provision in relation to relevant instruments of a particular class, may specify the class by reference to any common characteristic of the instruments concerned,

(c) in the case of an order that makes provision in relation to rights held by a particular class of persons, may specify the class by reference to any common characteristic of the persons concerned, and

(d) may be expressed to have retrospective effect to a date falling after 30 July 2009.

(4) If the Minister considers that an order under *subsection (2)* contains matter that is commercially sensitive, he or she may direct—

(a) that the obligations in relation to the order under section 3(1) of the Statutory Instruments Act 1947 are to be taken to be satisfied by the printing, sending to the institutions mentioned in section 3(1)(a) of that Act, publication and sale of a version of the order from which the commercially sensitive matter is omitted, or

(b) if the preparation of such a version would be impracticable, or would result in the version being seriously misleading, that the order is exempt from the operation of section 3(1) of that Act.

(5) A version of an order prepared in accordance with a direction given by the Minister under *subsection (4)(a)* shall indicate that matter has been omitted from the version of the order and the general nature of that matter.

(6) A direction given by the Minister under *subsection (4)* shall be published in *Iris Oifigiúil* as soon as practicable.

(7) Evidence of a direction given by the Minister under *subsection (4)* may be given by the production of a copy of *Iris Oifigiúil* purporting to contain the direction.

NOTES AND COMMENTARY

This section allows the Minister for Finance to remove, by statutory instrument, a particular relevant instruments or classes of relevant instrument from the scope of s.110. Before making such an order the Minster must be satisfied that the application of s.110 would lead to undue unfairness or hardship in a particular case or class of cases. Under s.110(4) the Minister must also have regard to the nature of the instrument and the consequences for NAMA's ability to perform its functions before making such an order. Under subs.(3)(d) an order under this section may be retrospective in effect to July 30, 2009—the date on which the public consultation draft of the Act was published.

Subsections (4)–(7) permit the Minster to direct that a statutory instrument made under this section should be published only in redacted form if the instrument contains commercially sensitive material. The wording of these subsections is identical in form to that utilised in s.9 of the Anglo Irish Bank Corporation Act 2009 but would appear to be otherwise without precedent on the Irish statute book. Significantly, no guidance is given on the meaning of the term "commercially sensitive". Where the Minister makes a direction under subs.(4), this fact must be published. Where a redacted version is published the "general nature" of the redacted matter must be indicated in the published version.

PART 7

CHAPTER 1

Expert Reviewer

Appointment and functions of expert reviewer

112.—(1) The Minister may appoint as the expert reviewer for the purposes of this Chapter a suitably qualified person who, in the Minister's opinion, has the experience necessary to perform the functions conferred on the expert reviewer under this Chapter.

(2) The terms and conditions of the appointment of the expert reviewer (including remuneration and reimbursement for expenses incurred) shall be as the Minister determines at the time of appointment.

(3) The functions of the expert reviewer are to review the objections referred to him or her under *section 85(3)* and to advise the Minister in accordance with *section 116*.

(4) Without prejudice to *subsection (3)*, the expert reviewer may, if he or she thinks that it is appropriate to do so, conduct the review of all or some of the objections from a participating institution on the basis of a sample of the bank assets that were the subject of objections referred to him or her under *section 85(3)* and if he or she does so, the advice to the Minister under *section 116* shall be based on that sample and shall be as valid, for all purposes of this Chapter, as if it had been based on a review of each bank asset that was the subject of an objection.

NOTES AND COMMENTARY

Subsection (1) authorises the Minister for Finance to appoint an expert reviewer. Read literally, the term "may" indicates that the Minister is not obliged to make an appointment; however since the reviewer is needed for the operation of important sections of the Act it is suggested that this provision must be read purposively in order to avoid an absurd result (see s.5(1) of the Interpretation Act 2005) and that the Minister is required to make an appointment.

No time limit is specified for the making of the appointment. In contrast to the appointment of members of the Board of NAMA under s.19 and the appointment of the valuation panel under s.119, the qualifications for appointment are at the discretion of the Minister and are not specified by the statute. There is no provision governing the resignation, replacement or term of office of the reviewer and these matters are presumably left to the discretion of the Minister when setting the terms and conditions of the reviewer's appointment under subs.(2).

The functions of the expert reviewer are set out in subss.(3) and (4). Subsection (3) permits the reviewer to provide the Minister with advice regarding the eligibility of particular bank assets for inclusion within the NAMA scheme. Under s.117 the expert reviewer's advice is binding on the Minister.

The reviewer's role is confined to resolving disputes between NAMA and the participating institutions under s.85. Subsection (4) permits the reviewer to conduct a review of all or some of the references from a given institution on the basis of a sample. It is not clear whether the reviewer is under an obligation to separately review each individual objection or whether the effect of s.(4) is to permit the reviewer to decide on a group of objections by selecting suitable sample objections and making a decision on them.

Procedure of expert reviewer

113.—(1) The Minister may make regulations providing for the procedures of the expert reviewer.

(2) Subject to any regulations made by the Minister under *subsection (1)*, the expert reviewer shall determine, in his or her sole discretion, procedures for—

    (*a*) the form and type of submissions to be made to the expert reviewer,

    (*b*) the means by which confidential information will be protected from public disclosure, and

    (*c*) the performance of any of the expert reviewer's functions.

NOTES AND COMMENTARY

This section gives the Minister a discretionary power to make regulations specifying the procedures which are to be followed by the expert reviewer in the performance of his functions. Any regulations made need not be laid before the Houses of the Oireachtas but they would have to be published in the normal manner provided by s.3(1) of the Statutory Instruments Act 1947. To date no regulations have been made under this section.

Subject to any regulations made by the Minister, subs.(2) requires the expert reviewer to determine his own procedures for the matters specified in paras (a)—(c). It is not clear whether the reviewer may amend the procedures from time to time; however the mention of the making of submissions would appear to indicate that the review is to be conducted in accordance with the rules of the natural justice, which would in any event, place restrictions on the reviewer's discretion. The reviewer's powers to determine its own procedures also appear to be subject to the provisions of s.115 relating to the materials to be made available to the reviewer.

It would appear from the language of para.(b) that the reviewer is required to adopt procedures for the protection of confidential information. The Act defines confidential information under s.202 and makes its unauthorised disclosure a criminal offence under s.(7). It is not an offence for a person to refuse or neglect to comply with the expert reviewer's procedures.

Objections to proposed acquisition of bank assets

114.—A participating institution may object to the proposed acquisition of a bank asset only as provided for in *section 80*.

NOTES AND COMMENTARY

Section 80(3) provides that where a participating institution is of the view that an asset is not an eligible bank asset it must state that this is its view, state that it objects to the acquisition of the asset and state the reason why it has formed this view.

Section 85(3) provides that where an objection has been made under s.80(3), NAMA may agree not to acquire the asset or may continue the acquisition process and refer the matter to the expert reviewer.

Materials, etc., to be made available to expert reviewer

115.—(1) A participating institution shall provide to the expert reviewer and to NAMA, no later than 7 days after NAMA notifies the participating institution under *section 85(4)*, all the material on which it bases its objection and any comments it may wish to make regarding the objection.

(2) For the purposes of the expert reviewer's review of NAMA's decision to acquire a bank asset, NAMA shall make available to the expert reviewer and the participating institution concerned, no later than 7 days after NAMA refers the objection to the expert reviewer under *section 85(3)(b)*, all the material that was before NAMA when it made its decision and any comments it may wish to make on the objection.

(3) NAMA and the participating institution shall each be allowed an opportunity to respond to the other's material and comments, and shall furnish any such responses to the expert reviewer and to the participating institution or NAMA, as the case may be, no later than 4 days after that material and those comments have been made available.

(4) The expert reviewer may request NAMA or a participating institution to provide additional information in relation to a bank asset that NAMA proposes to acquire. NAMA or a participating institution shall comply with any such request without delay.

NOTES AND COMMENTARY

This section imposes detailed requirements on NAMA and on any participating institution involved in a referral to the expert reviewer. The section requires that documentation be exchanged between NAMA, the institution and the reviewer and provides a timetable for the provision and exchange of the information. The effect of this section appears to limit the power of the reviewer to set down in s.113(2)(a) to regulate the form and type of submissions which are to be made to the reviewer. Since both NAMA and the participating institution are permitted to include "any comments it may wish to make" in the information to be provided to the reviewer, it is difficult to see how the reviewer could prevent submissions of a particular type from being made to him or her.

The obligation to provide information and material to the expert reviewer attaches to each and every objection relating to any bank asset. The reviewer is not empowered to relieve either NAMA or a participating institution from the obligation to provide relevant material even if the reviewer has elected to decide on the eligibility of a particular asset based on the outcome of a sample of assets under s.112(4).

Opinion of expert reviewer

116.—(1) In forming his or her opinion, the expert reviewer shall take into account the material, comments, responses and any additional information provided by the participating institution and NAMA under *section 115*.

(2) The expert reviewer shall advise the Minister, no later than 5 days after receiving the material, comments, responses and information under *section 115*, whether he or she is of the opinion that the bank asset is or is not an eligible bank asset.

(3) The Minister may, if he or she considers that to do so is warranted by exceptional circumstances, specify a longer period within which the expert reviewer is to provide advice under *subsection (2)*.

NOTES AND COMMENTARY

This section provides for the formulation of the expert reviewer's opinion and its transmission to the Minister. Under subs.(1) the reviewer is obliged to take account of the material provided to him or her under s.115; however it is unclear whether this is not exhaustive. There is nothing to indicate that the expert reviewer may not also take account of any relevant matter in addition to the material provided. It is not entirely clear how the requirement to take into account the material provided in relation to each asset sits with the reviewer's power to decide cases on the basis of a sample of the objections made by a particular institution under s.112(4).

Subsection (2) and (3) provide a timescale for the formulation of the expert reviewer's opinion and its transmission to the Minster. In the ordinary course this time period is five days which establishes a period of 12 days for the expert review process beginning with the date on which NAMA refers the matter to the reviewer. Section (3) permits the Minister to extend the timeframe in exceptional circumstances. No guidance is provided as to what might constitute exceptional circumstances and it would seem that the Minister has a broad discretion in this regard.

Confirmation by Minister of acquisition, etc.

117.—(1) The Minister shall, in accordance with the advice of the expert reviewer under *section 116* in relation to a bank asset, and no later than 5 days after receipt of that advice—

    (*a*) confirm that the bank asset may be acquired by NAMA, or

    (*b*) direct NAMA not to acquire the bank asset on the grounds that it is not an eligible bank asset.

(2) The Minister shall send copies of his or her confirmation or direction under *subsection (1)* to NAMA and to the participating institution concerned.

NOTES AND COMMENTARY

The Minister's role in the expert review process is limited to notifying the parties of the outcome of reviewer's decision and directing NAMA to act in accordance with it within the specified time limit. The Minister plays no role in the making of the reviewer's decision.

Costs

118.—(1) The costs of a review under this Chapter are payable as follows:

    (*a*) in a case where the Minister's decision is one referred to in *section 117(1)(a)*, the costs of both parties are payable by the participating institution; and

    (*b*) in any other case, neither of the parties pays costs and each of the parties bears its own costs.

(2) If a participating institution withdraws an application for the review under this Chapter, it is liable for the costs incurred up to the time of the withdrawal unless NAMA agrees otherwise.

(3) If NAMA and the participating institution concerned cannot reach agreement on costs, the costs of the review shall be determined by a Taxing Master of the Court. For that purpose, the Taxing Master has all the functions for the time being conferred on him or her under any enactment or in any rules of court (with any necessary modifications) in relation to the taxation of costs to be paid by one party to another in proceedings before the Court.

(4) The Taxing Master may direct that the costs of all reviews under this Chapter in relation to a participating institution shall be dealt with together after the service on the participating institution of a completion notice.

NOTES AND COMMENTARY

This section varies slightly from the costs rules associated with the valuation panel process under s.128.

See Ord.99 of the Rules of the Superior Courts in relation to the taxation of costs.

CHAPTER 2

Review of Valuations

Appointment of valuation panel

119.—(1) There shall be a valuation panel to adjudicate on disputes referred to it by NAMA under *section 122(3)*.

(2) The valuation panel shall consist of persons that the Minister appoints to be members of it. The Minister may determine how many members there shall be, but there shall not be more than 12 members.

(3) The Minister shall appoint a person as a member of the valuation panel only if the Minister is of the opinion that the person has relevant expertise or specialist knowledge.

(4) Without prejudice to the generality of *subsection (3)*, a person has relevant expertise or specialist knowledge if he or she is qualified, or has experience at a senior level, in any one or more of the following:

    (*a*) finance and economics;

    (*b*) law;

    (*c*) accountancy and auditing;

    (*d*) public administration;

    (*e*) project finance;

    (*f*) construction and land development;

    (*g*) property management and sale;

    (*h*) valuation;

    (*i*) urban and land planning;

    (*j*) banking and investment;

    (*k*) insolvency and restructuring.

(5) The terms and conditions of appointment (including remuneration and reimbursement of expenses incurred) of a member of the valuation panel shall be as the Minister determines.

NOTES AND COMMENTARY

The Minister must establish the valuation panel under this section though there is no timeframe specified within which a panel must be constituted. Unlike the expert reviewer appointed under s.112, subs.(4) sets out criteria for appointment to the valuation panel. These criteria are similar, though not identical, to those required for appointments to the Board of NAMA under s.19. There is no minimum size requirement for the review panel. A plain reading of the language of the section seems to indicate that there must be a least two people appointed to the panel but under s.18 of the Interpretation Act, 2005, words importing the plural are to be read as though also importing the singular and thus it would seem that a single member valuation panel could be validly appointed. The Minister for Finance indicated during the Dáil Debates that his intention was to appoint 12 members to the valuation panel and that panels would sit in blocks of three. Curiously, the legislation makes no express provision for the valuation panel to sit in chambers or to take an action other than *en banc*. (23 *Dáil Debates: Special Committee on Finance and the Public Service* Col. 1129 (October 29, 2009))

As with the expert reviewer appointed under s.112, the Act makes no provision for the resignation, removal or term of office of members appointed to the valuation panel. These matters are presumably left to the discretion of the Minister when setting the terms and conditions of the reviewer's appointment under subs.(5).

Procedure of valuation panel

120.—(1) The Minister may make regulations providing for the procedure of the valuation panel and any matters relating to the review to be carried out.

(2) Subject to any regulations made by the Minister under *subsection (1)*, the valuation panel shall determine, in its sole discretion, procedures for—

    (*a*) the form and type of submissions to be made to the valuation panel,

    (*b*) the means by which confidential information will be protected from public disclosure, and

    (*c*) the performance of any of the valuation panel's functions.

(3) Without prejudice to *subsection (1)*, the valuation panel may, if it thinks that it is appropriate to do so, conduct a review of the valuation of an acquired portfolio on the basis of a sample of the bank assets in the acquired portfolio concerned and if it does so, the advice to the Minister under *section 124* shall be based on that sample and shall be as valid, for all purposes of this Chapter, as if it had been determined in relation to all the assets in the acquired portfolio.

NOTES AND COMMENTARY

This section grants powers for the Minister to regulate the procedure of the valuation panel. As with the power to regulate the procedures of the expert reviewer under s.113, the Minister may make secondary legislation under this section without laying it before the Oireachtas. The Minister's power under this section is slightly broader than the corresponding power under s.113 in that regulations may govern "any matters relating to the review" and is not confined to regulating the procedures of the valuation panel.

Subject to any regulations made by the Minister, subs.(2) requires the valuation panel to determine its own procedures for the matters specified in paras (a)–(c). It is not clear whether the panel may amend the procedures from time to time; however the mention of the making of submissions would appear to indicate that the review is to be conducted in accordance with the rules of the natural justice which would in any event place restrictions on the panel's discretion. The panel's powers to determine its own procedures also appear to be subject to the provisions of s.123 relating to the materials to be made available to the panel.

It would appear from the language of para.(b) that the panel is required to adopt procedures for the protection of confidential information. The Act defines confidential information under s.202 and makes its unauthorised disclosure a criminal offence under s.(7). It is not an offence for a person to refuse or neglect to comply with the valuation panel's procedures.

Subsection (3) corresponds to s.113(4) and permits the use of a sampling approach in the panel's decision making. The panel has discretion as to when it is appropriate for this approach to be used.

Objection to value placed on bank assets acquired from participating institution

121.—(1) If, after the service on a participating institution of an acquisition schedule, a participating institution objects to the acquisition value specified in that schedule in relation to a bank asset, the participating institution shall serve on NAMA a notice in writing of its objection invoking the provisions of this Chapter within 14 days after the service on it of the acquisition schedule.

(2) On receipt of a notice under *subsection (1)*, NAMA may—

    (*a*) remove the bank asset concerned from the relevant acquisition schedule,

(*b*) revoke the acquisition schedule, or

(*c*) continue with the acquisition in accordance with the acquisition schedule.

(3) NAMA shall notify the participating institution as soon as may be of its decision under *subsection (2)*.

(4) Where NAMA continues with an acquisition in accordance with the acquisition schedule concerned, the participating institution may dispute only the total portfolio acquisition value and may do so only as provided for and in accordance with *section 122*, and is not otherwise entitled to dispute the valuation of any particular acquired bank asset.

(5) A participating institution is not entitled to challenge any valuation of NAMA including a total portfolio acquisition value, other than in accordance with this Chapter.

NOTES AND COMMENTARY

Sections 121 and 122 provide the only mechanisms by which participating institutions can challenge the valuation placed on bank assets by NAMA in accordance with the valuation methodology set out in Pt V. Section 121 permits participating institutions to notify NAMA of a dispute relating to the value placed on individual bank assets during the course of the acquisition process while s.122 provides for the resolution of dispute over the total value of the portfolio of assets acquired from a particular institution provided certain conditions are satisfied. Subsection (4) provides that valuations may not be challenged by any other means. The two sections should be distinguished from s.85(3) which permits a participating institution to object to the acquisition of a particular asset *in toto* on the basis that it is not eligible for acquisition by NAMA. Section 121 provides for notification of disputes over the valuation of particular eligible bank assets which NAMA has included on an acquisition schedule. Section 122 provides a means of resolving dispute over the valuation of the total portfolio of assets from a particular institution.

Subsection (1) provides that where a participating institution objects to the valuation of a specific bank asset it must notify NAMA of its objection within 14 days of service of the relevant acquisition schedule. There is no provision for an extension of this time limit. The service of a notice of objection is a key step in challenging a valuation under both ss.121 and 122.

On receipt of a notice of objection NAMA is entitled to withdraw the particular bank asset, revoke the acquisition schedule or continue with the acquisition process. These powers would seem to be additional to NAMA's power under s.89 to amend an acquisition schedule at any time prior to the acquisition date. It would appear that the s.89 power could be used by NAMA to proceed with the acquisition at an amended value.

Dispute over total portfolio acquisition value

122.—(1) If, after service of a completion notice on a participating institution, the participating institution wishes to dispute the total portfolio acquisition value, it shall do so only if—

(*a*) it is of the opinion that the aggregate market value of the acquired portfolio exceeds the total portfolio acquisition value, and

(*b*) it has served a notice or notices under *section 121* in relation to acquired bank assets comprising at least 12.5 per cent by value of the total portfolio acquisition value.

(2) A participating institution that wishes to dispute the total portfolio acquisition value shall serve on NAMA a notice in writing, in the form (if any)

that the Minister prescribes by regulation, no later than 14 days after the service of the relevant completion notice, specifying the reasons for its opinion.

(3) If a participating institution serves notice under *subsection (2)*, NAMA shall refer the dispute to the valuation panel for review.

(4) The service of notice by a participating institution under *subsection (2)* does not affect the acquisition by NAMA of the bank assets concerned.

NOTES AND COMMENTARY

This section provides for the referral of disputes of the total acquisition value of a portfolio of assets to the valuation panel. The section envisages the referral of a single dispute between NAMA and participating institution which is to occur at the end of the acquisition process. There is no mechanism whereby an objection to the valuation of one or more specific assets can be referred to the panel.

Subsection (1) provides a two-part test for admissibility of a dispute. The participating institution must be able to show that the total acquisition value of the portfolio of assets transferred to NAMA is less than the market value of the assets. Second it must show that it has served objections under s.121 in respect of individual bank assets which in aggregate amount to at least 12.5 per cent of the total acquisition value of the portfolio. Market value is defined by s.72(2)(b).

As with s.121 an objection must be served on NAMA within 14 days of the service of a completion notice. NAMA is required to refer the dispute to the valuation panel but there is no time limit during which this must be done.

Material, etc., to be made available to valuation panel

123.—(1) A participating institution that has served a notice under *section 122(2)* shall provide to the valuation panel and to NAMA, no later than 28 days after service of the relevant completion notice, all the material on which its dispute is based and any comments it wishes to make regarding the disputed total portfolio acquisition value.

(2) For the purposes of the valuation panel's review, NAMA shall make available to the valuation panel and the participating institution concerned, no later than 28 days after service on it of the relevant notice under *section 122(2)*, the information on which NAMA based its determination of the market value of bank assets in the acquired portfolio concerned and any comments it wishes to make on the dispute.

(3) NAMA and the participating institution shall each be allowed an opportunity to respond to the other's material and comments, and shall furnish any such responses, no later than 7 days after that material and those comments have been made available, to the valuation panel and to the participating institution or NAMA, as the case may be.

(4) The valuation panel may request NAMA or a participating institution to provide additional information in relation to the total portfolio acquisition value of the acquired portfolio concerned. NAMA or a participating institution shall comply with any such request without delay.

(5) The valuation panel shall take into account the material, comments, responses and any relevant additional information provided by the participating institution and NAMA.

This section parallels s.115 which provides for the provision of materials to the expert reviewer. The time limits are significantly longer than those provided for under s.115.

The effect of this section appears to limit the power of the panel to set down in s.120(2)(a) to regulate the form and type of submissions which are to be made to the panel. Since both NAMA and the participating institution are permitted to include "any comments it may wish to make" in the information to be provided to the panel, it is difficult to see how the panel could prevent submissions of a particular type from being made to it.

The obligation to provide information and material to the expert panel attaches to each and every objection relating to any bank asset. The panel is not empowered to relieve either NAMA or a participating institution from the obligation to provide relevant material even if the panel has elected to decide on the eligibility of a particular asset based on the outcome of a sample of assets under s.120(3).

Review by valuation panel

124.—(1) The function of the valuation panel is to review whether the aggregate market value of an acquired portfolio is correct. In carrying out that review, the test to be applied by the valuation panel is whether the participating institution concerned has established, as a matter of probability, and taking into account the degree of expertise and specialist knowledge possessed by NAMA, and taking the process as a whole, that the determination of the aggregate market value was vitiated by a serious and significant error or a series of such errors.

(2) For the avoidance of doubt, for the purposes of a review under *subsection (1)*, the market value of an acquired bank asset is its market value as at the date or event specified by NAMA under *section 73*.

(3) The valuation panel shall advise the Minister of its determination, including of the aggregate market value, and the reasons for it.

(4) The panel shall give its advice to the Minister in relation to a dispute under *section 122* no later than 90 days after receiving the material, comments, responses and any additional information under *section 123*, or a longer period specified by the Minister by notice in writing, if he or she considers that to do so is warranted by exceptional circumstances.

This section sets out the test to be used by the valuation panel in deciding disputes about the acquisition value under s.122. The wording of the test suggests that the valuation panel should observe a degree of deference to the specialised knowledge and expertise possessed by NAMA when assessing valuation decisions. The wording of subs.(1) is based on the decision of Keane C.J. in *Orange Ltd v Director of Telecoms (No.2)* [2000] 4 I.R. 159 at 184–5. In considering the approach which the court should adopt in an appeal from the decision of a specialist regulator, Keane C.J. stated:

> "In the case of this legislation at least, an applicant will succeed in having the decision appealed from set aside where it establishes to the High Court as a matter of probability that, taking the adjudicative process as a whole, the decision reached was vitiated by a serious and significant error or a series of such errors. In arriving at a conclusion on that issue, the High Court will necessarily have regard to the degree of expertise and specialised knowledge available to the first defendant."

This standard has been applied by the courts in a number of statutory appeals in banking and financial matters and these cases may assist in the interpretation of this section. See *Carrickdale Hotel v Controller of Patents, Designs and Trademarks* [2004] 2 I.L.R.M. 410; *Ulster Bank Investment Funds Ltd v Financial Services Ombudsman* [2006] IEHC 323; *Quinn Direct Insurance Ltd v Financial Services Ombudsman* [2007] IEHC 323; *Bus Éireann v*

Controller of Patents, Designs and Trademarks [2008] 1 I.L.R.M. 428; *Square Capital v Financial Services Ombudsman* [2009] IEHC 407; and *Rye v Competition Authority* [2009] IEHC 140.

Once the valuation panel have completed the review, their determination, together with the reasons for it must be communicated to the Minister. This differs slightly from the role of the expert reviewer under s.115(2), who is not obliged to communicate reasons to the Minster. Under subs.(3) the valuation panel must deliver its determination within a 90-day-period subject to the possibility of an extension in exceptional circumstances. The Act seems to anticipate that proceedings before the valuation panel will be considerably more complex than those before the expert reviewer for whom only a 15-day-period is provided.

Minister's determination

125.—(1) The Minister shall consider the advice of the valuation panel under *section 124* in relation to the acquired portfolio concerned and shall, no later than 28 days after receipt of that advice—

> (*a*) confirm the aggregate market value of the acquired portfolio as advised by the valuation panel, or
>
> (*b*) if the valuation panel's determination of the aggregate market value is greater than the total portfolio acquisition value and he or she considers that the advice of the valuation panel is wrong in a material respect, remit the matter to the valuation panel for reconsideration setting out his or her reasons for doing so.

(2) Where the Minister remits the matter to the valuation panel under *subsection (1)(b)*, *subsections (4)* and *(5)* of *section 123* and *section 124* apply to the reconsideration with any necessary modifications.

(3) The Minister shall send copies of his or her determination under *subsection (1)* to NAMA and to the participating institution concerned.

(4) Where the Minister confirms that the aggregate market value of the acquired portfolio is greater than the total portfolio acquisition value as determined by NAMA, the Minister shall direct NAMA to compensate the participating institution by, at NAMA's option, doing either of the following (or both in any combination)—

> (*a*) returning to the participating institution bank assets equal in value to the difference between the total portfolio acquisition value determined by NAMA and the aggregate market value determined by the Minister, or
>
> (*b*) giving further consideration to the participating institution (in the form of cash, securities or Government-guaranteed securities or in any other form that NAMA considers appropriate) equal to the difference referred to in *paragraph (a)*.

(5) The amount of compensation payable to a participating institution under *subsection (4)* is to be no greater than the amount by which the total portfolio acquisition value determined by NAMA is less than the aggregate market value of the portfolio as confirmed by the Minister.

(6) The value of a bank asset to be returned under *subsection (4)(a)* is its acquisition value.

(7) The payment for, or transfer of, bank assets under *subsections (4)* to *(6)* is subject to the laws of the European Communities governing State aid.

This section provides the Minister with a limited decision making power in relation to the implementation of the advice of the valuation panel. This should be contrasted with the position in respect of the expert reviewer under s.117 where the Minister's role is confined to implementing the advice received.

Subsection (1) gives the Minister a 28-day time period within which the Minister can affirm the advice of the valuation panel or can remit the matter back to the panel for further consideration. The latter option is available only where

(a) The panel has advised that the market value of the bank assets concerned is less than the total acquisition value; and

(b) The Minister considers that the advice of the panel is wrong in any material respect.

There is no provision for the Minister to receive representations or comments either from NAMA or the participating institution concerned regarding the quality of the advice. Nor is there any provision for the Minister to have access to the materials provided to the valuation panel under s.123. It would seem that the valuation panels will have to provide the Minister with an extensive set of reasons for their advice in order for the Minister to discharge his or her functions under this section. If the Minister chooses to not to affirm the advice of the panel, he or she must refer the matter back to the valuation panel together with their reasons for doing so. The Minister has no power to vary the panel's advice or to substitute a different market value to that advised by the panel.

Where the Minister remits advice to the valuation panel for reconsideration, subs.(2) permits the panel to request additional information from NAMA or the participating institution concerned. The section does not explicitly provide for how the panel is to reach a determination on a dispute which is remitted to it by the Minister but it is suggested that the question would be governed by the test in s.124(1). There is no time limit imposed on the panel for its second set of deliberations. It would seem that this is a matter which the panel may regulate in its own regulations under s.120(2).

If the Minister confirms the advice of the panel, then recompense may be paid to the participating institution concerned using either mechanism provided by subs.(4).

Withdrawal of dispute

126.—A participating institution may withdraw a notice served under *section 122* at any time before the Minister sends a copy of his or her determination to it under *section 125* in relation to the review of the total portfolio acquisition value of the acquired portfolio concerned.

It is not entirely clear whether a participating institution can withdraw a dispute once the Minister has given notice of a decision under s.125(1) to remit a dispute to the valuation panel for reconsideration. There is no analogous provision in relation to the expert review process.

Costs of review of valuations

127.—(1) The costs of a review under this Chapter are payable by the participating institution concerned unless the Minister's determination under *section 125* entitles the participating institution to compensation under that section.

(2) If a participating institution withdraws a notice under *section 126*, it is liable for the costs incurred up to the time of the withdrawal unless NAMA agrees otherwise.

(3) If NAMA and the participating institution concerned cannot reach

agreement on costs, the costs of the review shall be determined by a Taxing Master of the Court. For that purpose, the Taxing Master has all the functions for the time being conferred on him or her under any enactment or in any rules of court (with any necessary modifications) in relation to the taxation of costs to be paid by one party to another in proceedings before the Court.

NOTES AND COMMENTARY

This section imposes a slightly different rule to that imposed by s.118 in relation to the expert reviewer. Under s.118, a participating institution is liable to pay NAMA's costs in the event that NAMA is permitted to acquire the bank asset. In all other cases both NAMA and the participating institutions are to pay their own costs. It is unclear from subs.(1) whether a participating institution that is compensated under s.125 is required to pay its own costs. No express provision is made for the Minister's costs by the section.

See also Ord.99 of the Rules of the Superior Courts in relation to the taxation of costs.

PART 8

RELATIONSHIP BETWEEN NAMA AND PARTICIPATING INSTITUTIONS

Definition (*Part 8*)

128.—In this Part "relevant service" includes management, administration, restructuring and enforcement services in relation to bank assets, including any activity specified as part of a direction by NAMA or an arrangement or agreement to which NAMA or a NAMA group entity is a party.

NOTES AND COMMENTARY

The definition of relevant services partially defines the scope of NAMA's power to engage service providers under s.44. Section 131 requires participating institutions to continue to provide relevant services in respect of eligible assets until otherwise directed by NAMA or its group entities.

Participating institutions to act in utmost good faith

129.—(1) A participating institution shall act in utmost good faith at all times in its dealings with the Minister, NAMA, NAMA group entities, their agents, the expert reviewer and the valuation panel pursuant to this Act.

(2) A participating institution shall inform the Minister, NAMA and any NAMA group entity concerned of any fact or thing that may impede—

    (*a*) the achievement of the purposes of this Act,

    (*b*) the performance by the Minister of his or her functions, or NAMA of its functions, under this Act, or

    (*c*) the fulfilment by the participating institution of its obligations under this Act.

(3) If a participating institution identifies such an impediment the participating institution shall take all reasonable steps to address the impediment in a manner that best furthers the achievement of the purposes of the Act.

NOTES AND COMMENTARY

This section imposes a catch-all utmost good faith obligation on participating institutions in their dealings under the Act. Several sections of the Act impose specific obligations on participating institutions to act in good faith or utmost good faith when carrying out certain activities. See, for example, ss.66(1), 68(1), 71(1), 80(7), 81(7) etc. Under s.64(4), the obligation to act in the utmost good faith is extended to include disclosures by applicant institutions. The functions of the Act are set out in s.2, while the functions of NAMA are listed in s.10.

Breach of statutory requirements

130.—A participating institution that fails to comply with any obligation under this Act is liable to NAMA and any NAMA group entity concerned in damages in addition to any other consequence of the failure under this Act.

NOTES AND COMMENTARY

This section permits NAMA and its group entities to recover damages from a participating institution for breach of any obligation imposed by the Act. Liability under the section appears to be strict. It is not necessary for NAMA and its group entities to show that the obligation breached imposed a duty which was owed to NAMA; however it is unclear how damages would be assessed in such a case. The right to recover damages applies only to participating institutions and does not affect applicant institutions, though there seems to be no barrier to NAMA or its group entities recovering damages from a participating institution for a breach of duty while that institution was an applicant institution.

Servicing of acquired bank assets by participating institutions

131.—(1) For the purposes of this section, in the event of a conflict between—

(*a*) a direction by NAMA, and

(*b*) a term of an arrangement or agreement to which NAMA or a NAMA group entity is a party in relation to the provision of a relevant service,

then a direction by NAMA, a term of such an arrangement and a term of such an agreement shall have effect in that order of priority.

(2) The participating institution from which NAMA or a NAMA group entity has acquired or intends to acquire a bank asset shall, until NAMA or the NAMA group entity directs otherwise, continue to perform relevant services in respect of the bank asset. NAMA or the NAMA group entity shall reimburse the participating institution in respect of the agreed cost of such service.

(3) NAMA may direct a participating institution to perform a relevant service in connection with a bank asset that NAMA or a NAMA group entity has acquired or intends to acquire from that participating institution or any other participating institution. NAMA or the NAMA group entity shall reimburse the participating institution for the agreed cost of such service.

(4) A direction under *subsection (3)*—

(*a*) may require a participating institution to enter into an arrangement or agreement that includes an obligation to provide access for and permit the use by NAMA or a NAMA group entity of facilities, books, records and systems, and

(*b*) may require a participating institution concerned to provide a relevant service for the benefit of a NAMA group entity.

(5) NAMA may at any time amend, suspend or revoke a direction pursuant

to this section.

(6) A participating institution shall—

    (*a*) comply with a direction, and any amendment, suspension or revocation of a direction, pursuant to this section, and

    (*b*) ensure that any subsidiary to which such a direction extends also complies with it.

(7) A participating institution shall ensure that it and each of its subsidiaries—

    (*a*) obtains and maintains in effect any authorisation, consent, approval, resolution, licence, exemption, filing, notarisation or registration required (in the State or in any other place) in connection with the provision of the services required by a direction pursuant to this section, and

    (*b*) complies with the terms and conditions of, and any requirement of or under any law in relation to, any such authorisation, consent, approval, resolution, licence, exemption, filing, notarisation or registration.

(8) NAMA may give a debtor, associated debtor, guarantor or surety in relation to a bank asset in which NAMA or a NAMA group entity has acquired an interest, or any other person, notice of any direction given pursuant to this section. However, NAMA and the NAMA group entity are not liable to any debtor, associated debtor, guarantor or surety or any other person for failure to give such a notice.

(9) Any receivable or other amount received or recovered by a participating institution pursuant to the performance by it of a relevant service shall be held by that participating institution on trust absolutely for and to the order of NAMA or a NAMA group entity, as the case may be, and any amount so held shall be accounted for to NAMA or the NAMA group entity as NAMA from time to time directs. A trust constituted by this subsection—

    (*a*) does not form part of the assets of the participating institution whether for the purposes of laws generally applicable to winding up, reorganisations, liquidations or otherwise,

    (*b*) is effective for all purposes, and

    (*c*) shall not be taken to constitute or create a security.

NOTES AND COMMENTARY

Under s.44 NAMA may engage a participating institution, or any other persons to provide relevant services. Subsections (1) and (3) of this section permits NAMA to issue directions to participating institutions regarding the performance of a relevant service; under subs.(1) such an instruction is to have priority over anything contained in an agreement between the participating institution and NAMA. The subsection does not have the effect of abrogating any agreement between NAMA and the participating institution.

Institutions are obliged to service eligible bank assets at various stages during the acquisition process. Such obligations commence when the institution applies to become a participating institution under s.66. The obligations are continued following designation as a participating institution under s.71 and continued again after the service of an acquisition schedule under s.94. Subsection (3) provides that the participating institution will continue to provide relevant services relating to such assets until otherwise directed by NAMA. Under subs.(3) NAMA is required to pay for the performance of such services by a participating institution. Payment is owed in respect of services for assets which NAMA has "acquired or intends to acquire". Under s.85, NAMA is to indicate the assets which it proposes to acquire by serving acquisition schedules on the participating institution. Thus it seems that participating institutions are entitled to recompense for relevant service performed after the date of service. Participating institutions are entitled to recover "the agreed cost of such service". This envisages an agreement as to cost between NAMA and the institution concerned. The section is silent as to when this agreement is to be made and there is no dispute resolution procedure in the event that the parties do not agree on the cost.

Subsection (9) imposes a statutory trust for the benefit of NAMA and its group entities over any monies recovered by participating institutions in the course of providing relevant services. Paragraph (a) of this section gives statutory force to the existing position of trust property in Irish company law (see *Shanahans Stamp Auctions Ltd v Farrelly* [1962] I.R. 386 and *Re Money Markets International Stockbrokers Ltd (No.1)* [1999] 4 I.R. 267).

Other servicing arrangements

132.—(1) Where in relation to an acquired bank asset NAMA or a NAMA group entity has arranged with a service provider other than the participating institution from which the bank asset was acquired for the provision of relevant services in respect of an acquired bank asset, then—

   (*a*) the terms of the bank asset shall be taken to require each debtor, associated debtor, guarantor or surety in respect of a bank asset to deal with the service provider concerned,

   (*b*) NAMA or the NAMA group entity may give such a debtor, associated debtor, guarantor or surety notice of any arrangement for the provision of a relevant service in respect of that bank asset, and

   (*c*) NAMA and the NAMA group entity concerned are not liable to any such debtor, associated debtor, guarantor or surety or any other person for failure to give such a notice.

(2) Where NAMA or a NAMA group entity has arranged with a service provider for the provision of relevant services in respect of a bank asset that has been acquired or is to be acquired by NAMA or the NAMA group entity, the participating institution from which the bank asset is to be or was acquired shall do all such acts or things that NAMA or the NAMA group entity directs to facilitate the provision by the service provider of those relevant services.

Notes and Commentary

This section makes provision for situations in which NAMA has exercised its power under s.44 to engage a service provider other than the participating institution to provide relevant services in respect of an acquired bank asset. Subsection (1)(a) has the effect of altering any agreement between the listed parties and the participating institution so as to enable the service provider to carry out its functions. Subsection (1) only takes effect after the acquisition of the bank asset by NAMA or its group entities. Subsection (2) imposes a duty on participating institutions to cooperate with a service provider engaged by NAMA and its group entities. Subsection (2) appears to take effect from the date of service of the acquisition schedule. Although this section confers rights on NAMA group entities, it should be noted that the engagement of service providers under s.44 is a matter for NAMA alone and that NAMA group entities are not authorised by that section to engage service providers.

NAMA may give directions about certain bank assets not acquired

133.—(1) Where NAMA or a NAMA group entity has acquired a bank asset from a participating institution NAMA may, for the furtherance of the achievement of its purposes under this Act, direct the participating institution to deal in a specified way with any part of the bank asset not acquired, being a way in which the participating institution may lawfully deal, or has the authority to deal, with the bank asset or part.

(2) A participating institution shall comply with a direction by NAMA under *subsection (1)*.

NOTES AND COMMENTARY

A direction under this section may only be given by NAMA and not by a NAMA group entity. The remedy for non-compliance is set out in s.130.

Additional payment on servicing of acquired bank assets

134.—(1) With the consent of the Minister, NAMA or a NAMA group entity may agree with a participating institution on an arrangement in relation to the servicing of acquired bank assets.

(2) Without prejudice to the generality of *subsection (1)*, an arrangement referred to in that subsection may provide for—

(*a*) an adjustment to the total portfolio acquisition value,

(*b*) performance fees, and the reimbursement of costs and expenses, on terms approved by the Minister, or

(*c*) any combination of the things mentioned in *paragraphs (a)* and *(b)*.

NOTES AND COMMENTARY

This section provides for payments to participating institutions for servicing of acquired bank assets. It is not clear whether this section contemplates an additional payment to that provided for under s.131(2) or whether it merely provides the means by which payment is to be made. Subsection (1) appears to contemplate a payment pursuant to an agreement for the serving of bank assets so it would seem more likely that this section relates to an additional payment. The consent of the Minister is required for entering an agreement to make a payment under the section. This would appear to limit NAMA's powers to engage participating institutions under s.44. No ministerial approval is required for NAMA to enter an agreement under s.44, however it is difficult to imagine an agreement under s.44 which would not involve the making of a payment under this section.

Participating institutions to indemnify NAMA

135.—(1) If NAMA so directs, a participating institution shall indemnify NAMA or a NAMA group entity and each of their officers against any liability or loss (however arising, and regardless of any default on the part of NAMA or a NAMA group entity)—

(*a*) arising from any error, omission or misstatement in any information, explanation, instrument, document, record, book or certificate provided to NAMA or the NAMA group entity by or on behalf of the participating institution,

(*b*) in respect of any claim, award, payment or damages which NAMA or the NAMA group entity becomes liable to pay to any person by reason of the operation of the European Communities (Protection of Employees on Transfer of Undertakings) Regulations 2003 (S.I. No. 131 of 2003) where the liability arises in connection with a cause of action accruing before the relevant acquisition date (or any proportion of the liability or loss is attributable to a period before the relevant acquisition date) including any claim made by or on behalf of such a person that relates to an act or omission of the participating institution in connection with that person's employment before the acquisition date, and

(*c*) in respect of any redundancy payment, or any other severance payment, paid by NAMA or the NAMA group entity, or that NAMA or the NAMA group entity is ordered to pay, to any person whose employment transfers to NAMA or the NAMA group entity by reason of the operation of those Regulations and whose employment is terminated by NAMA or the NAMA group entity by reason of redundancy.

(2) Where the Court determines ownership of a bank asset in favour of a third party and as a result NAMA or a NAMA group entity is obliged to transfer the bank asset to the third party or pay damages in lieu, the participating institution shall indemnify NAMA or the NAMA group entity against that liability and all losses suffered by it.

(3) The Court and any other court or tribunal in which legal proceedings are brought in respect of a matter referred to in *subsection (1)* shall not make NAMA or a NAMA group entity a party to the proceedings in any capacity where the liability is that of the participating institution.

(4) If NAMA or a NAMA group entity so directs, and without prejudice to *section 105*, a participating institution shall indemnify NAMA or the NAMA group entity and its officers against any liability or loss in respect of a legal or equitable wrong referred to in that section.

NOTES AND COMMENTARY

Subsections (1) and (4) provide that NAMA or a NAMA group entity may direct a participating institution to provide an indemnity from liability or loss arising from the matters listed in the respective subsections. The two powers differ slightly in that NAMA may require an indemnity under subs.(1) even where the losses or liabilities arise from the default on the part of NAMA or its group entities. The subs.(4) power is narrower in scope. A direction under subs.(4) to grant an indemnity to NAMA or its group entities would seem to have no real effect since s.105 purports to grant immunity to NAMA and its group entities. A direction under subs.(4) could be used to obtain an indemnity for NAMA's officers against liabilities otherwise covered under s.105.

Participating institutions to be agent of subsidiaries, etc.

136.—(1) A participating institution is for all purposes of this Act the agent of each other legal entity in its group with full power to bind each other such entity.

(2) The service of a notice on, or any communication with, a participating institution referred to in *subsection (1)* is for all purposes of this Act effective as service of the notice on, or communication with, any other entity in the participating institution's group.

(3) In this section "group", in relation to a participating institution, means—

(*a*) the participating institution,

(*b*) any subsidiary of the participating institution, and

(*c*) any entity of which the participating institution is a subsidiary.

NOTES AND COMMENTARY

This section creates an agency relationship between participating institutions and their subsidiaries. The section is limited to granting authority to the participating institution as agent and does not confer additional contractual capacity on the subsidiary. The section is not limited to subsidiaries which are designated participating subsidiaries under s.67. Accordingly the section applies to a subsidiary company excluded from designation under s.67(6).

PART 9

POWERS OF NAMA IN RELATION TO ASSETS

CHAPTER 1

Definitions

Definitions (*Part 9*)

137.—In this Part—

"charged land" means land that is subject to a charge that is part of an acquired bank asset;

"convey" and "conveyance" have the same meanings respectively as in the Land and Conveyancing Law Reform Act 2009, and "conveyed" shall be construed accordingly;

"vesting order" means an order under *section 153*.

NOTES AND COMMENTARY

> Section 3 of the Land and Conveyancing Law Reform Act 2009 states:
> "'conveyance' includes an appointment, assent, assignment, charge, disclaimer, lease, mortgage, release, surrender, transfer, vesting certificate, vesting declaration, vesting order and every other assurance by way of instrument except a will; and 'convey' shall be read accordingly;".

CHAPTER 2

General Powers of NAMA in Relation to Assets

Interpretation (*Chapter 2*)

138.—For the purposes of this Chapter, a reference in this Chapter to NAMA shall be construed, in relation to a bank asset that has been acquired by a NAMA group entity, as a reference to either NAMA or the NAMA group entity unless the contrary intention appears.

NOTES AND COMMENTARY

This section confirms that the powers in this part are conferred on NAMA group entities as well as on NAMA unless a contrary intention appears. Under s.12(6), NAMA may exercise any of its powers for the benefit of a NAMA group entity.

NAMA's powers to dispose of bank assets

139.—NAMA may validly transfer, assign, convey, sell on or otherwise dispose of an acquired bank asset to any person notwithstanding—

    (*a*) any restrictions on such a disposal at law or in equity,

    (*b*) any contractual requirement, or any requirement under any enactment, for the consent of, for notice to, or for a document from, any person to such a disposal, or

    (*c*) any provision of any enactment that would otherwise prohibit or restrict such a disposal.

NOTES AND COMMENTARY

This section gives NAMA a wide ranging power to sell or transfer acquired bank assets. The power applies to the bank assets themselves and the section conferred does not alter NAMA's powers in respect of enforcing any security underlying a particular asset. It is clear that the section overrides non-assignment clauses which might otherwise make it impossible for the asset to be assigned. In *Dellway Investments v NAMA* [2011] IESC 14, Finnegan J. noted that para.(b) of this section combined with s.101 has the effect of depriving the mortgagor of the ability to enforce his rights by specific performance against NAMA. Finnegan J. did not consider whether there is a possibility of obtaining damages against the participating institution for breach of such a covenant under s.101(2).

Similarly, assignment of leaseholds which would normally require the consent of the landlord is avoided by the section (e.g. s.66 of the Landlord and Tenant (Amendment) Act 1980). The section would also appear to exempt NAMA from the operation of the Statute of Frauds requirements in respect of land (see s.51 of the Land and Conveyancing Law Reform Act 2009).

The Code of Practice on the Commercial Interests of Non-Participating Institutions, issued under s.35, states that powers under this section will not be used in the context of a syndicated loan without the approval of other members of the syndicate. NAMA is also committed to addressing the position of other loans secured on the property and ensuring that the rights of other secured creditors are not degraded (see [3.11(d)]). This is in line with a commitment given by the Irish authorities to the European Commission (see European Commission, Communication regarding State Aid N725/2009 Ireland of February 26, 2010, C(2010)1155 final, 18).

Power to discharge prior charge

140.—Where an acquired bank asset is secured by a charge (including a charge that is a collateral security), but the charge is a second or subsequent charge, NAMA may redeem or discharge any one (or more) of the prior charges in accordance with its terms.

NOTES AND COMMENTARY

This section gives NAMA the power to discharge a prior secured creditor. The power is likely to be used where the prior charge is held by a creditor other than a participating institution or where the prior charge is not itself connected with an acquired bank asset. It would seem likely that the section will be used alongside s.142, which enables NAMA to sell charged land free of any charge or mortgage which does not have priority to NAMA's interest in the land. The section has the effect of permitting NAMA to discharge or redeem prior charges notwithstanding anything in the charge documents which would prevent this result from being achieved. All other rights of the chargee are retained since redemption or discharge is "in accordance with it terms".

The section is silent as to who is to provide any funds necessary to secure redemption or discharge. Where funds are supplied by NAMA, it would seem to follow logically that such monies would be recoverable from the chargor but the section does not expressly confer a right of recovery on NAMA.

Power of entry to protect value or condition of land or buildings

141.—(1) Where an acquired bank asset is secured by a charge over land (including a charge that is a collateral security), and any one or more of the following paragraphs applies:

(*a*) the land or any building or structure on it has been abandoned;

(*b*) the land is or has become overgrown;

(*c*) the land or any building or structure on it is or has become infested with vermin;

(*d*) any building or structure on the land has fallen, or there is a serious risk of the building or structure falling, into disrepair;

(*e*) the land or any building or structure on it is at risk from trespassers or vandalism;

then NAMA may apply to a judge of the District Court for the time being assigned to the District Court district in which any part of the land concerned is situated, on notice to the owner and any occupier of the land, for an order (in this section referred to as an "entry and maintenance order") authorising it to enter (by force, if the order so provides) upon the land or any building or structure on it for any one or more of the following purposes:

(i) to fence or otherwise secure the boundary of the land;

(ii) to clear the land of overgrown vegetation;

(iii) to clear or treat the land or any building or structure on it in a manner designed to remove vermin;

(iv) to repair or make secure any building or structure on the land.

(2) NAMA shall serve a copy of an application under *subsection (1)* on every person it knows to have an interest in the relevant land.

(3) The District Court may make an order in accordance with an application under *subsection (1)* and if it does so shall specify the period, being not greater than 6 months beginning on the date of the order, for which the order shall have effect.

(4) NAMA shall give each owner and, where the relevant land is occupied, each occupier of the relevant land at least 24 hours' notice of its intention to enter on the land or any building or structure on it under the authority of an entry and maintenance order.

(5) An entry and maintenance order does not authorise forcible entry on the land, building or structure concerned unless the order expressly so provides.

(6) If NAMA enters on land or a building or structure under the authority of an entry and maintenance order, NAMA shall not be taken to be a mortgagee in possession of the land or any building or structure on it.

(7) Any cost, expense or liability that NAMA incurs pursuant to this section—

(*a*) is a debt due under the bank asset concerned, and

(*b*) is recoverable from the debtor, associated debtor, guarantor or surety concerned,

and the repayment of any such cost, expense or liability stands secured against the land.

Section 141 gives NAMA a power to take steps to preserve the value of land which constitutes the security for bank assets acquired by it. The section appears to be modelled on s.98 of the Land and Conveyancing Law Reform Act 2009 which permits a mortgagee to apply to the District Court for an order authorising him or her to go into possession of mortgaged premises. Under the 2009 Act, the mortgagee must satisfy the court that the mortgagor has abandoned the property and that "urgent steps are necessary to prevent" deterioration or damage to the property or entry onto it by trespassers or other persons. Since s.91 of the Act will place NAMA in the position of a mortgagee in many cases, it would seem that this section gives additional powers to those conferred by s.98 of the 2009 Act.

Under s.141, NAMA may obtain an order from the District Court in a broader range of circumstances than under the 2009 Act. In particular there is no requirement for NAMA to show urgency and subs.(1) expands the somewhat vague notion of "abandonment" to include specific examples of the sort of matters which justify making an order. The list of grounds appears to be exhaustive.

In contrast to the 2009 Act, the effect of an order under this section is not to place NAMA in possession of the land. The order is restricted to granting NAMA a right of entry to carry out the works specified in the order. The scope of the order is confined to the matters listed in subparas (i)–(iv) of subs.(1). Orders made under the section cannot exceed six months in duration. The order may authorise NAMA to make a forcible entry onto the property concerned. If authorisation is not expressly included in the order, the use of force is unlawful under the Forcible Entry and Occupation Act 1976. Subsection (4) requires NAMA to give the owner and any occupier 24 hours' notice before acting on foot of an order. Subsection (4) cannot be dispensed with by the court when making its order and it would appear to apply to persons who are in unlawful occupation of the premises as well as any tenant or licensee.

Subsection (2) requires copies of applications under this section to be served on all persons who have an interest in the land concerned. No timeframe is provided for this obligation and it is not clear whether other interested parties are entitled to be heard at the hearing of the application.

Subsection (7) allows NAMA to recover costs, expenses and liabilities incurred under this section from the debtor under the bank asset concerned. Under s.17 NAMA and its group entities are immune from suit in respect of a decision to exercise or not to exercise any of its powers under Pt 9. The immunity does not extend to the manner in which NAMA carries out its powers. Thus damages may be awarded against NAMA for any negligence or breach of duty by its agents when implementing an order under this section. Such damages may be recovered from the debtor as a "liability" under subs.(7). Subsection (7) states that any costs etc., are to be regarded as a debt secured against the land. The section is silent as to the priority of the resulting statutory security and the wording should be contrasted with s.98(3)(c) of the 2009 Act which makes costs incurred under an abandoned property order recoverable as part of the mortgage debt.

Certain instruments by NAMA to be taken to be deeds

142.—(1) In relation to any land in which NAMA has an interest, whether legal or beneficial, an instrument under seal of NAMA or the common seal of the NAMA group entity concerned that is expressed to convey that interest or any part of that interest in the land concerned to another person shall be taken for all purposes to be a deed of conveyance of the land executed under seal by the owner of the interest in the land concerned.

(2) An instrument referred to in *subsection (1)* extinguishes the interest of any other chargee or mortgagee in the land concerned other than a charge that has priority to the interest of NAMA concerned and has not been redeemed or discharged under *section 140*.

(3) Where the interest of a chargee or mortgagee in land is extinguished by

the operation of this section the interest attaches to the proceeds of the sale concerned.

(4) Where the interests of more than one chargee or mortgagee are extinguished by the operation of this section the interests so extinguished attach to the proceeds of the sale concerned in the same order of priority as those interests had before the extinguishment.

NOTES AND COMMENTARY

This section enables NAMA to sell or convey interest in land over which it acquires an interest through acquisition of a bank asset. The sale can be executed by way of an instrument under the seal of NAMA or a NAMA group entity. Subsection (2) provides that the purchaser shall take free of any other mortgages or charges except charges which have priority to NAMA's interests. Under s.140, NAMA has a separate power to redeem or obtain a discharge of such interests and in combination the two sections give NAMA an ability to sell land free of incumberances.

Where a junior secured creditor's interests are extinguished by subs.(2), subss.(3) and (4) provide that their interests re-attach to the proceeds of sale. If the proceeds of sale are insufficient to pay off the debts owed to NAMA, then in effect the charge-holders concerned will lose security for their advances.

For the formalities and effect of deeds generally see Ch.3, Pt 9, Land and Conveyancing Law Reform Act 2009.

Overreaching for protection of purchasers

143.—(1) Subject to *subsection (2)*, a conveyance by NAMA (including a conveyance by way of an instrument referred to in *section 142*) to a purchaser of a legal estate or legal interest in land overreaches any equitable interest in the land so that the equitable interest ceases to affect that estate or interest, whether or not the purchaser has notice of the equitable interest.

(2) *Subsection (1)* does not apply to an equitable interest—

    (*a*) to which the conveyance is expressly made subject,

    (*b*) that arises by virtue of an equitable mortgage related to the land concerned,

    (*c*) that, before the conveyance, is registered against the land in the Registry of Deeds or the Land Registry, or

    (*d*) that—

        (i) in the case of an interest in registered land, is a burden of a kind referred to in section 72(1)(*j*) of the Registration of Title Act 1964, or

        (ii) in the case of an interest in unregistered land, would take effect as such a burden if the land were registered land.

(3) Where an equitable interest is overreached under this section it attaches to the proceeds arising from the conveyance, and effect shall be given to it accordingly.

(4) NAMA shall discharge any obligations under *subsection (3)* as soon as is practicable.

(5) For the avoidance of doubt, overreaching in accordance with *subsections (1)* and *(2)* has effect in relation to land that is or includes a person's principal private residence.

(6) In this section "equitable mortgage" means a mortgage created by—

(*a*) the deposit of documents of title relating to the legal estate or legal interest in the land concerned, or

(*b*) an undertaking by a solicitor to hold the documents of title relating to the legal estate or legal interest in the land concerned in trust for a credit institution and which undertaking, where applicable, has been registered as a charge under section 99 or 111 of the Companies Act 1963.

NOTES AND COMMENTARY

Sections 140 and 142 taken together enable NAMA to sell land free from other mortgages and charges. Under this subs.(1) a conveyance of a legal interest by NAMA overreaches any other equitable interests binding on that legal interest. The section is clearly modelled on s.21 of the Land and Conveyancing Act Reform Act 2009. As with junior mortgagees or chargeholders, overreached interests attach to the proceeds of the sale and NAMA is required to discharge such interests as soon as practicable. The priority position of equitable interests attached to the purchase money is unclear. Arguably, NAMA's duty to discharge such obligations "as soon as practicable" has the effect of granting them priority to NAMA's interest in the proceeds.

Subsection (2)(d) exempts the interests of persons in actual occupation or in actual receipt of rents from the effect of overreaching. For consideration of the interests which fall with s.72(1)(j), see A. Lyall, *Land Law in Ireland*, 3rd edn (Dublin: Round Hall, 2010), p.948. Subsection (5) allows for the overreaching of an interest in a principal private residence. It is not clear whether this subsection would overreach spousal rights arising under the Family Home Protection Act 1976. By contrast, s.21(6) of the Land and Conveyancing Law Reform Act 2009 expressly excludes rights under the 1976 Act from the operation of overreaching.

Effect of certain assurances of land

144.—An assurance of charged land or a right or interest in charged land before the acquisition by, or vesting in, NAMA of the relevant charge (whether or not the land was charged at the date of the assurance) shall be taken to have created, for the benefit of the charged land, any easement or *profit à prendre* over any land retained by the grantor of the assurance that it is reasonable to assume, in the circumstances of the case, was within the contemplation of the parties at the date of the assurance as being included in it, or would have been within that contemplation at that time if they had adverted to the matter.

NOTES AND COMMENTARY

This section creates easements or profits à prendre over land retained by the grantor of an assurance which is not acquired by NAMA. The easement or profit is created for the benefit of land over which NAMA has acquired a charge through the acquisitions process. The general law of easements and profits has been modified by Ch.1, Pt 8 of the Land and Conveyancing Law Reform Act 2009. For an account of the general law see J.C.W. Wylie, *Irish Land Law,* 4th edn (Bloomsbury Professional, 2010), Ch.6.

An easement or profit is conferred on land by this section where either of the tests set out in the section are satisfied. First, if it is reasonable to assume that the parties to an assurance of the relevant land actually had an easement or profit in contemplation at the time the assurance was made. Second, an easement or profit will arise where it is reasonable to assume that the parties would have had a grant in mind had they "adverted to the matter".

Certain receivers not obliged to sell property, etc.

145.—(1) A receiver of the rents and profits of property appointed by NAMA pursuant to its powers as a chargee of the property is not obliged to sell the property at any particular time or at all, but is accountable for all profits and other monetary benefits arising directly from possession of the property.

(2) A receiver appointed to the property of a company by NAMA in its capacity as a creditor of the company is not obliged to sell any property of the company at any particular time or at all, but is accountable for all profits and other monetary benefits arising directly from possession of the property of the company.

Notes and Commentary

This section relates to receivers appointed by NAMA under s.108 of the Land and Conveyancing Law Reform Act 2009 or under powers contained in a charge document. A similar provision is made for statutory receivers appointed in Pt 9, Ch.3 by s.151 of the Act. The effect of the section is to confirm that a receiver appointed by NAMA may act as a receiver-manager but is subject to a duty of account for any profits and monetary benefits which may arise.

There is considerable uncertainty regarding the duties of receiver-managers. In *Kinsella v Somers,* unreported, High Court, Budd J., November 23, 1999, the court cited with approval the judgment of Lord Templeman in *Downsview Nominees v First City Corporation* [1993] 2 W.L.R. 86 at 99, in which the Privy Council held that a receiver-manager who acts in good faith and with the object of preserving and realising assets for the debenture-holder is subject to no additional liability.

Subsequently in *Medforth v Blake* [2000] 1 Ch 86 at 102, Scott V.C. suggested that a receiver-manager owes a broader set of equitable duties to the company. Scott V.C. summarised these in the following terms:

"In my judgment, in principle and on the authorities, the following propositions can be stated. (1) A receiver managing mortgaged property owes duties to the mortgagor and anyone else with an interest in the equity of redemption. (2) The duties include, but are not necessarily confined to, a duty of good faith. (3) The extent and scope of any duty additional to that of good faith will depend on the facts and circumstances of the particular case. (4) In exercising his powers of management the primary duty of the receiver is to try and bring about a situation in which interest on the secured debt can be paid and the debt itself repaid. (5) Subject to that primary duty, the receiver owes a duty to manage the property with due diligence. (6) Due diligence does not oblige the receiver to continue to carry on a business on the mortgaged premises previously carried on by the mortgagor. (7) If the receiver does carry on a business on the mortgaged premises, due diligence requires reasonable steps to be taken in order to try to do so profitably."

In *Moorview Developments v First Active Plc* [2009] IEHC 214, Clarke J. declined to definitively decide whether *Medforth* or *Downsview* represents the law in this jurisdiction. He noted that the *Downview* approach has the advantages of avoiding the difficult question of identifying the scope of a receiver-manager's duty to the company as well as avoiding the problem of a potential conflict between the receiver-manager's duty to the debenture-holder and his or her duty to the company.

Powers of NAMA to enforce securities, etc.

146.—The enforcement of a security by NAMA is not subject to the restrictions in the Conveyancing Act 1881 or the Land and Conveyancing Law Reform Act 2009.

NOTES AND COMMENTARY

Under this section, NAMA is not bound by the restrictions on the power of sale imposed on mortgagees. Section 7 of the Family Home Protection Act 1976 is unaffected. Sections 18 and 19 of the Conveyancing Act 1881 was repealed and re-enacted as ss.100 and 108 of the Land and Conveyancing Law Reform Act 2009 which minor changes to the wording of the section.

Section 100 of the Land and Conveyancing Law Reform Act 2009 restricts the situations in which the power of sale arises. In particular, s.100 requires a two month default in the payment of instalments before the mortgagee acquires a power of sale and the mortgagor is entitled to 28 days' notice of the possibility of resort to the power of sale. Once a power of sale arises, s.100 imposes further restrictions on the exercise of the power of sale. Unless the mortgagor consents in writing to the sale, the power of sale is only exercisable on foot of a court order. Section 108 imposes similar restrictions on the mortgagee's power to appoint a receiver.

Section 97 of the Land and Conveyancing Law Reform Act 2009 prevents the mortgagee from taking possession of the mortgaged property without the consent of the mortgagor or an order from the court. Finnegan J. in *Dellway Investments v NAMA* [2011] IESC 14, noted that the effect of s.146 is to put NAMA in the position of a mortgagee prior to the enactment of the Land and Conveyancing Law Reform Act 2009 by enabling it to take possession of the mortgaged property without the consent of the mortgagor and without recourse to court.

CHAPTER 3

Statutory Receivers

NAMA's power to appoint statutory receivers

147.—(1) Where any of the following occurs under the terms of an acquired bank asset:

(*a*) a power of sale becomes exercisable;

(*b*) a power to appoint a receiver becomes exercisable;

then NAMA may appoint any person, including an officer of NAMA, as a statutory receiver of the property the subject of the bank asset.

(2) NAMA may remove a statutory receiver and may appoint a new statutory receiver in the place of a statutory receiver removed.

(3) The appointment of a statutory receiver is not subject to the restrictions in the Conveyancing Act 1881 or the Land and Conveyancing Law Reform Act 2009 on the appointment of a receiver.

(4) NAMA may fix the remuneration of a statutory receiver. A maximum rate imposed by law (including that specified in section 24(6) of the Conveyancing Act 1881 or prescribed by regulations under section 108(7) of the Land and Conveyancing Law Reform Act 2009) does not apply.

(5) NAMA's power to appoint a statutory receiver under this Chapter does not affect any powers to appoint a receiver pursuant to any contractual power in any bank asset acquired by NAMA.

(6) The powers of NAMA under this section are exercisable by NAMA (and only by NAMA) in relation to a bank asset held by a NAMA group entity.

NOTES AND COMMENTARY

This section permits NAMA to appoint a statutory receiver with expanded powers in place of an ordinary receiver. Under subs.(1) the power to appoint a statutory receiver is aligned to the power of appointment under the terms of the relevant bank asset. Since s.146 disapplies the restrictions on the power of sale under s.100 of the Land and Conveyancing Law Reform Act 2009 it may be possible for NAMA to appoint a receiver earlier than would have been possible under the original charge documentation.

Subsection (3) removes the restrictions on the appointment of a receiver under s.108 of the 2009 Act. In *Dellway Investments v NAMA* [2010] IEHC 364, it was argued that this section had the effect of excluding a receiver's duty to obtain the best price for any asset sold under NAMA's powers. At [7.40], the court adopted the view expressed in JCW Wylie, *Land and Conveyancing Law Reform Act 2009: Annotations and Commentary* (Bloomsbury Professional, 2009), p.285, to the effect that s.103 of the 2009 Act is simply declaratory of the general law. As such, subs.(3) does not relieve statutory receivers from the obligation to obtain the best possible price when selling assets. In the Supreme Court, Finnegan J. noted that a statutory receiver has wide powers beyond those normally associated with receivership under the Companies Acts or under the Land and Conveyancing Law Reform Acts.

The section is silent on the qualifications needed to serve as a statutory receiver. Section 315 of the Companies Act 1963 disqualifies undischarged bankrupts, persons who have been officers or employees of the company within 12 months before the appointment of the receiver and certain connected persons from acting as receiver. NAMA may set remuneration without regard to any prescribed limits and may remove a statutory receiver at will, though a dismissed receiver would be entitled to a remedy for loss of office.

Under subs.(6) only NAMA may appoint a statutory receiver. This is unusual since NAMA group entities may hold title to the relevant bank assets and thus NAMA may not actually be a creditor when making the appointment. It is unclear whether or how this will affect the duties of a statutory receiver. In particular, it may possible to argue that since a statutory receiver is appointed under the provisions of the Act, he or she is not solely the agent of NAMA and must consider the interests of all creditors when performing his or her duties. See *Parsons v Sovereign Bank of Canada* [1913] 1 A.C. 160 at 167.

Powers of statutory receivers

148.—(1) A statutory receiver has the powers, rights and obligations that a receiver has under the Companies Acts, and the powers, rights and obligations specified in *Schedule 1*.

(2) In *Schedule 1* a reference to a secured asset is, in relation to a particular statutory receiver, a reference to land or property that is subject to a charge or other security that is included in the bank asset pursuant to which the statutory receiver was appointed.

(3) Where a charge provides for a receiver appointed under it to have any power in addition to those referred to in *subsection (1)*, a statutory receiver appointed in relation to the property subject to the charge also has that additional power. However, a statutory receiver exercising any such additional power is taken to do so by virtue of his or her appointment under this Chapter and is not bound by any restriction on its exercise specified in the charge.

(4) A statutory receiver is not subject to the restrictions on the powers of a receiver in the Conveyancing Act 1881 or the Land and Conveyancing Law Reform Act 2009.

(5) The enforcement of a security by a statutory receiver is not subject to the restrictions in the Conveyancing Act 1881 or the Land and Conveyancing Law Reform Act 2009.

(6) Section 100(2) of the Land and Conveyancing Law Reform Act 2009 does not apply to the exercise of a power of sale by NAMA or a statutory receiver.

(7) A statutory receiver, in selling property the subject of a charge in favour of NAMA, shall exercise all reasonable care to obtain the best price reasonably obtainable for the property at the time of sale.

(8) If joint statutory receivers are appointed, each one severally may exercise any power or carry out any function of a statutory receiver.

NOTES AND COMMENTARY

This section grants statutory receivers all the powers which would ordinarily arise under Pt VIII Companies Act 1963, as amended, as well as powers arising under the charge documentation. These powers are in addition to the extremely extensive powers conferred on statutory receivers by subs.(1) and Sch.1. Subsection (3) has the effect of broadening the language of the charge documentation by removing any constraints on any powers conferred on the receiver which are in addition to his powers under the Act. Given the breadth of power conferred by Sch.1, it is suggested that statutory receivers will only have to rely on subs.(3) in very unusual cases.

Subsections (4)–(6) exempt statutory receivers from restrictions arising under Pt 10 Ch.3 of the Land and Conveyancing Law Reform Act 2009. Subsection (5) exempts statutory receivers from compliance with the 2009 Act when enforcing security. It is not clear whether this extends to the application of the proceeds of sale under s.107 of the 2009 Act. If it does so, then there seems to be a lacuna in the NAMA legislation in that no provision is made for the application of proceeds.

Subsection (7) imposes a duty of care on a statutory receiver when selling property. In *Dellway Investments v NAMA* [2010] IEHC 364, the High Court held that this provision does not "imply that the ordinary legal duty on either a mortgagee selling property or a receiver selling property, having been appointed on foot of a debenture is in any way diminished or reduced".

Statutory receiver to be agent of chargor, etc.

149.—(1) A statutory receiver shall be taken to be the agent of the chargor for all purposes.

(2) The chargor is solely responsible for the remuneration, contracts, engagements, acts, omissions, defaults and losses of a statutory receiver and for liabilities incurred by a statutory receiver. NAMA does not incur any liability (either to the chargor or to any other person) by reason of the appointment of a statutory receiver or for the actions or inactions of a statutory receiver.

(3) A statutory receiver shall be taken to have been irrevocably appointed as an attorney of the chargor (with full powers of substitution and delegation) and to have the authority in the chargor's name, on the chargor's behalf and as the chargor's act and deed, to—

(*a*) sign, seal, execute, deliver and perfect and do all deeds, instruments, acts and things that the chargor could do or ought to do pursuant to any bank asset that has been acquired by NAMA or a NAMA group entity,

(*b*) generally in the chargor's name and on the chargor's behalf exercise all or any of the powers, authorities and discretions—

(i) conferred by any enactment, or the common law or pursuant to any agreement forming part of any acquired bank asset, or

(ii) that NAMA or the statutory receiver thinks fit for carrying into effect a sale, lease, charge, mortgage or dealing by NAMA, the relevant NAMA group entity concerned or the statutory receiver,

and

(*c*) generally to use the chargor's name in the exercise of any power, authority or discretion conferred on a statutory receiver.

Notes and Commentary

Subsection (1) creates a statutory agency between statutory receivers and NAMA.

Subsection (2) is an effective re-enactment of s.24(2) of the Conveyancing Act 1881. Subsection (2) exempts NAMA from any liability arising from the appointment of a statutory receiver. There is English authority suggesting that a mortgagee may be liable to the mortgagor for the acts of the receiver where the mortgagee directs the activities of the receiver (see *American Express International Banking Corporation Ltd v Hurley* [1985] 3 All E.R. 564 at 571). Subsection (2) prevents any such liability attaching to NAMA even where an officer of NAMA is appointed to act as statutory receiver.

Subsection (2) also appears to make the statutory receiver personally immune from suit in relation to the matters listed in the first sentence. This should be contrasted with the position under s.316(2) of the Companies Act 1963.

Subsection (3) confers powers on statutory receivers. These powers are in addition to those conferred by s.148.

Appointment of liquidator or examiner to companies whose assets are under control of statutory receiver

150.—(1) Notwithstanding any provision of the Companies (Amendment) Act 1990, the appointment of an examiner to a company whose assets or any part of them are under the control of a statutory receiver does not—

    (*a*) displace the statutory receiver or affect his or her powers, authority or agency,

    (*b*) prevent the statutory receiver from enforcing any security held by NAMA or a NAMA group entity, or

    (*c*) cause the de-crystallisation of any charge created as a floating charge over assets that are under the control of the statutory receiver.

(2) The appointment of a liquidator to a company whose assets or any part of them are under the control of a statutory receiver does not displace the statutory receiver and does not affect his or her powers, authority and agency.

NOTES AND COMMENTARY

In relation to the effect of examinership on the appointment of a receiver under contractual powers or under the Land and Conveyancing Law Reform Act (see s.5(2)(b) of the Companies (Amendment) Act 1990, as amended). In relation to de-crystallisation of floating charges on the appointment of an examiner see *Re Holidair Ltd* [1994] 1 I.R. 416. This section does not apply to receivers other than statutory receivers appointed by NAMA or a NAMA group entity, as a result it would seem advisable for NAMA to use statutory receivership in preference to any other right to appoint a receiver which it may have or acquire.

Statutory receiver not obliged to sell property, etc.

151.—A statutory receiver is not obliged to sell a charged property at any particular time or at all, but is accountable for all profits and other monetary benefits arising directly from possession of the property.

NOTES AND COMMENTARY

This section applies the duty to account for profits and monetary benefits arising from possession created for ordinary receivers under s.145 to statutory receivers appointed under Ch.3. The statutory receiver's duty to account under this section is a derogation from the statutory indemnity provided by the chargor under s.149(2).

CHAPTER 4

Vesting Orders

Application to Court

152.—(1) NAMA may apply to the Court for a vesting order if—

(*a*) an acquired bank asset includes a charge over land,

(*b*) the chargee's power of sale has become exercisable, and

(*c*) NAMA forms the view that it is unlikely that the sum secured by the charge can be recovered by a sale within 3 months after the application.

(2) An application under *subsection (1)* shall, where there is a charge secured over the land concerned that has priority to the charge referred to in *paragraph (a)* of that subsection, contain an undertaking by NAMA to discharge that charge in accordance with *section 154*.

(3) An application under *subsection (1)* shall be supported by an affidavit to which is exhibited evidence—

(*a*) as to the price likely to be realised, within 3 months after the application, by a sale of the land concerned, and

(*b*) of any other interests in the land, including any prior charge referred to in *subsection (2)*.

(4) NAMA shall serve notice of the application on—

(*a*) the chargor concerned,

(*b*) any chargee (whether prior or subsequent), and

(*c*) any guarantor of the relevant credit facility.

(5) NAMA shall publish a notice of an application for a vesting order in at least one daily newspaper circulating generally in the State.

(6) The Court shall set down an application under *subsection (1)* for preliminary hearing, at which it shall give directions for the taking of accounts in relation to the credit facility concerned. At the preliminary hearing the Court may stay the proceedings if a subsequent chargee wishes to offer to redeem in full the charge held by NAMA or a NAMA group entity.

(7) At a preliminary hearing under *subsection (6)*, the Court may direct that notice of the application shall be given to any other person.

(8) The Court may, in any application under this Chapter where it seems to the Court appropriate to do so, direct that evidence be given on affidavit. The Court may deal with the application summarily on consideration of any affidavits presented to it.

NOTES AND COMMENTARY

This section permits NAMA to apply to court to have land which is the subject of a charge vested in NAMA. Under s.155 the effect of a vesting order is, inter alia, to extinguish the chargor's equity of redemption in the land. In the Commission's State aid approval for the NAMA scheme (see European Commission, Communication regarding State Aid N725/2009 Ireland of February 26, 2010, C(2010)1155 final, 31), it was suggested that the rationale for the inclusion of provision for vesting orders is as follows:

> This remedy would allow NAMA to hold the land concerned rather than putting it up for sale immediately and then would avoid flooding the market with fire sales. The Commission recognises that the ability to work out a loan and its security over

a longer time horizon is central to the valuation process of the assets and in line with requirements of the Impaired Assets Communication.

Before NAMA may apply for a vesting order, the chargee's power of sale must have arisen. Under s.148(6) the provisions of the Land and Conveyancing Law Reform Act 2009 do not apply to the exercise of a power of sale by NAMA. Thus, it would appear that an application may be made under this section at any time after a default event which triggers a power of sale under the charge has occurred.

Subsection (2) requires NAMA to give an undertaking to discharge any prior charge-holder in accordance with s.154. There is nothing to prevent NAMA from exercising its power to discharge prior charge-holders under s.140 in advance of making an application under this section.

Subsection (3) requires NAMA to exhibit certain evidence on an affidavit in support of the application. The section does not require that the affidavit be sworn by any particular person.

Subsections (4) and (5) are concerned with publicising of NAMA's intention to make an application under the section. No time limit is specified for the service of notice, nor for the advertising of the petition. The Act is silent on whether or not an application under the section can proceed in circumstances where NAMA has failed to comply with its obligations under subss.(4) and (5). The range of persons entitled to notice under subs.(4) is narrower than that imposed on initial notices of compulsory purchase under s.160(2).

Under subs.(6) the court must order a taking of accounts at the preliminary hearing of the application. On the taking of accounts generally, see RSC Ord.33 rr.2–11. The interests of a subsequent charge-holder in the land would be extinguished by the making of a vesting order—see s.155(1)(c). A subsequent charge-holder's rights to proceed against the debtor are preserved by s.155(2).

A vesting order is similar to the equitable relief to grant foreclosure which was formally abolished (the jurisdiction had in any event become obsolete by the early twentieth century) by s.96(2) of the Land and Conveyancing Law Reform Act 2009. At pp.7–8 of his judgment in *Dellway Investments v NAMA* [2011] IESC 14, Finnegan J. suggested (though expressly reserving a definitive decision to later case) that there are a number of differences between NAMA's right to apply for a vesting order and foreclosure:

> The provisions of Part 9 Chapter 4 of the NAMA Act are even more disadvantageous to a mortgagor than foreclosure. The court has no power to make an order for sale in lieu. There were circumstances in which foreclosure could be reopened. Where within a reasonable time after foreclosure the mortgagor is in a position to redeem the foreclosure could be reopened. Again foreclosure could be reopened where the mortgagee sold the lands shortly after obtaining the order. If after foreclosure the mortgagee, claiming that the property is insufficient to satisfy the mortgaged debt, sued the mortgagor on his covenant for payment the foreclosure was reopened and the mortgagor became entitled to redeem. If the mortgagee sold the property he could not sue the mortgagor or a guarantor of the mortgagor's covenant. A mortgagor in respect of whom a vesting order is made is accordingly in a worse position than a mortgagor against whom a foreclosure order was made. The mortgagor, notwithstanding any increase in value of the land in the hands of the mortgagee, and the receipt of an income stream by the mortgagee, can still be sued on his covenant. If a sale by the mortgagee after a vesting order is made achieves a price which together with the income stream enjoyed exceeds the liability on the mortgage the mortgagor still remains liable to be sued on his covenant for the excess of the mortgage debt over the valuation fixed by the court. ...
>
> ... The courts of equity regarded foreclosure orders as oppressive of mortgagors, a view with which it seems the legislature concurs having abolished the remedy. For the reasons which I have mentioned the making of a vesting order is even more oppressive. It is no answer that the mortgagor whether on the exercise of a power of sale or on the making of a vesting order gets the benefit of the market value of the lands and so is not adversely affected by the additional power conferred upon NAMA. This is not so. The availability of a vesting order enables NAMA to proceed in a manner in which a prudent mortgagee in its own interest would not. A prudent mortgagee with a mortgagor in the appellants position as to the value of the mortgaged land and as to the excess

of the income stream over liability for interest would have a strong incentive not to exercise a power of sale but to appoint a receiver and delay a sale to abide an expected improvement in land values and in the interim obtain the benefit of the income stream in satisfaction of interest as it falls due with the excess going towards reduction of capital. NAMA has no incentive to do this and on the contrary has the incentive to avail of a vesting order. Having regard to NAMA's Business Plan it is more than a mere possibility that NAMA would exercise its right to obtain a vesting order.

Vesting orders

153.—(1) If the Court is satisfied, after considering the accounts and other relevant matters, that—

> (*a*) it is unlikely that the sum secured by the charge would be recovered were the land to be sold within 3 months after the application, and
>
> (*b*) there is no reasonable prospect of the chargor redeeming the charge concerned,

the Court shall make an order (in this Part referred to as a "vesting order") vesting in NAMA, or a NAMA group entity nominated by NAMA, the interest of the chargor, subject to any undertaking under *section 152(2)*, in the land concerned.

(2) If the Court makes a vesting order, the Court shall also—

> (*a*) determine the amount likely to be realised were the land to be sold within 3 months after the application, and
>
> (*b*) make an order for possession of the land concerned in favour of NAMA or the nominated NAMA group entity.

NOTES AND COMMENTARY

Once the two elements of the burden of proof under subs.(1) are established, the court must make a vesting order. There is no residual discretion and performance of an undertaking to discharge a prior charge-holder is on the only condition which the court may place on a vesting order.

Once a vesting order is made under subs.(1), the court must then decide the amount which a sale would be likely to realise within three months of the date after the application. The phrase "after the application" appears to indicate a period of three months after the conclusion of the application and this will need to be borne in mind when preparing affidavits under s.152(3) since the court will need to have sufficient evidence available to decide this issue.

The court is not required to consider the interests of any person other than a prior charge-holder. The section is silent as to the rights of anyone other than the chargor and charge-holders who may have an interest in the land. Where there are other equitable interests in the land it may be more appropriate for NAMA to proceed by utilising its power of sale under s.139, which would enable such interests to be overreached by s.143.

The Code of Practice on the Commercial Interests of Non-Participating Institutions, issued under s.35, states that powers under this section will not be used in the context of a syndicated loan without the approval of other members of the syndicate. Under para.3.11(a) of the code, NAMA must get the approval of holders of equivalent charges, in ranking and priority, before using its powers under this section. This is in line with a commitment given by the Irish authorities to the European Commission when obtaining state aid approval for NAMA (see European Commission, Communication regarding State Aid N725/2009 Ireland of February 26, 2010, C(2010)1155 final, 18).

Prior chargee's right to payment

154.—(1) In this section "value" means the amount determined by the court under *section 153(2)(a)*.

(2) Where the Court makes a vesting order in relation to land that is subject to a charge that is either prior to, or ranks equally with, that held by NAMA or the NAMA group entity concerned, the Court shall also order NAMA or the NAMA group entity—

> (*a*) if there is only one such chargee, to pay to that chargee whichever is the lesser of the amount secured by its charge and the value, or
>
> (*b*) if there is more than one such chargee, to pay to each such chargee, in the order of their priority, whichever is the lesser of—
>
>> (i) the amount secured by its charge, and
>>
>> (ii) the value or the remainder of the value, as the case requires.

NOTES AND COMMENTARY

This section requires the court to make an additional order concerning prior charge-holders where a vesting order is made. The court can only make an order under this section where there are charges which rank before or equal to NAMA's charge.

Where there is one such charge, the court must order NAMA to pay the lesser of the value of the property, as determined by the court under s.153(2)(a), or the amount secured by first charge. Where the other charge ranks equally with NAMA's this amounts to a modification of the ordinary rule that where charges equally ranked charges are treated *pari passu* (*Usborne v Trustees of Limerick Market* [1899] 1 I.R. 229; *Bowen v Brecon Railway Co* (1867) LR 3 Eq 541). In effect, NAMA's claim is subordinated to that of the other chargee.

Effect of vesting order

155.—(1) Notwithstanding any other enactment or rule of law, a vesting order—

> (*a*) extinguishes the chargor's equity of redemption in the land concerned,
>
> (*b*) vests title to the land in NAMA or the NAMA group entity nominated by NAMA for that purpose,
>
> (*c*) extinguishes the interest in the land of any other chargee, and
>
> (*d*) satisfies the requirements of the Land Registration Rules 1972 to 2008.

(2) The extinguishing of the interest of a chargee by *subsection (1)(c)* does not extinguish the debt secured by the charge concerned.

However, a payment ordered to be made under *section 154(2)* shall be applied in reduction of the debt secured by the relevant charge.

(3) The debt or debts owed by the chargor to NAMA or the NAMA group entity shall be reduced by the extent, if any, to which the value (within the meaning given by *section 154*) of the charged land exceeds the amount paid under that section.

(4) NAMA shall cause a vesting order to be sent to the Property Registration Authority under the Registration of Title Act 1964 and the Registration of Deeds and Title Act 2006. The Property Registration Authority shall cause NAMA or the nominated NAMA group entity, as the case requires, to be registered as owner of the land in accordance with the order.

(5) For the avoidance of doubt, the making of a vesting order in relation to land does not impose on NAMA or any NAMA group entity any obligation to sell the land within any particular period or at all.

This section vests ownership of land which is the subject of a vesting order in NAMA or a nominated NAMA group entity. Under s.(3) the value of the land as determined by the court under s.153(2) less any amount paid by NAMA to other charge-holders is deducted from the debts owed to NAMA by the chargor.

The effect of a vesting order on a title to affected land is set out in subss.(1) and (4). Under subs.(1)(d) a vesting order is deemed to satisfy the Land Registration Rules. This subsection is designed to facilitate NAMA's registration of its interest in the relevant land under subs.(4). There seems to be a minor drafting error in subs.(1)(d). The wording refers to the Land Registration Rules 1972 to 2008. By the time the NAMA Act had received the President's signature on November 22, 2009, the Land Registration Rules 2009 (S.I No. 349 of 2009) had been introduced. Rule 1(2) of the 2009 rules state that the 2009 rules are to be construed "together as one" with the existing corpus of land registration rules.

Subsection (4) requires NAMA to register a vesting order with the Property Registration Authority and requires the authority to cause NAMA or the nominated entity "to be registered as owner of the land". The Act does not define the term owner. The term owner may refer to outright ownership of the legal title to the land in question, or may refer to ownership of whatever interest in the land was formerly held by the chargor. It is suggested that the second interpretation is to be preferred.

If NAMA were to be registered as a freehold owner of land where the chargor only held a leasehold interest then the reversionary interests in the land would be effectively overreached. Section 155 makes no provision for the overreaching of interests belonging to persons other than the chargor. By contrast, when providing a power of sale for NAMA under s.139, the Oireachtas specifically provided for overreaching under s.143. The other reason for ascribing a limited meaning to the word "owner" in subs.(4) is that the Registration of Title Acts 1964 and 2006 provide for the registration of different classes of ownership depending on whether the land in question is freehold or leasehold land.

Title of purchaser not impeachable

156.—(1) The title of a purchaser from NAMA or a NAMA group entity of land in relation to which NAMA has obtained a vesting order is not impeachable on the ground of any irregularity in the vesting order or any irregularity or impropriety in the obtaining of it.

(2) No purchaser from NAMA or a NAMA group entity, and no subsequent purchaser, of land referred to in *subsection (1)* is either required or entitled to raise any requisition or make any objection on title specific to the vesting order.

This section ensures that any title acquired by NAMA under a vesting order is unaffected by any irregularity in the making or obtaining of the vesting order. Subsection (2) prohibits the validity of the vesting order from being raised as an objection or requisition on a subsequent conveyance of the land. Unlike the somewhat similar s.105 of the Land and Conveyancing Law Reform Act 2009, this section makes no provision for damages to be paid to any person who suffers loss as a result of an improper use by NAMA of its powers under this Chapter. It should be noted that NAMA has a general immunity from suit from claims arising from a decision to utilise its powers under Pt 9 provided that the decision to do so is made in good faith (see s.17 and the notes accompanying that section).

CHAPTER 5

Compulsory Acquisition of Land

Definitions (*Chapter 5*)

157.—(1) In this Chapter—
"acquisition order" means an order under *section 163*;
"compulsory transfer order" means an order under *section 167*;
"initial notice" means a notice referred to in *section 160*.
   (2) In this Chapter—
   (*a*) a reference to charged land includes land in relation to which a vesting order has been made, and
   (*b*) a reference to the nominated NAMA group entity in relation to land is a reference to the NAMA group entity nominated by NAMA under *section 163(1)* in relation to the land.

NOTES AND COMMENTARY

Section 4 imports the definition of land from s.3 of the Land and Conveyancing Law Reform Act 2009.

NAMA's powers to acquire land compulsorily

158.—(1) NAMA may compulsorily acquire land if in its opinion it is necessary to do so—
   (*a*) to enable NAMA to perform the functions referred to in *section 10(1)(b)* and *(c)*,
   (*b*) to enable a building constructed on charged land to be used or enjoyed for the purpose for which it was developed, or
   (*c*) to enable NAMA or a NAMA group entity to vest in a prudent and experienced purchaser good and marketable title to charged land but only if the land sought to be acquired is only of material benefit to the owner in so far as it affects the use or development of charged land.
   (2) In addition, NAMA may compulsorily acquire land where—
   (*a*) the land is owned by a person who is a debtor, associated debtor, guarantor or surety in relation to an acquired bank asset, and that person is in material default of his or her obligations to NAMA or a NAMA group entity and the default has caused, or is likely to cause, NAMA or the NAMA group entity substantial loss,
   (*b*) the land was intended to form part of a security in relation to a credit facility provided by a participating institution but was not included in the security through an error or omission, or
   (*c*) a debtor, associated debtor, guarantor or surety in relation to an acquired bank asset is using or intends to use his or her ownership of the land to materially impede the disposition, at a fair and reasonable price, of land by NAMA or a NAMA group entity.
   (3) NAMA may compulsorily acquire land only if it has first made a reasonable attempt to acquire the land by agreement.

155

Subsection (3) requires NAMA to make an attempt to acquire land by agreement before utilising its compulsory purchase powers. No guidance is given on the meaning of the words reasonable attempt. A similar restriction is to be found in ss.22 and 23 of the Forestry Act 1946. Under s.163(2)(a)(ii) the court must be satisfied that this obligation has been complied with before it can make an acquisition order following a contested application.

Subsections (1) and (2) list the circumstances in which NAMA may utilise compulsory purchase powers. Under subs.(1), NAMA may compulsorily acquire land only where it is necessary for the purposes listed in paras (a)–(c).

Paragraph (1)(a) gives NAMA a power to acquire land where this is necessary for achieving its statutory purposes under s.10. Section 10(1)(a) and (b) gives NAMA the function of expeditiously managing assets acquired by it and of protecting or enhancing the value of those assets in the interest of the State.

Paragraph (1)(c) envisages a situation in which NAMA proposes to transfer charged land to a "prudent and experienced person" for development purposes. A power arises for NAMA to compulsorily acquire additional land and to transfer it to the developer where this would enhance the use or development or the charged land.

During the Committee Stage debate in the Dáil, the Minister indicated that paras (1)(b) and (c) were included purely to enable NAMA to acquire "ransom strips" connected with charged lands. He stated that the necessity test had been included in subs.(1) in order to ensure that the power could not be used to acquire land for the State's commercial advantage (23 *Dáil Debates: Special Committee on Finance and the Public Service* Cols 1139–1141 (October 29, 2009)).

The Code of Practice on the Commercial Interests of Non-Participating Institutions, issued under s.35, states that the power to seek a compulsory purchase order under para.(1)(a) will only be used where there are "issues concerning ransom strips or access or related issues" and where the case cannot be dealt with under the other grounds for seeking compulsory purchase. Paragraph [3.11(b)] of the Code defines a ransom strip as "any estate or interest in or over land…whatsoever without which, in line with good conveyancing practice in Ireland, there is a material impediment or physical impediment to the use or sale of the land for its intended use or purpose or a material impediment to the vesting good and marketable title in the land."

These restrictions are in line with commitments given by the Irish authorities to the European Commission when obtaining state aid approval for NAMA. Under the terms of the Commission's approval for NAMA, NAMA is committed to advising and consulting the Commission in the event it seeks to utilise the power under para.(1)(a) outside the context of ransom strips (see European Commission, Communication regarding State Aid N725/2009 Ireland of February 26, 2010, C(2010)1155 final, 18).

Subsection (2) creates an additional power of compulsory purchase. In contrast to subs.(1), the exercise of this power is not contingent on use of the power being necessary. The subs.(2) power is confined to land which is owned by a debtor, associated debtor, guarantor or surety in relation to acquired bank assets. Secondly, the owner of the land must be in "material default" and must have caused or be likely to cause "substantial loss" to NAMA. No guidance is given on how "material default" is be interpreted. Nor does the legislation specify what is to be considered "substantial loss". The magnitude of the loss is presumably to be measured by reference to the size of the debtor's obligation to NAMA. If measured against the size of the NAMA portfolio as a whole, it is difficult to imagine this condition ever being satisfied.

The third condition presents two alternatives. First, NAMA may show that the land was intended to form part of the security for the credit facility but did not do so owing to an error or omission. Alternatively NAMA may show that the present owner of the land is using or intends to use their ownership to impede the disposition of land by NAMA at a reasonable price.

The first of these alternatives seems to relate to a situation where land has not been taken as security owing to some failure to comply with a formal requirement such as registration, use of written documentation etc. This follows from the fact that an intention to create a mortgage or charge will result in the creation of an equitable charge provided the property subject to the charge is adequately specified (see *Re Valley Ice Cream (Ireland) Ltd,* unreported, High Court, July 22, 1998). It is not a requirement of the section that the error or omission be made by any party to the security. The second alternative seems to relate to ransom strips owned by a debtor or associated person.

Application to Court for acquisition order

159.—(1) If NAMA proposes to compulsorily acquire any land, NAMA shall apply to the Court for an order (in this Chapter called an "acquisition order") authorising it to acquire the land.

(2) The application under *subsection (1)* shall be accompanied by the maps, plans and books of reference to be deposited in accordance with *section 161*.

NOTES AND COMMENTARY

For procedural controls governing applications under this section see ss.160 and 161.

Initial notice of acquisition

160.—(1) NAMA shall publish a notice (in this Chapter called the "initial notice"), in the form (if any) prescribed by the Minister by regulations, of an application under *section 159* in a daily newspaper circulating in the State generally.

(2) NAMA shall serve a copy of an initial notice on every person who appears to NAMA to have an estate or interest in the land concerned, so far as it is reasonably practicable to ascertain those persons. However, failure to serve an initial notice on every such person does not invalidate the acquisition order concerned.

(3) An initial notice—

    (*a*) shall include a statement that persons claiming an estate or interest in the land concerned have the right to lodge with the Court, within 21 days after the publication of the notice, an objection to the making of an acquisition order in relation to the land, and

    (*b*) shall specify the times and places where the maps, plans and books of reference deposited in accordance with *section 161* can be inspected.

NOTES AND COMMENTARY

The Minister has not specified a form for the initial notice under subs.(1). No time period is specified for the publication of the initial notice, but a period of at least 21 days is required in light of subs.(3).

The initial notice must be served on all persons who NAMA believes to have an interest in the land. This should be contrasted with the position in relation to applications for vesting orders under s.152. Subsection (2) makes it clear that an acquisition order cannot be overturned in the event that it is discovered that notice was not served on a relevant party after an order has been made under s.163 . It is unclear whether an application to court under s.159 may proceed in the event that a mistake in service is discovered prior to the application being heard.

Maps, plans and books to be deposited

161.—(1) NAMA shall cause maps, plans and books of reference to be deposited in accordance with this section.

(2) The maps and plans shall be sufficient in quantity and character to show the land at an adequate scale.

(3) The books of reference shall so far as practicable contain the names of the owners or reputed owners, lessees or reputed lessees, and occupiers of the land that is proposed to be acquired.

(4) The maps, plans and books of reference shall be deposited at such place or places as NAMA considers suitable and shall remain so deposited for at least 21 days after publication of the initial notice. While so deposited, they shall be open to inspection, free of charge, between 10 o'clock in the morning and 4 o'clock in the afternoon on every day except Saturdays, Sundays and public holidays.

NOTES AND COMMENTARY

This is a standard requirement in respect of compulsory purchase schemes. For analogous provisions see s.31 and Sch.2 to the National Sports Campus Development Authority Act 2002; s.17 and Sch.2 to the Air Navigation and Transport (Amendment) Act 1998; s.16 and Sch.4 to the Harbours Act 1996; and s.76 and Sch.3 to the Housing Act 1966.

Consideration by Court of objections

162.—(1) A person claiming an estate or interest in land in relation to which an initial notice has been published and served may lodge with the Court, within 21 days after the publication of the initial notice, an objection to the making of an acquisition order in relation to the land, setting out the grounds on which the objection is based.

(2) In determining an application by NAMA under this Chapter, the Court shall consider any objection lodged with the Court in accordance with *subsection (1)*.

(3) The Court is not obliged to consider any objection—

(*a*) that is not lodged within the period allowed by *subsection (1)*, or

(*b*) that does not show on its face the objector's estate or interest in the land concerned.

(4) In considering an objection under *subsection (1)*, the Court shall have regard to the nature of the objector's estate or interest in the land.

NOTES AND COMMENTARY

It should be noted that the court is not prohibited from hearing an objection which has not been lodged within the 21 day time limit or which does not show the objector's interest in the land. Subsection (3) gives the court a residual discretion in this regard.

Acquisition order

163.—(1) If no objection to NAMA's application is lodged with the Court within the period referred to in *section 162(1)*, the Court shall make an order authorising NAMA or a NAMA group entity nominated by NAMA to acquire the land concerned compulsorily in accordance with the terms of its application.

(2) If an objection to NAMA's application is lodged with the Court within the period referred to in *section 162(1)* the Court shall make an order referred to in *subsection (1)* if the Court is satisfied that—

(*a*) one of the following applies:

(i) NAMA has reasonably formed the opinion referred to in *section 158(1)*;

      (ii) a condition set out in *section 158(2)* is satisfied;

   (*b*) NAMA has complied with the obligation in *section 158(3)*, and

   (*c*) it is just and equitable to make the order.

(3) The Third Schedule to the Housing Act 1966 applies to an acquisition order subject to the following modifications:

   (*a*) references to a sum of money shall be construed as references to the equivalent sum in euro;

   (*b*) references to a housing authority or an authority shall be construed as references to NAMA;

   (*c*) references to the Minister shall be construed as a reference to the Court in the exercise of its functions under this Chapter;

   (*d*) the omission of Article 4, paragraphs (1) to (4) of Article 5 and Article 5(5)(*d*).

NOTES AND COMMENTARY

As with the provisions in relation to vesting orders the court has no discretion regarding the making of an acquisition order under this section beyond the grounds of refusal provided in the section itself. Under subs.(1) an uncontested application must result in the court making an order.

Under subs.(2) the court must first assess NAMA's compliance with s.158 before considering whether it just and equitable for the order to be made. This will presumably involve detailed consideration of the nature of the objections placed before the court under s.162. The court appears not to be prevented from considering other matters when assessing para.(c).

Subsection (3) applies the provisions of Sch.3 to the Housing Act 1966 to the making of an acquisition order under this section.

Notice to treat

164.—(1) Where an acquisition order has been made, NAMA may serve a notice (referred to as a notice to treat) on every owner, lessee and occupier of the land (except tenants for a month or a shorter period).

(2) A notice to treat—

   (*a*) shall state that NAMA is willing to treat for the purchase of the several interests in the land, and

   (*b*) shall require each owner, lessee and occupier—

      (i) to state within a specified period (not less than one month from the date of service of the notice to treat) the exact nature of the interest in respect of which he or she claims compensation and details of the compensation claimed, and

     (ii) if NAMA so requires, to distinguish separate amounts of that compensation in such manner as NAMA specifies in the notice to treat and show how each such amount is calculated.

(3) A notice to treat served under *subsection (1)* shall be taken to be a notice to treat for the purposes of the Acquisition of Land (Assessment of Compensation) Act 1919.

NOTES AND COMMENTARY

A notice to treat need be served only on owners, lessees and occupiers. This notice requirement appears to be narrower than the requirement to service an initial notice of acquisition under s.160.

Although the verb "may" is used in connection with the service of a notice to treat, it is suggested that service is mandatory. In *Doyle v Hearne* [1987] I.R. 601, the Supreme Court held that the word "may" can be treated as "shall" where the context so requires.

Subsection (2) imposes minimum information requirements which a notice to treat under this section must meet. For details of the consequences of failing to abide by statutory requirements when drafting a notice to treat, see S. McDermott and R. Woulfe, *Compulsory Purchase and Compensation: Law and Practice in Ireland* (Butterworths, 1992), p.173.

NAMA's power to take possession

165.—(1) At any time after the making of an acquisition order and before conveyance or ascertainment of price, NAMA or the NAMA group entity nominated by NAMA under *section 163(1)* may, subject to *subsection (2)*, enter on and take possession of the land to be acquired.

(2) NAMA or the nominated NAMA group entity referred to in *subsection (1)* shall not enter on or take possession of land under this section without giving any occupier or owner of the land at least 14 days' notice in writing of its intention to do so.

Notes and Commentary

This is a standard provision in legislative schemes providing for compulsory purchase. For analogous provisions see s.31 and Sch.2 to the National Sports Campus Development Authority Act 2002; s.17 and Sch.2 to the Air Navigation and Transport (Amendment) Act 1998; s.16 and Sch.4 to the Harbours Act 1996; and s.76 and Sch.3 to the Housing Act 1966.

In contrast to s.141 NAMA has no means of obtaining power to enter onto land by force under this section.

Determination of compensation

166.—(1) The amount of the price to be paid by NAMA for land shall, in default of agreement, be fixed under and in accordance with the Acquisition of Land (Assessment of Compensation) Act 1919.

(2) Section 63 and sections 69 to 79 of the Lands Clauses Consolidation Act 1845 apply to the price and, subject to *sections 167* and *169* of this Act, to the land acquired. For the purpose of the application of those sections a reference to the promoters of an undertaking shall be construed as a reference to NAMA.

(3) If NAMA or a NAMA group entity exercises its power of entry under *section 165*, NAMA is liable to pay compensation as if the provisions of the Lands Clauses Acts (within the meaning given by the Schedule to the Interpretation Act 1937) relating to entry on lands had been complied with and to pay interest upon that compensation from the date of entry at the rate applicable to compulsory purchase orders by local authorities in accordance with the provisions of the Housing Act 1966.

Notes and Commentary

The Land Clauses Acts are defined in the Interpretation Act 1937 as meaning:
"the Lands Clauses Consolidation Act, 1845, the Lands Clauses Consolidation Acts Amendment Act, 1860, the Railways Act (Ireland), 1851, the Railways Act (Ireland), 1860, the Railways Act (Ireland), 1864, the Railways Traverse Act, the Acquisition of Land (Assessment of Compensation) Act, 1919, and every statute for the time being in force amending those Acts or any of them."

The Interpretation Act 1937 has now been repealed by the Interpretation Act 2005. The 2005 Act does not contain a definition of the Land Clauses Act.

Court may make compulsory transfer order

167.—(1) Where NAMA or a NAMA group entity has entered on and taken possession of land in accordance with *section 165* and the Court is satisfied that—

(a) the several estates or interests in the land have not been conveyed or transferred to NAMA or the nominated NAMA group entity,

(b) it is necessary, in connection with the purposes for which NAMA has been authorised to acquire the land compulsorily, that the acquisition of the land should be completed, and

(c) NAMA has made an offer in writing to each person having an estate or interest in the land who has furnished sufficient particulars of that estate or interest to enable NAMA to make an offer for it,

then the Court may make an order (in this Chapter referred to as a "compulsory transfer order") vesting the land in NAMA or the nominated NAMA group entity subject to any terms and conditions that the Court thinks fit.

(2) After the Court makes a compulsory transfer order, NAMA shall within 7 days after having received notification from the Court of the making of the order—

(a) publish in a newspaper circulating in the area of the land to which the order relates a notice stating that the order has been made, describing the land and naming a place where a copy of the order may be seen at all reasonable times, and

(b) serve on every person appearing to NAMA to have an estate or interest in the land a notice that the order has been made and the effect of the order.

NOTES AND COMMENTARY

This is a standard requirement in respect of compulsory purchase schemes. For analogous provisions see s.31 and Sch.2 to the National Sports Campus Development Authority Act 2002; s.17 and Sch.2 to the Air Navigation and Transport (Amendment) Act 1998; s.16 and Sch.4 to the Harbours Act 1996; and s.76 and Sch.3 to the Housing Act 1966. It is worth noting that unlike many of the analogous examples, it is not necessary for NAMA to show that there is an urgent need to complete the transaction before obtaining a completion order.

NAMA to inform Revenue Commissioners if certain liabilities exist

168.—Where NAMA becomes aware, before the making of a compulsory transfer order, that a person from whom an estate or interest in the land is to be transferred by the order is subject to a liability for estate duty, succession duty or inheritance tax, NAMA shall notify the Revenue Commissioners of the Court's intention to make the order.

NOTES AND COMMENTARY

Legislation establishing compulsory purchase schemes frequently requires that bodies such as the Land Commission or the Commissioner for Public works be informed of the proposed orders. For analogous provisions see s.31 and Sch.2 to the National Sports Campus

Development Authority Act 2002; s.17 and Sch.2 to the Air Navigation and Transport (Amendment) Act 1998; s.16 and Sch.4 to the Harbours Act 1996; and s.76 and Sch.3 to the Housing Act 1966.

This section obliges NAMA to notify the Revenue Commissioners of the proposed order in the event NAMA becomes a liability to estate duty, succession duty or inheritance tax. NAMA has no discretion in making the notification. It appears that NAMA must have actual notice of a relevant liability before the obligation arises.

Form and effect of compulsory transfer order

169.—(1) A compulsory transfer order shall have attached to it a map of the land to which it relates.

(2) A compulsory transfer order vests in NAMA or the NAMA group entity nominated by NAMA under *section 163(1)* the land specified in it in fee simple free from encumbrances and all estates, rights, titles and interests of whatever kind (other than any public right of way) with effect from a date (not earlier than 21 days after the making of the order) specified in the order.

(3) NAMA shall cause a compulsory transfer order to be sent to the Property Registration Authority under the Registration of Title Act 1964 and the Registration of Deeds and Title Act 2006. The Property Registration Authority shall cause NAMA or the nominated NAMA group entity referred to in *section 163(1)* to be registered as owner of the land in accordance with the order.

NOTES AND COMMENTARY

This section is in broadly line with other statutory schemes for compulsory purchase. For analogous provisions see s.31 and Sch.2 to the National Sports Campus Development Authority Act 2002; s.17 and Sch.2 to the Air Navigation and Transport (Amendment) Act 1998; s.16 and Sch.4 to the Harbours Act 1996; and s.76 and Sch.3 to the Housing Act 1966.

The most significant difference between the wording of this section and its counterparts is that subs.(3) permits NAMA to register a compulsory transfer order in the Registry of Deeds. This reflects the fact that, unlike other public bodies, NAMA is exempt from the obligation to register title in Land Registry under s.107(7).

Effect of compulsory acquisition without compulsory transfer order

170.—(1) Upon the completion of a compulsory acquisition otherwise than by compulsory transfer order, all private rights of way and all rights of laying down, erecting, continuing or maintaining pipes, sewers, drains, wires or cables on, under or over the land concerned (together with the property in those pipes, sewers, drains, wires or cables) and all other rights or easements in or relating to the land shall (except so far as otherwise agreed by NAMA or the NAMA group entity nominated by NAMA under *section 163(1)* and the person entitled to the right) vest in NAMA or the nominated NAMA group entity without any conveyance or transfer.

(2) A person who suffers loss by the vesting, by virtue of *subsection (1)*, of a right or property is entitled to be paid compensation by NAMA.

(3) Compensation payable by virtue of *subsection (2)* shall be determined under and in accordance with the Acquisition of Land (Assessment of Compensation) Act 1919.

NOTES AND COMMENTARY

This section provides for the payment of compensation where NAMA compulsorily acquires rights in land other than by way of compulsory transfer order. The section appears to be based on s.83 of the Housing Act 1966. It provides for the payment of compensation to the owners of easements affected by a compulsory acquisition. Compensation is to be calculated by reference to the Acquisition of Land (Assessment of Compensation) Act 1919. For a helpful analysis of s.83 of the Housing Act 1966 (see S. McDermott and R. Woulfe, *Compulsory Purchase and Compensation: Law and Practice in Ireland* (Butterworths, 1992), p.277).

Service of notices

171.—(1) A notice under this Chapter may be served on a person by sending it by registered post in an envelope addressed to him or her at his or her usual or last known address.

(2) If for any reason the envelope cannot be so addressed, it may be served on the person for whom it is intended by—

    (*a*) sending it by registered post in an envelope addressed to "the occupier" without stating his or her name, at the land to which the notice relates, or

    (*b*) affixing a copy of the notice prominently on the land.

NOTES AND COMMENTARY

This section governs the service of notices under this Chapter. Affected notices include: initial notices under s.160, notices to treat under s.164 and notices of compulsory transfer orders under s.167. In contrast to the position of participating institutions under s.136, separate notices must be given to each company within a group of companies.

CHAPTER 6

General Powers in Relation to Land

Limitations on certain dealings in land, etc.

172.—(1) If a person owns charged land and—

    (*a*) the person—

        (i) owns other land (in this subsection referred to as the "relevant land") or holds an option to acquire such land, or

        (ii) holds an interest in other land, or an option to acquire such an interest,

    and

    (*b*) unless the relevant land, the interest or the option were owned or held (as the case requires) by NAMA, the charged land would be unable to realise its full value for development, sale, leasing or any other use,

the person shall not deal with the relevant land, the interest or the option without giving reasonable written notice to NAMA.

(2) A dealing in contravention of *subsection (1)* is voidable at NAMA's option except against a person who has in good faith and for value acquired an interest in the land concerned.

(3) A person who is the debtor in relation to an acquired bank asset, who is a person referred to in any of *subparagraphs (i), (ii), (iii), (v) or (vi)* of *section*

70(1)(b) or who is a person on whose behalf the debtor or the person referred to in one of those subparagraphs acts as a nominee or trustee in relation to an acquired bank asset shall not, if any of those persons is in default in relation to any acquired bank asset, acquire from NAMA or a NAMA group entity, any legal or beneficial interest in property comprised in the security forming part of any acquired bank asset in relation to which the default has occurred.

(4) The Minister may, if in the opinion of the Minister it is necessary to do so having regard to the purposes of this Act and, in particular, to the interests of taxpayers and the nature and extent of the default, make regulations—

    (*a*) prohibiting or restricting the acquisition by a person who is in a prescribed class of debtors, or of persons directly or indirectly connected to debtors, of any legal or beneficial interest in property comprised in the security forming part of any acquired bank asset or any acquired bank asset of a prescribed class of acquired bank assets, where the debtor concerned is in material default of any payment obligation to NAMA or a NAMA group entity for which a satisfactory arrangement to remedy the default has not been made, and

    (*b*) prescribing the requirements which such persons would be required to meet in order to acquire property comprised in the security forming part of any acquired bank asset or any acquired bank asset of a specified class of acquired bank assets from NAMA or a NAMA group entity.

(5) A draft of every regulation proposed to be made under *subsection (4)* shall be laid before each House of the Oireachtas and the regulation shall not be made until a resolution approving of the draft has been passed by each such House.

NOTES AND COMMENTARY

Subsection (1) prevents certain dealings with land which is not subject to a charge held NAMA by persons who also own charged lands. The subsection only applies to land which is not subject to a charge and which would impact on the value of charged lands were it not transferred to NAMA. Any person holding such land must give NAMA notice of an intention to deal with the land. NAMA has no power to prevent dealings with the land; however such a notice would give NAMA an opportunity to consider exercising its compulsory purchase powers under Ch.5 of this Part.

Subsection (3) contains a prohibition on debtors and certain associated persons from acquiring land from NAMA or a NAMA group entity. Subsection (3) applies to land which forms the security for a bank asset which is in default. Persons affected by the section include:

(a) The debtor under the relevant bank asset;

(b) Any body corporate which was a subsidiary or related company of the debtor;

(c) A nominee of the debtor;

(d) Any person acting as a declared or undeclared trustee for any person lists in (a)–(c) above;

(e) A body corporate of which the debtor is the sole member;

(f) A body corporate which is controlled by the debtor;

(g) Any person acting as a nominee or trustee for any of the persons listed in (a)–(f) above.

Subsection (4) allows the Minister to make regulations to prevent debtors or classes of persons who are connected to debtors, from acquiring any property which is part of the security for any acquired asset. The power only applies where the debtor is in "material default of a payment obligation" to NAMA. There is no definition of what constitutes material default.

Set-off of compensation

173.—Where a person is indebted to NAMA or a NAMA group entity (whether under an acquired bank asset or otherwise) the amount of any compensation payable by NAMA or any other payment due by NAMA or a NAMA group entity to that person under this Act may, without prejudice to any other right of set-off arising as a matter of law, be applied towards satisfaction of the debt due to NAMA or the NAMA group entity.

NOTES AND COMMENTARY

In relation to set-off generally see J. Breslin, *Banking Law,* 2nd edn (Dublin: Round Hall, 2007), paras.[9-78]–[9-113].

CHAPTER 7

Powers in Relation to Development of Land

Interpretation (*Chapter 7*)

174.—For the purposes of this Chapter, a reference in this Chapter to NAMA shall be construed, in relation to a bank asset that has been acquired by a NAMA group entity, as a reference to either NAMA or the NAMA group entity unless the contrary intention appears.

Application (*Chapter 7*)

175.—This Chapter applies where an acquired bank asset includes a charge over development land and—
  (*a*) the Court has made a vesting order in relation to the land, or
  (*b*) the chargee's power of sale has become exercisable, or
  (*c*) a statutory receiver has been appointed.

NOTES AND COMMENTARY

See Chs 3 and 4 of Pt 9 in relation to the appointment of statutory receivers and the making of vesting orders. Under s.146 NAMA is not bound by the conditions on the chargee's power of sale set out in s.100 of the Land and Conveyancing Law Reform Act 2009. It is arguable that those conditions must be fulfilled before the chargor's power of sale would be exercisable under this section.

Development of land

176.—(1) Where this Chapter applies, NAMA may enter into an agreement (including an agreement with the person who was the debtor in relation to the bank asset concerned) for the purpose of developing the land.

(2) NAMA's objective in entering into an agreement under *subsection (1)* shall be the orderly development of the land concerned to secure the best return reasonably possible.

NOTES AND COMMENTARY

Section 12(2)(ab) gives NAMA a power to "undertake development for the purpose of realising the full value of any asset". This section permits NAMA to enter agreements in furtherance of the s.12 power. Subsection (1) appears to be an unnecessary provision. Under s.12(2)(ae) the Board of NAMA has a general power to "do all such other things as the Board considers incidental to, or conducive to the achievement of, any of NAMA's purposes". NAMA would thus have capacity to enter into an agreement for the development of land without reference to s.176.

Subsection (2) imposes a limit on the aims and objectives of NAMA when exercising its development powers. NAMA's motive for entering an agreement under subs.(1) must be connected with achieving the best return reasonably possible. There is no reference to furthering "the social and economic development of the State" which is among the purposes of the Act as set out in s.2(b)(viii).

NAMA to have certain contractual rights of land developers

177.—(1) Where this Chapter applies, NAMA has, without prejudice to any rights arising at law, the same rights as the participating institution and the debtor and any associated debtor, guarantor or surety in relation to the acquired bank asset concerned in relation to any breach of contract or obligation (including defective design or workmanship in any building or other structure constructed or to be constructed, or works to be carried out, on, in or under the land concerned). All such rights shall be taken to have been assigned to NAMA by the acquisition by NAMA of the bank asset, subject to—

(*a*) any obligations or liabilities of the participating institution under the relevant bank asset, and

(*b*) any exclusion of obligations and liabilities from the acquisition set out in the relevant acquisition schedule.

(2) Where under *subsection (1)* NAMA acquires a right in relation to any breach of contract or obligation, NAMA may, by certificate under its seal, confer that right on another person.

NOTES AND COMMENTARY

Subsection (1) transfers any rights which a participating institution or debtor under a bank asset had in relation to breach of contract or obligation. The obligations of the participating institutions are not affected and NAMA can exclude particular rights from the operation of this section through the acquisition schedule under s.87(3)(b). The subsection only operates where this Chapter is applicable under s.175.

Subsection (2) permits NAMA to assign a right acquired under subs.(1) by instrument under its seal. The seal to be used is the seal of NAMA which is provided for in s.29. In contrast to other sealed documents (see ss.108, 142, 190) issued under the Act, it would appear that a NAMA group entity may not affix its common seal to a certificate under subs.(2).

Designs and planning documents for land development

178.—(1) Where—

(*a*) this Chapter applies, and

(*b*) there is an agreement with a person in relation to the development of the land concerned,

then—

(i) the person shall deliver to NAMA, on demand, a copy of the agreement (and, if under the agreement any design, plan or other document has been prepared for the purposes of the development of the land, a copy of the design, plan or other document prepared), and

    (ii) NAMA may elect to continue, in accordance with its terms, the agreement (with or without entering into a further agreement with the person) as it thinks fit and if it does continue the agreement, NAMA shall assume the rights and obligations under that agreement.

(2) Where an agreement referred to in *subsection (1)(b)* creates a lien over any design, plan or document prepared for the purposes of the development, the lien is void as against NAMA, without prejudice to the claim underlying the lien.

(3) Without prejudice to *subsection (1)(b)(ii)*, where an agreement referred to in *subsection (1)(b)* confers a right to do so on a participating institution, NAMA may direct the participating institution to assign the agreement to NAMA and when NAMA does so, the participating institution shall comply with the direction.

(4) Where an agreement referred to in *subsection (1)(b)* is assigned to NAMA in accordance with a direction under *subsection (3)*, or NAMA makes an election under *subsection (1)(b)(ii)*, NAMA is not liable for any breach of the agreement that occurs, or liability that arises, before the assignment or the election to continue the agreement.

(5) Where a participating institution cannot assign to NAMA any licence that it holds, then NAMA, at its option, shall, by virtue of this section, be taken to hold a licence from the person referred to in *subsection (1)(b)*—

    (*a*) authorising the reproduction, making available, adaptation, distribution and use by NAMA of any intellectual property of the person in any drawings, designs, plans or other documents referred to in that subsection, and

    (*b*) authorising NAMA to grant a sub-licence of that licence.

(6) Where a licence held by a participating institution—

    (*a*) does not authorise the reproduction, making available, adaptation, distribution and use by the participating institution of any intellectual property of the person referred to in *subsection (1)(b)* in any drawings, designs, plans or other documents referred to in that subsection, or

    (*b*) does not authorise the participating institution to grant a sub-licence of the licence,

then, at its option, NAMA shall, by virtue of this section, be taken to hold a licence from the person authorising it to do the things mentioned in *paragraphs (a)* and *(b)*.

(7) Nothing in this section deprives a person of—

    (*a*) fair and reasonable remuneration for work already done, or

    (*b*) a fair and reasonable licence fee in relation to a licence referred to in *subsection (5)*.

NOTES AND COMMENTARY

This section enables NAMA to continue or terminate pre-existing agreements regarding the development of land. The section only applies where this Chapter is applicable under s.175. The section gives NAMA powers to demand copies of agreements, designs, plans documents etc. from persons who may not be participating institutions, debtors, associated debtors and who may not have any other connection whatsoever to NAMA.

Under subs.(1)(ii) NAMA has an absolute discretion whether to continue operating a relevant agreement. Subsection (2) renders any contractual lien created by an agreement void against NAMA. Aside from subs.(2) there is no provision enabling NAMA to amend the agreement, though NAMA could utilise its power under s.176 to enter into a new agreement with the consent of the counterparty. Where NAMA elects not to continue the agreement, the counterpart has a right to remuneration under subs.(7)(a) for work already carried out. It is not clear whether this right is to be asserted against NAMA or the original party from whom NAMA has taken over the agreement. The section makes no provision for compensation to a counterparty for loss of future benefits under an agreement which is not continued under subs.(1)(ii).

Subsection (5) creates a statutory licence for NAMA to use and sublicense the use of any intellectual property subsisting in drawings, designs etc. delivered to NAMA under subs.(1). The owner of such property is entitled to compensation under subs.(7).

Limitation of right to renewal of certain business tenancies

179.—Section 16 of the Landlord and Tenant (Amendment) Act 1980 does not apply in relation to a tenancy (other than a renewal of an existing tenancy) granted by NAMA or a NAMA group entity of a tenement (within the meaning given by section 5 of that Act) unless NAMA or the NAMA group entity specifies otherwise in writing.

NOTES AND COMMENTARY

This section excludes leases granted by NAMA or a NAMA group entity from the right of renewal arising from s.16 of the Landlord and Tenant (Amendment) Act 1980. Existing leases are not affected. On a literal reading of s.175 is seems that the operation of s.179 is limited to situations where Ch.9 is applicable. There is no obvious reason for this restriction.

PART 10

LEGAL PROCEEDINGS

CHAPTER 1

Interpretation

Interpretation (*Part 10*)

180.—In this Part:
"Court" means the High Court;
"court" includes an arbitrator;
"defendant" includes a respondent in arbitration proceedings;
"plaintiff" includes an applicant in arbitration proceedings.

NOTES AND COMMENTARY

Section 4(1) applies the same definition of "Court" to the entirety of the Act.

CHAPTER 2

Legal Proceedings Commenced on or after 30 July 2009

Application (*Chapter 2*)

181.—(1) The provisions of this Chapter apply in relation to legal proceedings commenced on or after 30 July 2009 by a person who is a debtor, associated debtor, guarantor or surety in relation to a bank asset, or a participating institution in connection with a bank asset if the bank asset is specified (whether at the commencement of the proceedings or afterwards) in an acquisition schedule.

(2) The provisions of this Chapter apply in relation to legal proceedings referred to in *subsection (1)* on and from the time at which the bank asset concerned is specified in an acquisition schedule.

NOTES AND COMMENTARY

The definition of "legal proceedings" in s.4(1) extends the application of Ch.2 to arbitration and any other form of binding dispute resolution. July 30, 2009 was the date on which the Public Consultation Draft of the Bill was published.

Damages to be only remedy for certain claims

182.—(1) Subject to *subsection (2)*, a claim to which this Chapter applies gives rise only to a remedy in damages or other relief that does not in any way affect the bank asset, its acquisition, or the interest of NAMA or the NAMA group entity or (for the avoidance of doubt) any property the subject of any security that is part of such a bank asset.

(2) A person may apply for an order that the person may apply for a remedy other than or in addition to that permitted by *subsection (1)* in relation to a claim to which this Chapter applies.

(3) An application for an order mentioned in *subsection (2)* shall be made only by leave of the Court. An application for such leave may be made *ex parte*.

(4) Leave shall not be granted to apply for an order under *subsection (2)* unless the Court is satisfied that the application raises a substantial issue for the Court's determination and—

    (*a*) the application for leave is made to the Court within 30 days after the later of—
- (i) the notification by the participating institution to the relevant debtor, associated debtor, guarantor or surety under *section 96*, and
- (ii) the accrual of the cause of action in respect of which the legal proceedings arose,

    or

    (*b*) the Court is satisfied that—
- (i) there are substantial reasons why the application was not made within that period, and
- (ii) it is just and equitable in all the circumstances to grant leave having regard to the interests of any affected person.

(5) If the Court grants leave to apply for an order under *subsection (2)*, the applicant shall serve on NAMA the order granting leave and the application.

(6) The Court shall make an order under *subsection (2)* if and only if the Court is satisfied that if the applicant's claim were established, damages would not be an adequate remedy.

(7) For the avoidance of doubt, this Chapter applies to proceedings in being at the time of specification in an acquisition schedule of a relevant bank asset.

(8) Nothing in this section prevents a party—

(*a*) defending proceedings *in rem* in respect of a bank asset instituted against it by NAMA, a NAMA group entity, a participating institution or a statutory receiver, in a manner which might affect the bank asset, its acquisition by NAMA or a NAMA group entity or any property the subject of any security, or

(*b*) in the defence of such proceedings, making any claim in relation to such a bank asset.

(9) Nothing in the section affects the operation of the Family Home Protection Act 1976.

NOTES AND COMMENTARY

This section ensures that any litigation initiated in relation to a bank asset which has been specified in an acquisition schedule will not affect NAMA's rights in relation to that asset in the absence of an order under the section. Subsection (6) states than an order can only be made where damages would not be an adequate remedy for the applicant.

It further ensures that a party who purchases an asset from NAMA does so with certainty that any outstanding litigation will not affect their title to the asset, unless an order has been made under the section.

Subsection (7) provides that Ch.2 applies in relation to proceedings in being at the time of specification in an acquisition schedule of a relevant bank asset. Where proceedings are already in being, a plaintiff who has sought a relief other than damages must apply to the court for an order under this section to maintain those proceedings in their existing form within the time constraints imposed by subs.(4).

A plaintiff in proceedings in the Circuit Court which fall within the scope of this chapter must apply to the High Court for an order under this section, rather than to the court which is dealing with the case. As the definition of "legal proceedings" in s.4(1) extends the application of Ch.2 to arbitration and any other form of binding dispute resolution, an applicant in such binding dispute resolution proceedings must apply for an order under s.182 to the High Court, not the arbitrator, if they wish to seek a remedy other than damages, or maintain proceedings which seek such a remedy.

CHAPTER 3

Legal Proceedings Generally

Application (*Chapter 3*)

183.—This Chapter applies in relation to all legal proceedings—
(*a*) to which NAMA or a NAMA group entity is or becomes a party,
(*b*) relating to a designated bank asset or acquired bank asset, or
(*c*) otherwise relating to NAMA.

NOTES AND COMMENTARY

The broad scope of this section extends the application of this Chapter to all litigation that relates to NAMA or a bank asset acquired by NAMA or a NAMA group entity.

It does not, however, extend to litigation which does not relate to NAMA, but which relates to a bank asset where NAMA or a NAMA group entity has not yet either: (i) acquired the bank asset or an interest in it; or (ii) specified the bank asset in an acquisition schedule that has been served on a participating institution.

The definition of "legal proceedings" in s.4(1) extends the application of Ch.3 to arbitration and any other form of binding dispute resolution.

Conduct of legal proceedings in relation to acquired bank assets

184.—(1) Where NAMA or a NAMA group entity is a party to any legal proceedings affecting an acquired bank asset, the participating institution from which the bank asset was acquired shall, without prejudice to any other obligation arising under this Act, if NAMA or the NAMA group entity so requests, provide NAMA or the NAMA group entity with any assistance reasonably required by NAMA or the NAMA group entity for the purpose of the proceedings, including—

(*a*) the provision of documents or information,

(*b*) the making available of witnesses, and

(*c*) the provision of evidence by affidavit or otherwise.

(2) A participating institution has, and shall be taken always to have had, as part of its functions and objects, the power and capacity to give the assistance required by *subsection (1)*.

NOTES AND COMMENTARY

The obligations imposed on a participating institution by this section only extend to the provision of assistance reasonably required by NAMA or a NAMA group entity where the legal proceedings affect an acquired bank asset and NAMA or the NAMA group entity are a party to those proceedings.

The obligations imposed by this section are placed on the institutions themselves, rather than on individual officers or employees of those institutions. While the section requires the participating institutions to make witnesses available, this section does not impose any obligations on individual witnesses.

Subsection (1) imposes the requirement of co-operation, whereas subs.(2) empowers and authorises that co-operation on the part of the participating institutions.

Effect of acquisition, etc., of bank assets on legal proceedings — participating institution plaintiff, etc.

185.—(1) If legal proceedings were in being in relation to a bank asset immediately before the time when it was acquired under this Act, and the participating institution concerned was a plaintiff in those proceedings, those proceedings shall continue. After the bank asset is acquired, NAMA or the NAMA group entity concerned may elect to be substituted for the participating institution, in its capacity as plaintiff, in the proceedings.

(2) If NAMA or a NAMA group entity is substituted under *subsection (1)*, subject to this section it assumes all of the rights and obligations in relation to the relevant proceedings that the participating institution had immediately before that time, other than the obligations in relation to the defence of or liability for any counterclaim or cross-claim. The participating institution has full rights in relation to, and is solely liable for any remedy awarded in relation to, any such counterclaim or cross-claim.

(3) Notwithstanding *subsection (1)*, where NAMA or a NAMA group entity is substituted under *subsection (1)*, the participating institution remains a party to the proceedings as defendant or respondent to any counterclaim or cross-claim in the proceedings.

(4) Where NAMA or a NAMA group entity is substituted under *subsection (1)*—

(*a*) the court may order the participating institution to make discovery or answer interrogatories as if it were still a party to the proceedings, and

(*b*) NAMA or the NAMA group entity shall not be ordered to make discovery or answer interrogatories unless the court considers it necessary to do so for any special reason in the interests of justice.

(5) Notwithstanding *subsection (1)*, an election by NAMA or a NAMA group entity to be substituted under *subsection (1)* does not render NAMA or the NAMA group entity liable in relation to any counterclaim or cross-claim, or claim to set off, in those proceedings.

(6) Where NAMA or a NAMA group entity has elected to be substituted under *subsection (1)*, NAMA or the NAMA group entity shall as soon as may be file a notice in the court concerned of the election and shall serve a copy of the notice on the participating institution and each other party to the proceedings. No amendment to the proceedings is to be required.

(7) Where NAMA or a NAMA group entity is substituted under *subsection (1)*, without prejudice to any application for costs by the participating institution against any person other than NAMA or a NAMA group entity, the participating institution continues to be liable for—

(*a*) its own costs in the proceedings before the substitution of NAMA or the NAMA group entity as a party and any potential costs liability incurred to other parties to the proceedings as a result of the participating institution being a party to the proceedings before that substitution, and

(*b*) any subsequent costs that it may incur in any capacity in which it remains a party to the proceedings.

(8) A party to legal proceedings referred to in this section is not entitled to join NAMA or a NAMA group entity as a party to the proceedings.

(9) The provisions of this section apply with any necessary modifications to arbitration proceedings.

NOTES AND COMMENTARY

The provisions of this section which permit NAMA to be substituted as a plaintiff in proceedings in place of a participating institution, while leaving the participating institution solely liable for any remedy awarded in relation to any counterclaim or cross-claim are somewhat one-sided.

They create the possibility that NAMA could be given judgment against a defendant, who in turn is successful in their counterclaim against the participating institution for the full amount of the judgment in question.

This asymmetry is further extended in s.187, which deals with circumstances where a participating institution is a party other than the plaintiff in legal proceedings in relation to a bank asset. Under that section, where the participating institution has brought a counterclaim NAMA may elect to be substituted for the participating institution as counterclaimant but does not become liable in respect of the plaintiff's claim.

Subsection (9) provides that the provisions of this section apply with any necessary modifications to arbitration proceedings. Furthermore, "legal proceedings" is defined by s.4(1) to include arbitration and any other form of binding dispute resolution and s.180 defines "court" as including an arbitrator, "defendant" as including a respondent in arbitration proceedings and "plaintiff" as including an applicant in arbitration proceedings.

Effect of acquisition of bank assets on legal proceedings — NAMA, etc., may enforce judgment

186.—(1) Where a participating institution has obtained judgment in legal proceedings in relation to an acquired bank asset, the judgment so obtained shall be taken to have been assigned to NAMA or the NAMA group entity concerned.

(2) NAMA or the NAMA group entity concerned may enforce a judgment referred to in *subsection (1)* by any means (including by issuing execution). In particular, NAMA or the NAMA group entity may apply for a judgment mortgage pursuant to the judgment.

NOTES AND COMMENTARY

This section gives NAMA the benefit of any judgment obtained by a participating institution in relation to any acquired bank asset, including the right to enforce that judgement.

While the entitlement to apply for a judgment mortgage pursuant to a judgment is specifically mentioned, subs.(2) allows NAMA or a NAMA group entity to enforce a judgment referred to in subs.(1) by any means, which would include enforcement by the sheriff, cross-examination in aid of execution, the appointment of a receiver by way of equitable execution, application for a garnishee order, or application for an instalment order or bankruptcy in relation to a private individual or a winding-up order in relation to a company.

Effect of acquisition of bank assets on legal proceedings where participating institution not plaintiff

187.—(1) If the participating institution from which NAMA or a NAMA group entity acquires a bank asset is, at the time of acquisition of the bank asset, a party (otherwise than as plaintiff) in legal proceedings in relation to the bank asset, the participating institution remains a party to the proceedings in the same capacity.

(2) NAMA or a NAMA group entity may elect to become a party to any legal proceedings referred to in *subsection (1)*. In a case where the participating institution has brought a counterclaim NAMA or the NAMA group entity may at its election be substituted for the participating institution as counterclaimant but does not become liable in respect of the claim.

NOTES AND COMMENTARY

This section deals with circumstances where a participating institution is a party other than the plaintiff in legal proceedings in relation to a bank asset. Where the participating institution has brought a counterclaim, NAMA may elect to be substituted for the participating institution as counterclaimant but does not become liable in respect of the plaintiff's claim.

This is similar to the provisions of s.185 which permit NAMA to be substituted as a plaintiff in proceedings in place of a participating institution, while leaving the participating institution solely liable for any remedy awarded in relation to any counterclaim or cross-claim.

Conduct of proceedings

188.—If NAMA or a NAMA group entity elects not to be substituted for a participating institution in relation to legal proceedings, or elects only to be substituted as plaintiff under *section 185*—

(*a*) the participating institution shall conduct the proceedings with all due vigour in a way that protects the interests of NAMA and the NAMA group entity and in accordance with any directions given by NAMA or the NAMA group entity, and

(*b*) NAMA or the NAMA group entity may at its election join the proceedings as a notice party.

This section allows NAMA to direct a participating institution in its conduct of proceedings where it has elected not to be substituted for the participating institution in relation to those proceedings under ss.185 or 187.

It further empowers NAMA to elect to join such proceedings as a notice party.

Costs

189.—(1) At the conclusion of each interlocutory application in any legal proceedings to which this Chapter applies, the court concerned shall make orders as to costs in respect of the application and, having received submissions from the parties as to the levels of those costs, the court shall measure those costs.

(2) Costs measured under *subsection (1)* shall be enforceable against the party directed to pay those costs. If the party fails to discharge those costs within 30 days of the court order measuring those costs, the court may on the application of any party to the proceedings or of its own motion impose terms as to the continuation of the proceedings pending the discharge of the costs.

The provisions of this section are mandatory in so far as they require the court or arbitrator to make a costs order and measure costs in relation to each interlocutory application in any legal proceedings to which this Chapter applies, but the power to impose terms as to the continuation of the proceedings pending the discharge of outstanding costs is discretionary.

Evidence — amount of debt due

190.—In any proceedings for the recovery by NAMA or a NAMA group entity of money, a certificate in writing under the seal of NAMA or the common seal of the NAMA group entity that a specified sum of money was owing to NAMA or the NAMA group entity at the date of the certificate by a specified person on a specified account is, at any time within one month after the date of the certificate, evidence that the sum specified in the certificate is and remains owing to NAMA or the NAMA group entity by the person and on the account specified in the certificate.

This section provides that a certificate under the appropriate seal is evidence, rather than conclusive proof that the sum specified therein is and remains owing to NAMA or the NAMA group entity by the person and on the account specified in the certificate.

Evidence — application of Bankers' Books Evidence Act 1879

191.—(1) In this section "Act of 1879" means the Bankers' Books Evidence Act 1879.

(2) Where—

    (*a*) a copy of an entry in a bankers' book (within the meaning given by section 9(2) of the Act of 1879) falls to be produced in evidence,

    (*b*) the book is in the custody or under the control of NAMA or a NAMA group entity, and

    (*c*) an officer of NAMA or a NAMA group entity gives evidence (orally or by affidavit) that—

        (i) he or she truly believes that the book or record was kept in the ordinary course of the bank's business, and

        (ii) the book is in the custody or under the control of NAMA or the NAMA group entity,

then the requirement for proof in section 4 of the Act of 1879 shall be taken to have been satisfied.

(3) The Act of 1879 has effect in relation to the books and records of NAMA or a NAMA group entity as if—

    (*a*) NAMA or the NAMA group entity were a bank,

    (*b*) references to bankers' books in that Act were to the ordinary books and records of NAMA or the NAMA group entity, and

    (*c*) references in that Act to an officer of a bank were references to an officer of NAMA or the NAMA group entity.

NOTES AND COMMENTARY

Definitions and Cross References

Section 4 of the Bankers' Books Evidence Act 1879 provides as follows:
"A copy of an entry in a banker's book shall not be received in evidence under this Act unless it be first proved that the book was at the time of the making of the entry one of the ordinary books of the bank, and that the entry was made in the usual and ordinary course of business, and that the book is in the custody or control of the bank.

Such proof may be given by a partner or officer of the bank, and may be given orally or by an affidavit sworn before any commissioner or person authorised to take affidavits."

Section 9(2) of the Bankers' Books Evidence Act 1879 as amended by the Bankers' Books Evidence (Amendment) Act 1959 provides as follows:
"Expressions in this Act relating to "bankers' books"—

    (a) include any records used in the ordinary business of a bank, or used in the transfer department of a bank acting as registrar of securities, whether—

        (i) comprised in bound volume, loose-leaf binders or other loose-leaf filing systems, loose-leaf ledger sheets, pages, folios or cards, or

        (ii) kept on microfilm, magnetic tape or in any non-legible form (by the use of electronics or otherwise) which is capable of being reproduced in a permanent legible form, and

    (b) cover documents in manuscript, documents which are typed, printed, stencilled or created by any other mechanical or partly mechanical process in use from time to time and documents which are produced by any photographic or photostatic process."

Comments

This section extends the provisions of the Bankers' Book Evidence Act 1879 to allow NAMA to be treated as though it is a bank for the purposes of that legislation. The effect of the section is to permit copies of NAMA's books and records to be admissible in evidence as prima facie evidence of the original entries therein. It also subjects NAMA to the possibility of applications to inspect its books and records in the course of litigation under s.7 of 1879 Act as amended. See RSC Ord.63, r.17.

Limitation of power to grant injunctive relief

192.—(1) Where injunctive relief is sought on an interim or interlocutory basis in proceedings to which this Chapter applies—

(*a*) to compel NAMA or a NAMA group entity to take or refrain from taking any action, or

(*b*) to compel any other person to take or refrain from taking any action where the relief if granted would adversely affect NAMA or a NAMA group entity,

the Court shall have regard, in determining whether to grant such relief, to the public interest.

(2) In considering the public interest, the Court shall have regard to—

(*a*) the purposes of this Act, and

(*b*) the importance of permitting NAMA to discharge its functions in an expeditious and efficient manner.

(3) Unless the Court is satisfied that not granting injunctive relief would give rise to an injustice, the Court shall not grant such relief where a remedy in damages would be available to the person who seeks that relief.

(4) For the purposes of *subsection (3)*, the possibility that the action against which injunctive relief is sought would or might result in a person being declared bankrupt or ordered to be wound up or otherwise adversely affected is not, of itself, sufficient to establish that not granting such relief would give rise to an injustice.

NOTES AND COMMENTARY

The requirement in subs.(1) that the court have regard to the public interest only arises where injunctive relief is sought on an interim or interlocutory basis. There is no explicit provision which limits subs.(3) to occasions where the relief sought is an interim or interlocutory injunction, and when read in isolation subs.(3) appears to apply to the granting of injunctive relief in all its forms.

This section is similar in nature to s.182 which provides that damages are to be the only remedy available in certain claims relating to bank assets, subject to a mechanism which allows the court to permit a claim to be made for a remedy other than damages where it is satisfied that damages would not be an adequate remedy.

Indeed, by virtue of s.182, it would be necessary for a plaintiff (or applicant in binding dispute resolution proceedings) to apply to the High Court for permission to seek any form of injunctive relief in any proceedings commenced on or after July 30, 2009, by a person who is a debtor, associated debtor, guarantor or surety in relation to a bank asset, or a participating institution in connection with a bank asset if the bank asset is specified (whether at the commencement of the proceedings or afterwards) in an acquisition schedule.

Section 192, however, relates to a much wider range of legal proceedings, as defined in s.183.

Limitation of judicial review

193.—(1) Leave shall not be granted for judicial review of a decision under this Act unless—

(*a*) either—

(i) the application for leave to seek judicial review is made to the

    Court within one month after the decision is notified to the person concerned, or

  (ii) the Court is satisfied that—

    (I) there are substantial reasons why the application was not made within that period, and

    (II) it is just, in all the circumstances, to grant leave, having regard to the interests of other affected persons and the public interest,

and

  (*b*) the Court is satisfied that the application raises a substantial issue for the Court's determination.

(2) The Court may make such order on the hearing of the judicial review as it thinks fit, including an order remitting the matter back to the maker of the decision with such directions as the Court thinks appropriate or necessary.

(3) This section applies to NAMA and a NAMA group entity in the same manner as it applies to any other applicant for judicial review of a decision under or pursuant to this Act.

Notes and Commentary

This section reduces the period within which an application for leave for judicial review should be made to one month from the notification of the decision in question to the applicant.

While it provides that a court may make such order on the hearing of a judicial review as it thinks fit, including an order remitting the matter back to the maker of the decision with such directions as the court thinks appropriate or necessary, it provides no guidance as to how the court should reach its determination.

While the provisions of s.192(2), which deals with the concept of "the public interest", do not apply to an application for leave to seek judicial review, it is likely that the court would have regard to them in determining whether it would be in the public interest to extent time for the making of an application for leave to seek judicial review in accordance with s.193(1)(a)(ii)(II).

In *Dellway Investments v NAMA* [2010] IEHC at [3.6] the High Court considered the meaning of the phrase "substantial issue for the Court's determination". The court noted that similar language has been used in other statutes. The court adopted the interpretation provided by Carroll J. in *McNamara v An Bord Pleanála* [1995] 2 I.L.R.M. 125:

"In order for a ground to be substantial it must be reasonable, it must be arguable, it must be weighty. It must not be trivial or tenuous. However, I am not concerned with trying to ascertain what the eventual result will be. I believe I should go no further than satisfy myself that the grounds are 'substantial'. A ground that does not stand any chance of being sustained (for example, where the point has already been decided in another case) could not be said to be substantial."

Limitation of certain rights of appeal to the Supreme Court

194.—(1) The determination of the Court of an application for leave to apply for judicial review, of an application for judicial review, of an application for leave to apply for an order, or an application for an order, under section 182, is final and no appeal lies from the decision of the Court to the Supreme Court in either case, except with the leave of the Court.

(2) The Court shall grant leave under subsection (1) only if that Court certifies that its decision involves a point of law of exceptional public importance and that it is desirable in the public interest that an appeal should be taken to the

Supreme Court.

[(2A) On an appeal from a determination of the Court in respect of an application referred to in subsection (1), the Supreme Court—

    (*a*) has jurisdiction to determine only the point of law certified by the Court under subsection (2), and to make only such order in the proceedings as follows from that determination, and

    (*b*) shall, in determining the appeal, act as expeditiously as possible consistent with the administration of justice.]

(3) This section does not apply to a determination of the Court in so far as it involves a question as to the validity of any law having regard to the provisions of the Constitution.

AMENDMENT HISTORY

Subsection (2A) was inserted by s.75, Sch.1 Pt 5 of the Credit Institutions (Stabilisation) Act 2010.

NOTES AND COMMENTARY

This section constitutes a statutory exception to Art.34(4) of the Constitution, which provides that the Supreme Court (The Court of Final Appeal) shall have appellate jurisdiction from all decisions of the High Court, "with such exceptions and subject to such regulations as may be prescribed by law".

Article 34(4) further provides that: "No law shall be enacted excepting from the appellate jurisdiction of the Supreme Court cases which involve questions as to the validity of any law having regard to the provisions of this Constitution." This is reflected in s.194 by virtue of the fact that that section does not apply to a determination of the High Court in so far as it involves a question as to the constitutionality of any law.

This section only limits appeals to the Supreme Court in relation to rulings of the High Court in relation to four specified applications:

    (i)   For leave to apply for judicial review;

    (ii) For judicial review;

    (iii) For leave to apply for an order allowing a person to apply for a remedy other than damages under s.182; and

    (iv) For an order allowing a person to apply for a remedy other than damages under s.182.

The limitations on rights of appeal apply to all parties, including NAMA and NAMA group entities.

The test of whether a prospective appellant can obtain a certificate is one of whether the decision of the High Court involves a point of law of exceptional public importance and that it is desirable in the public interest that an appeal be permitted. This statutory formula appears in a number of other statutes (e.g. s.50 Planning and Development Act 2000; s.5 Illegal Immigrants (Trafficking Act) 2000; s.29 Courts of Justice Act 1924 as amended). The meaning of the terms "point of law of exceptional public importance" and "desirable in the public interest" has been explored in a wide range of contexts. In *Dellway Investments v NAMA* [2010] IEHC 375 the High Court adopted summaries of the existing jurisprudence set out in *Glancré Teo v An Bord Pleanála* [2006] IEHC 250 and *Arklow Holidays v An Bord Pleanála* [2007] 4 I.R. 112 at 115.

Subsection (2A) was inserted by s.75 of the Credit Institutions (Stabilisation) Act 2010. Similar provisions are to be found in ss.13(7) and 47(11) Planning and Development (Strategic Infrastructure) Act 2006 and s.92(10) Water Services Act 2007. The effect of the section is to restrict the scope of the right of appeal to the Supreme Court to the point of law certified by the High Court under subs.(2). The language is designed to prevent appellants from relying on the dictum of Walsh J. in *People (Attorney General) v Giles* [1974] I.R. 422 at 430 to the effect that the certificate permitting an appeal does not limit the scope of the appeal. This dictum was recently approved by a unanimous Supreme Court in *Clinton v An Bord Pleanála* [2007] 1 I.R. 272.

Lites pendentes to have no effect, etc.

195.—Where NAMA or a NAMA group entity has acquired a bank asset, a *lis pendens*, caution or inhibition registered on or after 30 July 2009 shall be of no effect against NAMA, a NAMA group entity or a person who acquires that bank asset from NAMA or a NAMA group entity, even if it is registered against the title to any registered land that forms part of the bank asset unless the party registering it has secured or secures an order under *section 182(2)*.

NOTES AND COMMENTARY

The structure of this section leaves it open to two competing interpretations.

The first is that a *lis pendens*, caution or inhibition, whether registered against the title to any registered land that forms part of the bank asset or otherwise, registered on or after July 30, 2009 shall be of no effect against NAMA, a NAMA group entity or a person who acquires that bank asset from NAMA or a NAMA group entity, unless the party registering it has secured or secures an order under s.182(2).

The second is that a *lis pendens*, caution or inhibition registered on or after July 30, 2009 shall never be of any effect against NAMA, a NAMA group entity or a person who acquires that bank asset from NAMA or a NAMA group entity under any circumstances, except that in the case of a *lis pendens*, caution or inhibition registered against the title to any registered land that forms part of the bank asset, in which case the *lis pendens*, caution or inhibition shall be of no effect against NAMA, a NAMA group entity or a person who acquires that bank asset from NAMA or a NAMA group entity, unless the party registering it has secured or secures an order under s.182(2).

While a strict interpretation of the section lends itself towards the second interpretation, logic would suggest the first, as it would be remarkable if the statute were to discriminate so decisively between a *lis pendens*, caution or inhibition registered against the title to any registered land and any other form of *lis pendens*, caution or inhibition.

PART 11

USE OF INFORMATION

Definition (*Part 11*)

196.—In this Part "adviser" includes an investment adviser, an investment banker, a property valuer, a solicitor, an accountant and any staff member or employee of, and any agent or other person acting on behalf of, an adviser.

Deemed consent to disclosure of information

197.—A participating institution shall be taken for all purposes to have consented to the disclosure of information in accordance with this Part.

NOTES AND COMMENTARY

Participating institutions are required to make disclosures of various matters to NAMA in the course of the acquisitions process under Pt 6, Chapter 1. This section deems these disclosures and any other information disclosed under the Act to be done with the consent of the participating institution concerned. The section does not apply to a disclosure of books and records to the Minister for Finance by an applicant institution under s.64.

Duty of confidentiality, etc., not contravened by provision of information or production of documents and books for inspection

198.—(1) Disclosure by a credit institution to NAMA or the NTMA of information or records about a bank asset, or about any person connected with a bank asset, made on or after 30 July 2009, does not contravene any duty of confidentiality to which the credit institution or any other person is subject.

(2) The production by a person to NAMA, a NAMA group entity or the NTMA of a document that a person could not have been compelled to produce to a court on the grounds of legal professional privilege does not constitute a waiver of that privilege from production in relation to the document.

NOTES AND COMMENTARY

Subsection (1) provides credit institutions with protection from suit for breach of confidence when making disclosures to NAMA. In the absence of the section compliance with the obligations on applicant and participating institutions might expose credit institutions to liability for breach of the banker's duty of confidentiality (see *Tournier v National and Provincial Union Bank of England* [1924] 1 K.B. 461 and *National Irish Bank v Radio Telefís Éireann* [1998] 2 I.R. 465). It would seem that this section creates a general immunity covering disclosures to NAMA and the NTMA and that a credit institution would not be liable were it to accidentally make a disclosure that was not strictly required by the Act.

Subsection (2) allows for a person to provide a document to NAMA, a NAMA group entity or the NTMA without waiving any legal professional privilege which protects that document from disclosure. This provision will be of assistance to individuals who wish to co-operate with NAMA, but who would otherwise be reluctant to disclose legal advice they had received from NAMA for fear that it might be used against them in future litigation.

Duty of confidentiality, etc., not contravened by provision of information to, or production of documents and books for inspection by, potential purchasers

199.—(1) The disclosure of information or a book, document or record in relation to a bank asset by NAMA or a NAMA group entity to a potential purchaser or to such a purchaser's agent or adviser does not contravene any duty of confidentiality to which NAMA or the NAMA group entity would otherwise be subject.

(2) The production of any book, document or record under *subsection (1)* that NAMA or a NAMA group entity could not have been compelled to produce to any court on the grounds of legal professional privilege does not constitute a waiver of that privilege.

(3) NAMA or a NAMA group entity may disclose confidential information to a participating institution, but only if to do so is necessary for the identification of bank assets, for the purposes of NAMA's making a decision whether or not to acquire bank assets, or for the proper management of acquired bank assets.

NOTES AND COMMENTARY

This section extends the immunity afforded to credit institutions under s.198(1) to NAMA when dealing with potential purchasers of bank assets. It should be noted that this section does not apply to the NTMA.

Subsection (2) is similar to s.198(2), and provides that the disclosure of a book, document or record in relation to a bank asset by NAMA or a NAMA group entity to a potential purchaser or to such a purchaser's agent or adviser does not constitute a waiver of any legal professional privilege which protects that document from disclosure.

Obligation to provide information, etc., to NAMA, etc., extends to provision to advisers

200.—An obligation under this Act of a person to provide information to NAMA or a NAMA group entity, to produce a book, document or record to NAMA or a NAMA group entity, or to provide facilities for the inspection of or taking copies from a book, document or record also has effect as an obligation of the person to provide such information, produce such a book, document or record or provide such facilities to an agent or adviser acting on behalf of NAMA or the NAMA group entity.

NOTES AND COMMENTARY

This section extends the obligations to provide information or documents to NAMA to include an obligation to provide the information or documentation in question to an agent or adviser acting on behalf of NAMA.

Operation of Data Protection Acts 1988 and 2003

201.—To avoid doubt, an obligation on a credit institution or any other person under this Act to disclose information to NAMA, a NAMA group entity or the NTMA extends to personal information, within the meaning of the Data Protection Acts 1988 and 2003.

NOTES AND COMMENTARY

This section clarifies that an obligation to disclose personal information to NAMA, a NAMA group entity or the NTMA extends to information regarded as personal within the meaning of the Data Protection Acts 1988 and 2003. There is no comparable provision to s.199 permitting NAMA to disclose personal information to a prospective purchaser of a bank asset.

Disclosure of confidential information

202.—(1) In this Act "confidential information" means—
  (*a*) information relating to the commercial or business interests of a participating institution or of a person who is or has been in a relationship with a participating institution,
  (*b*) information that is subject at law or in equity to a duty of confidentiality,
  (*c*) information that, if it were contained in a document, would have the result that a person could not be compelled to disclose the document in evidence,
  (*d*) information the disclosure of which would tend to place NAMA, a NAMA group entity or the NTMA at a commercial disadvantage, or
  (*e*) information about proposals of a commercial nature and tenders submitted to NAMA, a NAMA group entity or the NTMA.
  (2) Except as otherwise provided or authorised by this section or another

enactment, a person shall not, unless authorised by NAMA, a NAMA group entity or the NTMA or authorised or obliged by law to do so, disclose information that he or she knows is confidential information, or use, to the direct or indirect advantage of himself or herself or of another person (other than NAMA, a NAMA group entity or the NTMA), confidential information that he or she obtained—

    (*a*) while a member of the Board,

    (*b*) while an officer of NAMA or a staff member of the NTMA or otherwise performing duties on behalf of NAMA or the NTMA,

    (*c*) as a result of a disclosure to him or her permitted by *subsection (5)(d)* or *section 199(3)*, or

    (*d*) in the course of the provision (including the provision by another person) of a service to NAMA or the NTMA.

(3) A reference in *subsection (2)* to the disclosure or use of information includes the disclosure or use of a document containing the information.

(4) For the purposes of this section, it shall be presumed, unless the contrary is shown, that a person knew that information was confidential information, if that person reasonably ought to have known that it was confidential information.

(5) Nothing in *subsection (2)* prevents the disclosure of information—

    (*a*) to NAMA or a NAMA group entity, the NTMA or the Minister,

    (*b*) in the course of giving evidence before a court or tribunal having the power to examine witnesses on oath,

    (*c*) in the course of giving evidence before a House of the Oireachtas or a Committee of either or both such Houses, or

    (*d*) to an agent of NAMA, a NAMA group entity, the NTMA or the Minister.

(6) Notwithstanding *subsection (2)*, it is not an offence for a person, acting in good faith, to disclose confidential information to—

    (*a*) the Garda Síochána,

    (*b*) the Revenue Commissioners,

    (*c*) the Director of Corporate Enforcement,

    (*d*) the Competition Authority,

    (*e*) [the Central Bank],

    (*f*) any other body (whether within the State or not) responsible for the detection or investigation of criminal offences, or

    (*g*) any other body (whether within the State or not) responsible for the detection or investigation of contraventions of law (whether of the State or not) relating to taxation, companies, the regulation of financial services, or competition,

where that information gives rise to a reasonable suspicion that a participating institution, an employee or agent of a participating institution, a debtor in respect of a bank asset acquired by NAMA or a NAMA group entity or an employee or agent of such a debtor may have—

    (i) committed a criminal offence, or

    (ii) contravened a law relating to taxation, companies, the regulation of financial services, or competition.

NOTES AND COMMENTARY

Amendment History

In subs.(6)(e) the reference to "the Regulatory Authority" was substituted for "the Central Bank" by s.15(11), Sch.2 Pt 11 of the Central Bank Reform Act 2010 (No.23 of 2010).

Notes

Breach of the obligation under subs.(2) is a criminal offence under s.7 of the Act.

Subsection (1) defines confidential information. For the purposes of assessing compliance with subs.(2), there is a rebuttable presumption that a person knows that information is confidential information.

Subsection (2) applies to information obtained while performing functions listed in paras (2)(a)–(d). A person will be in breach of their obligations under the section if, without authorisation, they disclose any information which they know to be confidential information or they make use of the information for their own personal advantage or that of any person other than NAMA, a NAMA group entity or the NTMA. Disclosures may be authorised by NAMA, a NAMA group entity or the NTMA.

Subsection (6) provides an exception for good faith public interest disclosures to the authorities where the person making the disclosure has a reasonable suspicion that a criminal offence has been permitted. Subsection (5) creates further exceptions for disclosure without prior authorisation.

Obligation to pass certain information to law-enforcement authorities

203.—Where NAMA has reason to suspect that—

(*a*) a participating institution may have committed a criminal offence, or

(*b*) a participating institution may have contravened a law relating to taxation, companies, the regulation of financial services, or competition,

then NAMA shall report the information that leads it to form that suspicion to—

(i) the Garda Síochána,

(ii) the Revenue Commissioners,

(iii) the Director of Corporate Enforcement,

(iv) the Competition Authority,

(v) the [Central Bank],

(vi) any other body (whether within the State or not) responsible for the detection or investigation of criminal offences, or

(vii) any other body (whether within the State or not) responsible for the detection or investigation of contraventions of law (whether of the State or not) relating to taxation, companies, the regulation of financial services, or competition,

as the case appears to it to require.

NOTES AND COMMENTARY

Amendment History

In subs.(v) the reference to "Regulatory Authority" was substituted for "Central Bank" by s.15(11), Sch.2 Pt 11 of the Central Bank Reform Act 2010 (No.23 of 2010).

Notes

This section is mandatory in so much as it places an absolute obligation on NAMA to report information which has led it to suspect certain forms of illegality on the part of a participating institution to the relevant law-enforcement authority. This obligation arises where NAMA has reason to suspect the illegality in question.

This section only relates to suspicions of wrongdoing by a participating institution.

Provision of information to Revenue Commissioners

204.—(1) In this section—

"relevant person" means a debtor, associated debtor, guarantor, surety or chargor and includes a connected person (within the meaning given by section 10 of the Taxes Consolidation Act 1997) in relation to a debtor, associated debtor, guarantor, surety or chargor;

"tax" has the meaning given by section 960A of the Taxes Consolidation Act 1997.

[(2) Notwithstanding any provision of this Act or any other enactment—

(a) NAMA shall make available to the Revenue Commissioners details of each eligible bank asset,

(b) where the Revenue Commissioners require any information or documents, relating to any eligible bank asset or such other matters as may be necessary for the purposes of the performance of their duties, then they may require NAMA to provide such information as is in the possession or control of NAMA or of which it has knowledge, and such documents as are in the possession or control of NAMA or to make such documents available for inspection,

(c) the Revenue Commissioners may, for the purposes of the performance of their functions under Part 42 of the Taxes Consolidation Act 1997 and any regulations made under that Part, seek from NAMA information in relation to a named relevant person, and

(d) where NAMA is in possession of, or has knowledge of, information or has possession or control of documents referred to in paragraph (b) or (c), NAMA shall provide such information and documents to, or make such documents available for inspection by, the Revenue Commissioners.]

(3) Notwithstanding any other enactment, the Revenue Commissioners shall disclose to NAMA information in relation to a named relevant person that, in the opinion of the Revenue Commissioners or of NAMA, is required by NAMA for the purposes of the performance of its functions under this Act, and that is in the possession of the Revenue Commissioners, or of which the Revenue Commissioners have knowledge.

NOTES AND COMMENTARY

Amendment History

Subsection (2) was substituted by s.154 of the Finance Act 2010 (No.5 of 2010).

Notes

This section allows for the sharing of information between NAMA and the Revenue

Commissioners. Under subs.(2) NAMA is required to disclose details of eligible bank assets to the Revenue Commissioners and must provide additional information if requested to do so. The obligation is not confined to bank assets that NAMA in fact acquires and all information supplied by participating or applicant institutions under Pts 4 and 6 seems to be potentially subject to disclosure.

The Code of Practice on the Commercial Interests of Non-Participating Institutions, issued under s.35, states that NAMA will not utilise its powers under subs.(3) to obtain tax information from the Revenue Commissioners (see [3.11(e)]). This is in line with a commitment given by the Irish authorities to the European Commission when obtaining state aid approval for the NAMA scheme (see European Commission, Communication regarding State Aid N725/2009 Ireland of February 26, 2010, C(2010)1155 final, 18).

Disclosure by regulatory authorities

205.—(1) The Minister, the Governor and the [Central Bank] may, in accordance with applicable law, disclose to each other any information that any of them receives concerning a participating institution or any of its subsidiaries. The recipient shall treat any information disclosed pursuant to this section as confidential.

(2) Disclosure under *subsection (1)* is subject to the requirements of—

(*a*) the treaties governing the European Communities, and

(*b*) the ESCB Statute.

(3) In *subsection (1)* "information" includes information relating to a period before the participating institution concerned was designated under *section 67* as a participating institution.

(4) The Governor and the [Central Bank] may use information disclosed to either of them under *subsection (1)* in the performance of their functions.

Notes and Commentary

Amendment History

In subss.(1) and (4), the reference to "Regulatory Authority" was substituted for "Central Bank" by s.15(11), Sch.2 Pt 11 of the Central Bank Reform Act 2010 (No.23 of 2010).

Comments

This section allows for the discretionary sharing of information between the Minister for Finance and the Central Bank (and the Governor thereof). The requirement that each of the aforementioned parties treat any information disclosed pursuant to this section as confidential is mandatory.

PART 12

Conduct of Participating Institutions

Directions in relation to conduct of participating institutions

206.—(1) The [Central Bank] may, with the approval of the Minister, give a direction to a participating institution in order to achieve the purposes of this Act, as specified in *section 2*.

(2) A direction under *subsection (1)* may—

(*a*) restrict balance sheet growth,

(*b*) restrict the institution's ability to take over other credit institutions, (*c*) require balance sheet reduction, or

    (*d*) restrict or require consolidation and merger of participating institutions.

NOTES AND COMMENTARY

Amendment History

In subs.(1) the reference to "Regulatory Authority" was substituted for "Central Bank" by s.15(11), Sch.2 Pt 11 of the Central Bank Reform Act 2010 (No.23 of 2010).

Comments

This section gives significant powers to the Central Bank to give directions to a participating institution in order to achieve the purposes of the Act. A direction given under this section may be enforced under s.209.

Under this section, it is the Central Bank that gives the direction, but with the approval of the Minister. In contrast, a direction order under the Credit Institutions (Stabilisation) Act 2010 is made by the High Court on the application of the Minister.

Reporting by participating institutions

207.—(1) The [Central Bank] may direct a participating institution in writing to make any report that the [Central Bank] considers necessary to monitor the institution's compliance with its obligations under or by virtue of this Part.

(2) A direction under *subsection (1)* shall specify the information to be provided in the report and the period within which the report shall be submitted to the [Central Bank].

(3) A participating institution that is directed to make a report under *subsection (1)* shall comply with the direction.

(4) The Minister may direct the [Central Bank] to require such other reports from a participating institution as the Minister considers necessary.

(5) The Minister may make regulations providing for the making by participating institutions of periodic reports, the frequency and form of such reports and the matters that such reports shall address.

(6) If the Minister makes regulations under *subsection (5)*, the matters prescribed may include liquidity requirements, capital ratios, asset quality, risk exposures and funding costs.

NOTES AND COMMENTARY

Amendment History

In subss.(1), (2) and (4) the reference to "Regulatory Authority" was substituted for "Central Bank" by s.15(11), Sch.2 Pt 11 of the Central Bank Reform Act 2010 (No.23 of 2010).

Comments

This section authorises the Central Bank to require a participating institution to make a report containing specific information. It further empowers the Minister to direct the Central Bank to require such other reports from a participating institution as the Minister considers necessary.

Subsection (5) empowers the Minister to make regulations providing for the making by participating institutions of periodic reports of a specified form and frequency. Such regulations need not be tabled before the Houses of the Oireachtas.

Restructuring plans

208.—(1) The Minister, after consultation with the Governor and the [Central Bank], may direct a participating institution to draw up or amend, within a specified period, a restructuring plan for the purposes of this Act.

(2) A participating institution that is given a direction under *subsection (1)* shall submit a draft of the restructuring plan for the Minister's approval within the period specified in the direction.

(3) The Minister, after consultation with the Governor and the [Central Bank], may direct a participating institution to amend a draft restructuring plan in a specified respect. The direction shall specify a period within which the participating institution is required to do so.

(4) A participating institution that is directed under *subsection (3)* to amend a draft restructuring plan shall do so within the period specified in the direction.

(5) If the Minister approves a draft restructuring plan, the participating institution concerned shall put the plan into effect in accordance with a timetable directed by the Minister.

(6) The Minister, after consultation with the Governor and the [Central Bank], may direct a participating institution to submit to the Minister a business plan in accordance with this section.

(7) A participating institution that is given a direction under *subsection (6)* shall submit a draft of the business plan for the Minister's approval within the period specified in the direction.

(8) The Minister, after consulting with the Governor and the [Central Bank], may direct a participating institution to amend a draft business plan submitted to the Minister under *subsection (7)* in accordance with the direction.

(9) A participating institution that is directed to amend a draft business plan under *subsection (8)* shall comply with the direction within the period specified in the direction.

(10) A participating institution shall take all reasonable steps to ensure that any draft business plan submitted to the Minister accurately contains all relevant information. If the Minister approves a draft business plan, the participating institution shall take all reasonable steps to implement that plan.

(11) The Minister shall not approve a restructuring plan or business plan that does not comply with the law of the State and of the European Communities relating to competition and with the laws of the European Communities governing State aid.

NOTES AND COMMENTARY

Amendment History

In subss.(1), (3), (6) and (8) the reference to "Regulatory Authority" was substituted for "Central Bank" by s.15(11), Sch.2 Pt 11 of the Central Bank Reform Act 2010 (No.23 of 2010).

Comments

This section empowers the Minister to direct a participating institution to draw up or amend, within a specified period, a restructuring plan and/or a business plan for the purposes of this Act.

While the powers of the Minister are subject to having consulted with the Governor and the Central Bank there is no obligation on the Minister to follow the advice of the Governor and the Central Bank.

Compliance with directions

209.—(1) Where the [Central Bank] is of the opinion that a participating institution has not complied with a direction under this Part, the [Central Bank] may apply to the Court for an order that the institution comply with the direction.

(2) On hearing an application under *subsection (1)*, the Court may order the participating institution concerned to comply with the relevant direction or refuse the application, as it thinks fit.

(3) An application under *subsection (1)* shall be made summarily.

(4) When dealing with an application under *subsection (1)* the Court may make any interim or interlocutory order it considers appropriate.

(5) The Court shall not deny interim or interlocutory relief referred to in *subsection (4)* solely on the basis that the [Central Bank] would not suffer any damage if the relief were not granted pending conclusion of the proceedings.

(6) If the Court is satisfied that for reasons of commercial confidentiality a hearing under this section should be conducted otherwise than in public, the Court may so order.

NOTES AND COMMENTARY

Amendment History

In subss.(1), and (5) the reference to "Regulatory Authority" was substituted for "Central Bank" by s.15(11), Sch.2 Pt 11 of the Central Bank Reform Act 2010 (No.23 of 2010).

Comments

This section allows the Central Bank to apply to the High Court for an order compelling a participating institution to comply with a direction under this Part. This provision does not limit the Central Bank to applying only in respect of a failure to comply with a direction under this part made by the Central Bank, so the Central Bank could apply under this section for an order compelling a participating institution to comply with a direction under this Part made by the Minister, for instance a direction made under s.208.

The High Court may grant the application, make any interim or interlocutory order it thinks fit or refuse the application.

Guidelines regarding lending practices

210.—(1) The Minister may issue guidelines—

(*a*) regarding lending practices and procedures to facilitate the availability of credit to classes of borrowers or potential borrowers including small and medium sized enterprises, and

(*b*) relating to the review of decisions of participating institutions to refuse credit facilities.

(2) The Minister shall cause a copy of guidelines issued under *subsection (1)* to be laid before each House of the Oireachtas as soon as practicable.

(3) A participating institution shall comply with any guidelines issued under *subsection (1)*.

This section empowers the Minister for Finance to issue guidelines regarding lending practices and the review of the decisions of participating institutions to refuse credit facilities.

On March 26, 2010, the Minister for Finance exercised his powers under subs.(1) and issued Guidelines Regarding Lending Practices and Procedures and Relating to the Review of Decisions of Participating Institutions to Refuse Credit Facilities (S.I. No. 127 of 2010). The guidelines establish the Credit Review Office, and allow for a "SME", including a farm enterprise or sole trader, to apply to the Office for a review of a decision by a participating institution to refuse credit facilities, or to restructure existing credit facilities in relation to amounts ranging from €1,000 to €250,000.

"SME" is defined in the guidelines as "a business that meets one or more of the following criteria: it has fewer than 250 employees, it has an annual turnover of less than €50 million it has a balance sheet value of less than €43 million".

Under the Guidelines, the Credit Review Office is entitled to carry out such inquiries as it sees fit. The Guidelines stress that the review process is to be an informal one and that the Reviewer "is not bound by the rules of evidence" when carrying out inquiries.

At the conclusion of its inquiries the Credit Review Office may make a recommendation that credit be granted by the respondent participating institution. The recommendation is not binding. Where a participating institution declines to abide by a recommendation made under this section, it must provide an explanation to the Credit Review Office.

Under s.18 of the Finance Act 2011, the Credit Review Office is an accountable person for the purposes of Chap.1 of Pt 18 of the Taxes Consolidation Act 1997, as amended.

PART 13

MISCELLANEOUS

Avoidance of certain transactions

211.—(1) Where, on the application of NAMA or a NAMA group entity, it is shown to the satisfaction of the Court that—

    (*a*) an asset of a debtor or associated debtor, guarantor or surety was disposed of, and

    (*b*) the effect of the disposition was to defeat, delay or hinder the acquisition by NAMA or a NAMA group entity of an eligible bank asset, or to impair the value of an eligible bank asset or any rights (including a right to damages or any other remedy, a right to enforce a judgment and a priority) that NAMA or the NAMA group entity would have acquired or increased a liability or obligation but for that disposition,

the Court may declare the disposition to be void if in the Court's opinion it is just and equitable to do so.

(2) In deciding whether it is just and equitable to make a declaration under *subsection (1)*, the Court shall have regard to the rights of any person who has in good faith and for value acquired an interest in the asset the subject of the disposition.

(3) Nothing in this section affects the operation of section 14 of the Conveyancing Act 1634 or section 74(4)(*a*) of the Land and Conveyancing Law Reform Act 2009.

Section 211 allows for the High Court, on the application of NAMA or a NAMA group entity, to reverse the disposition of assets of a debtor, associated debtor, guarantor or surety made for the purpose of depriving NAMA of those assets.

The equivalent provision of the Land and Conveyancing Law Reform Act 2009, s.74 entitled "fraudulent dispositions", provides at subs.(3) that "any conveyance of property made with the intention of defrauding a creditor or other person is voidable by any person thereby prejudiced", but with a limitation in subs.(4) which completely excludes "any estate or interest in property conveyed for valuable consideration to any person in good faith not having, at the time of the conveyance, notice of the fraudulent intention" from the provisions of subs.(3).

In contrast, s.211 only requires the High Court to have regard to the rights of any person, who has in good faith and for value, acquired an interest in the asset in question when deciding whether or not it is just and equitable to make a declaration that the disposition of an asset is void. The High Court could, therefore, declare void a disposition of an asset to a bona fide third party purchaser for value where that disposition was detrimental to NAMA within the terms of subs.(1)(b).

Provision of tax information to NAMA

212.—(1) In this section "the Capital Gains Tax Acts" and "the Corporation Tax Acts" have the respective meanings given by section 1(2) of the Taxes Consolidation Act 1997.

(2) Where shares in a company are acquired by—

(*a*) NAMA,

(*b*) a company referred to in section 616(1)(*g*) of the Taxes Consolidation Act 1997, or

(*c*) a NAMA group entity,

and, as a consequence of the acquisition, the provisions of the Capital Gains Tax Acts, the Corporation Tax Acts or the Stamp Duties Consolidation Act 1999 as amended or extended impose a charge to tax or duty on the company by virtue of a clawback of a relief, the person from whom the shares are acquired shall inform NAMA, the acquiring company or the NAMA group entity of the charge and the amount of tax or duty due.

The relevant portion of s.1(2) of the Taxes Consolidation Act 1997 provides as follows:
"In this Act and in any Act passed after this Act, except where the context otherwise requires—
"the Capital Gains Tax Acts" means the enactments relating to capital gains tax in this Act and in any other enactment;
"the Corporation Tax Acts" means the enactments relating to corporation tax in this Act and in any other enactment, together with the Income Tax Acts"
Section 616 of the Taxes Consolidation Act 1997 provides that a group of companies is comprised of a principal company and all its 75 per cent subsidiaries. Subsection (1)(g) is inserted by s.240 of the National Asset Management Agency Act 2009 as specified in Pt 9 of Sch.3 of that Act, and it provides as follows:
"Notwithstanding paragraph (b)—
(i) a company (in this paragraph referred to as the 'first-mentioned company') shall be an effective 75 per cent subsidiary of the National Asset Management Agency where that Agency directly owns any part of the ordinary share capital of that company, and
(ii) any other company which is an effective 75 per cent subsidiary of the first-mentioned company shall be an effective 75 per cent subsidiary of the National Asset Management Agency."

NAMA, etc., not to make payments in certain circumstances

213.—(1) In this section—

"the Acts" has the meaning given by section 1095 of the Taxes Consolidation Act 1997;

"Collector-General" has the meaning given by section 2(1) of the Taxes Consolidation Act 1997;

"outstanding tax", in relation to a relevant person, means any obligation on the relevant person arising under the Acts in relation to the payment or remittance of any taxes, interest or penalties required to be paid or remitted under the Acts;

"relevant person" means a debtor, associated debtor, guarantor, surety or chargor and includes a connected person (within the meaning given by section 10 of the Taxes Consolidation Act 1997) in relation to a debtor, associated debtor, guarantor, surety or chargor.

(2) This section applies where in the exercise of any of its functions under this Act, NAMA or a NAMA group entity is obliged to pay an amount of money to a relevant person.

(3) Where this section applies, NAMA or the NAMA group entity concerned shall not make any payment to a relevant person until—

    (*a*) the relevant person delivers to NAMA, or to a person authorised by NAMA, a valid tax clearance certificate issued to the relevant person by the Collector-General, or

    (*b*) the Collector-General has confirmed to NAMA, following a request from NAMA, that it has no objection to the making of a payment to the relevant person.

(4) Where a relevant person is unable to produce a valid tax clearance certificate to NAMA because of any outstanding tax and NAMA or a NAMA group entity is obliged to pay an amount of money to the relevant person, the relevant person may issue a notice in writing to NAMA or the NAMA group entity directing it to forward to the Collector-General—

    (*a*) where the amount of money is greater than the outstanding tax, an amount of money equal to the amount of the outstanding tax, or

    (*b*) where the amount of money is equal to or less than the outstanding tax, that amount of money.

(5) On receipt by the Collector-General of an amount of money paid by NAMA or a NAMA group entity pursuant to *subsection (4)*, the Collector-General shall notify the relevant person.

NOTES AND COMMENTARY

This section ensures that NAMA will not be required to pay over funds to a debtor, associated debtor, guarantor, surety or charger who in turn owes outstanding tax to the Collector General.

This section does not, however, require any other party who is due to be paid money by NAMA to produce a tax clearance certificate.

Section 10 of the Taxes Consolidation Act 1997 deals with the concept of a "connected person", providing that any question whether a person is connected with another person shall be determined in accordance with subss.(3) to (8) of that section, which are as follows:

    "(3) A person shall be connected with an individual if that person is the individual's husband or wife, or is a relative, or the husband or wife of a relative, of the individual or of the individual's husband or wife.

(4) A person in the capacity as trustee of a settlement shall be connected with—

(a) any individual who in relation to the settlement is a settlor,

(b) any person connected with such an individual, and

(c) a body corporate which is deemed to be connected with that settlement, and a body corporate shall be deemed to be connected with a settlement in any accounting period or, as the case may be, year of assessment if, at any time in that period or year, as the case may be, it is a close company (or only not a close company because it is not resident in the State) and the participators then include the trustees of or a beneficiary under the settlement.

(5) Except in relation to acquisitions or disposals of partnership assets pursuant to bona fide commercial arrangements, a person shall be connected with any person with whom such person is in partnership, and with the spouse or a relative of any individual with whom such person is in partnership.

(6) A company shall be connected with another company—

(a) if the same person has control of both companies, or a person (in this paragraph referred to as "the first-mentioned person") has control of one company and persons connected with the first-mentioned person, or the first-mentioned person and persons connected with the first-mentioned person, have control of the other company, or

(b) if a group of 2 or more persons has control of each company, and the groups either consist of the same persons or could be regarded as consisting of the same persons by treating (in one or more cases) a member of either group as replaced by a person with whom such member is connected.

(7) A company shall be connected with another person if that person has control of the company or if that person and persons connected with that person together have control of the company.

(8) Any 2 or more persons acting together to secure or exercise control of, or to acquire a holding in, a company shall be treated in relation to that company as connected with one another and with any person acting on the direction of any of them to secure or exercise control of, or to acquire a holding in, the company."

Section 1095 of the Taxes Consolidation Act 1997 defines "the Acts" as:

"(a) the Tax Acts,

(b) the Capital Gains Tax Acts, and

(c) the Value-Added Tax Act, 1972, and the enactments amending or extending that Act,

and any instruments made thereunder"

NAMA exempt from certain taxes

214.—Income and gains arising to NAMA shall be exempt from income tax, corporation tax and capital gains tax.

NOTES AND COMMENTARY

This section exempts income and gains "arising to NAMA" from income tax, corporation tax and capital gains tax. The Act does not, however, provide whether income and gains made by a NAMA subsidiary or other NAMA group entity are considered to be "arising to NAMA", and, therefore, not subject to tax.

Disapplication of certain provisions of Competition Act 2002 and Credit Institutions (Financial Support) Act 2008

215.—(1) Parts 2 and 3 of the Competition Act 2002 do not apply with respect to the acquisition of bank assets under this Act.

(2) Section 7 of the Credit Institutions (Financial Support) Act 2008 does not apply with respect to the acquisition of bank assets under this Act.

Part 2 of the Competition Act 2002 deals with Competition Rules and Enforcement and includes the prohibition on anti-competitive agreements and abuse of dominant position; Part 3 deals with mergers and acquisitions.

Section 7 of the Credit Institutions (Financial Support) Act 2008 deals with certain mergers and acquisitions involving credit institutions.

NAMA, etc., not to be taken to be carrying on banking business, etc.

216.—(1) Except pursuant to the provisions mentioned or referred to in *subsection (2)*, neither NAMA nor a NAMA group entity shall be taken to be providing a service or carrying on an activity which would require it to be authorised or regulated by the Central Bank.

(2) The provisions referred to in *subsection (1)* are:

(*a*) Irish market abuse law, as defined in section 29(1) of the Investment Funds, Companies and Miscellaneous Provisions Act 2005;

(*b*) Irish prospectus law, as defined in section 38(1) of the Investment Funds, Companies and Miscellaneous Provisions Act 2005;

(*c*) transparency (regulated markets) law, as defined in section 19(1) of the Investment Funds, Companies and Miscellaneous Provisions Act 2006;

(*d*) regulations made under section 6A of the Markets in Financial Instruments and Miscellaneous Provisions Act 2007 if in those regulations the Minister declares that those regulations apply for the purposes of this section;

(*e*) any other provision that the Minister by regulation from time to time declares to apply to NAMA or a NAMA group entity.

This section exempts NAMA and NAMA group entities from all legal requirements of authorisation or regulation by the Central Bank for all activities other than those enumerated in subs.(2).

The natural consequence of the foregoing is that NAMA and NAMA group entities are subject to regulation by the Central Bank pursuant to the provisions listed in subs.(2).

Section 29(1) of the Investment Funds, Companies and Miscellaneous Provisions Act 2005 provides the following definition of "Irish market abuse law":

"(a) the measures adopted for the time being by the State to implement the 2003 Market Abuse Directive and the supplemental Directives (whether an Act of the Oireachtas, regulations under section 3 of the European Communities Act 1972 , regulations under section 30 or any other enactment (other than, save where the context otherwise admits, this Part)),

(b) any measures directly applicable in the State in consequence of the 2003 Market Abuse Directive and, without prejudice to the generality of this paragraph, includes the Market Abuse Regulation, and

(c) any supplementary and consequential measures adopted for the time being by the State in respect of the Market Abuse Regulation".

It further provides that "2003 Market Abuse Directive" means "Directive 2003/6/EC of the European Parliament and of the Council of 28 January 2003 on insider dealing and market manipulation (market abuse), including that Directive as it stands amended for the time being" and that "Market Abuse Regulation" means "Commission Regulation 2273/2003 of 22 December 2003".

Section 38(1) of the Investment Funds, Companies and Miscellaneous Provisions Act 2005 provides the following definition of "Irish prospectus law":

"(a) the measures adopted for the time being by the State to implement the 2003 Prospectus Directive (whether an Act of the Oireachtas, regulations under section 3 of the European Communities Act 1972, regulations under section 46 or any other enactment (other than, save where the context otherwise admits, this Part)),

(b) any measures directly applicable in the State in consequence of the 2003 Prospectus Directive and, without prejudice to the generality of this paragraph, includes the Prospectus Regulation, and

(c) any supplementary and consequential measures adopted for the time being by the State in respect of the Prospectus Regulation".

It further provides that "2003 Prospectus Directive" means "Directive 2003/71/EC of the European Parliament and of the Council of 4 November 20038, including that Directive as it stands amended for the time being" and that the "Prospectus Regulation" means "Commission Regulation (EC) No. 809/2004 of 29 April 2004 implementing Directive 2003/71/EC of the European Parliament and of the Council as regards information contained in prospectuses as well as the format, incorporation by reference and publication of such prospectuses and dissemination of advertisements".

Section 19(1) of the Investment Funds, Companies and Miscellaneous Provisions Act 2006 provides the following definition of "transparency (regulated markets) law":

"(a) the measures adopted for the time being by the State to implement the Transparency (Regulated Markets) Directive and any supplemental Directive (whether an Act of the Oireachtas, regulations under section 3 of the European Communities Act 1972 , regulations under section 20 or any other enactment (other than, save where the context otherwise admits, this Part)),

(b) any measures directly applicable in the State in consequence of the Transparency (Regulated Markets) Directive and, without prejudice to the generality of this paragraph, includes any Regulation or Decision made by the Commission pursuant to the procedure referred to in Article 27(2) of that Directive, and

(c) any supplementary and consequential measures adopted for the time being by the State in respect of any Regulation or Decision made by the Commission in consequence of the Transparency (Regulated Markets) Directive pursuant to the foregoing procedure".

It further provides that "Transparency (Regulated Markets) Directive" means "Directive 2004/109/EC 1 of the European Parliament and of the Council of 15 December 2004 on the harmonisation of transparency requirements in relation to information about issuers whose securities are admitted to trading on a regulated market and amending Directive 2001/34/EC, including the first-mentioned Directive as it stands amended for the time being".

Section 6A of the Markets in Financial Instruments and Miscellaneous Provisions Act 2007, as inserted by the Investment of the National Pensions Reserve Fund and Miscellaneous Provisions Act 2009, empowers the Minister to make regulations requiring persons who have entered into transactions in specified financial instruments or classes of financial instruments to disclose such information as may be specified in the regulations.

Application of laws in relation to netting agreements, etc.

217.—Nothing in this Act affects the operation of—

(*a*) the Netting of Financial Contracts Act 1995,

(*b*) the European Communities (Settlement Finality) Regulations 2008 (S.I. No. 88 of 2008),

(*c*) the European Communities (Financial Collateral Arrangements) Regulations 2004 (S.I. No. 1 of 2004), or

(*d*) regulation 30 of the European Communities (Reorganisation and Winding-Up of Credit Institutions) Regulations 2004 (S.I. No. 198 of 2004),

in relation to an agreement to which a participating institution is a party.

NOTES AND COMMENTARY

The Netting of Financial Contracts Act 1995 provides for the enforceability of netting agreements, notwithstanding anything contained in any rule of law relating to bankruptcy, insolvency or receivership, or in the Companies Acts or the Bankruptcy Act 1988.

For the purposes of the Act, "netting" means "the termination of financial contracts, the determination of the termination values of those contracts and the set off of the termination values so determined so as to arrive at a net amount due, if any, by one party to the other where each such determination and set off aforesaid is effected in accordance with the terms of a netting agreement between those parties".

The European Communities (Settlement Finality) Regulations 2008 (S.I. No. 88 of 2008) transposes the mandatory provisions of the Settlement Finality Directive (98/26/EC) on settlement finality in payment and securities settlement systems. The explanatory note appended to the regulations describes the primary aim of the Directive as "to reduce the legal risks associated with participation in settlement systems, in particular as regards the legality of netting agreements and the enforceability of collateral security."

The European Communities (Financial Collateral Arrangements) Regulations 2004 (S.I. No. 1 of 2004) give effect to Directive 2002/47/EC which deals with financial collateral arrangements and the provision of financial collateral. The Regulations were repealed and replaced by the European Communities (Financial Collateral Arrangements) Regulations 2010 (S.I. No. 626 of 2010) in December 2010.

Regulation 30 of the European Communities (Reorganisation and Winding-Up of Credit Institutions) Regulations 2004 (S.I. No. 198 of 2004) provides that "A netting agreement to which a credit institution is a party is to be governed solely by the law of contract that governs such an agreement."

Certain bank assets not invalidated

218.—(1) An acquired bank asset is not invalidated or rendered void or voidable as against NAMA or a NAMA group entity or their successors in title—

  (*a*) by section 60, 99, 100, 101, 111, 286 or 288 of the Companies Act 1963,

  (*b*) by section 29, 31 or 139 of the Companies Act 1990,

  (*c*) on the grounds that it was *ultra vires*,

  (*d*) by reason that the provider may not have been able to pay its debts as they fell due at the time the security was given or that the directors of that provider ceased to have the power to create that security,

  (*e*) by reason that the grant of the security may not have been duly authorised by the grantor or may not have been for the benefit of the grantor, or

  (*f*) by reason that the consent of a party required for the creation of the security may not have been obtained.

(2) Notwithstanding section 127(4) of the Stamp Duties Consolidation Act 1999, a charge or security that secures an acquired bank asset that is required to be stamped but has not been stamped or is insufficiently stamped is not rendered inadmissible in evidence or unenforceable only by reason that it is unstamped or insufficiently stamped.

(3) *Subsection (1)* shall not affect the existing priority of any other charge.

NOTES AND COMMENTARY

This section protects the ability of NAMA to acquire bank assets and provides certainty for those purchasing bank assets from NAMA. It is extraordinary in its breadth, allowing for

NAMA to enforce security even notwithstanding the fact that the consent of a party required for the creation of the security need not have been obtained, or that the granting of the security was ultra vires or not duly authorised by the grantor. Subsection (3) provides limited protection for third parties who have acquired rights under competing charges.

Section 60 of the Companies Act 1963, as amended, provides that it shall not be lawful for a company to give any financial assistance for the purpose of a purchase or subscription made for any shares in that company, or, where the company is a subsidiary company, in its holding company, unless authorised by a special resolution of the company passed not more than 12 months previously.

Section 99 of the Companies Act 1963, as amended, provides that certain charges created by a company are to be void against the liquidator and any creditor of the company, unless the prescribed particulars of the charge are delivered to the registrar of companies for registration in the manner required by the Act within 21 days after the date of the creation of the charge.

Section 100 of the Companies Act 1963, as amended, requires the registration of the particulars of every charge created by a company and of the issues of debentures as required by s.99 of that Act.

Section 101 of the Companies Act 1963, as amended, provides for the registration of pre-existing charges which affect property purchased by a company.

Section 111 of the Companies Act 1963 provides that the provisions of the relevant Part of that Act shall extend to charges on property in the State which are created by a company incorporated outside the State which has an established place of business in the State, and to judgment mortgages affecting property in the State and to receivers of property in the State of such a company.

Section 286 the Companies Act 1963, as amended, invalidates certain fraudulent preferences of its creditors by a company which is unable to pay its debts as they fall due.

Section 288 of the Companies Act 1963, as amended, sets out circumstances in which a floating charge made over the property of a company that is being wound up will be invalid.

Section 29 of the Companies Act 1990, as amended, requires the prior approval by way of a resolution of the company in a general meeting for any acquisition of "non-cash assets" by a director of the company from the company or by the company from a director.

Section 31 of the Companies Act 1990 prohibits companies from making loans to directors or to people connected to directors.

Section 139 of the Companies Act 1990 gives certain powers to the High Court in relation to the disposal of company property where the effect of the disposal was to perpetrate a fraud on the company, its creditors or members.

Nothing done under Act to be reorganisation or winding-up measure

219.—Nothing done under this Act constitutes a reorganisation or winding-up measure for the purposes of—

(*a*) the European Communities (Reorganisation and Winding- Up of Credit Institutions) Regulations 2004 (S.I. No. 198 of 2004), or

(*b*) the European Communities (Reorganisation and Winding- Up of Insurance Undertakings) Regulations 2003 (S.I. No. 168 of 2003).

NOTES AND COMMENTARY

Section 217 also provides that nothing in this Act affects the operation of reg.30 of the European Communities (Reorganisation and Winding-Up of Credit Institutions) Regulations 2004 (S.I. No. 198 of 2004).

The European Communities (Reorganisation and Winding-Up of Credit Institutions) Regulations 2004 (S.I. No. 198 of 2004) gives effect to Directive 2001/24/EC which deals with the reorganisation and winding up of credit institutions.

The European Communities (Reorganisation and Winding-Up of Insurance Undertakings) Regulations 2003 (S.I. No. 168 of 2003) give effect to Directive 2001/17/EC which deals with the reorganisation and winding-up of insurance undertakings.

Operation of certain provisions of Land Registration Rules 1972 to 2008

220.—(1) Notwithstanding anything in the Land Registration Rules 1972 to 2008, an officer of NAMA, an adviser acting on behalf of NAMA or a person nominated in writing by the Chief Executive Officer of NAMA may inspect and take copies of any document filed in the Land Registry on a dealing or transaction with the property of any person.

(2) This section applies only to documents relevant to an acquired bank asset.

(3) A person who seeks to inspect or take a copy of a document pursuant to *subsection (1)* shall produce to the Property Registration Authority evidence that he or she is a person authorised under that subsection to do so.

NOTES AND COMMENTARY

This section allows an officer, adviser or nominee of NAMA to inspect and take copies of any document filed in the Land Registry to do with a property transaction where those documents are relevant to an acquired bank asset.

Offence of lobbying NAMA, etc.

221.—(1) Subject to *subsections (3)* and *(4)*, if a person communicates, on behalf of another person, with NAMA, a NAMA group entity or a person providing services or advice to NAMA or a NAMA group entity with the intention of influencing the making of a decision in relation to the performance of the functions of NAMA or the NAMA group entity, the person commits an offence.

(2) Without prejudice to the generality of *subsection (1)*, a reference in that subsection to a decision relating to the performance of the functions of NAMA includes a decision relating to—

    (*a*) the lending of money,
    (*b*) the initiation of legal proceedings,
    (*c*) legal proceedings in being,
    (*d*) the engagement of the services of an expert adviser or other service provider,
    (*e*) any other matter that could give rise to an advantage or benefit to a person other than NAMA,
    (*f*) a tender, or
    (*g*) the purchase or sale of property.

(3) It is not an offence pursuant to *subsection (1)* if the communication concerned—

    (*a*) is made public at the time of the communication,
    (*b*) is made without an intention to benefit, or confer an advantage on, any specific person, or
    (*c*) is made in the public interest.

(4) It is not an offence pursuant to *subsection (1)* if the person who makes the communication concerned—

    (*a*) is acting in his or her professional capacity or in the course of his or her employment, and
    (*b*) does so in that capacity.

(5) A person who believes that he or she has been communicated with in contravention of *subsection (1)* shall, as soon as may be, report—

    (*a*) that the communication was made,

    (*b*) the details of the communication made, and

    (*c*) the name of the person who communicated with him or her,

to a member of the Garda Síochána.

(6) A person who fails to comply with *subsection (5)* commits an offence.

(7) A person who commits an offence under this section is liable on summary conviction to a fine not exceeding €1,000 or imprisonment for a term not exceeding 6 months or both.

NOTES AND COMMENTARY

This section ostensibly criminalises non-public lobbying of NAMA. The practical implications of the provision are, however, extremely limited.

On the one hand, this section only deals with communications made "on behalf of another person", on the other hand it excludes communications made by a person in their professional capacity or in the course of their employment.

As a consequence, subs.(1) only criminalises communications made on behalf of a person by another person who is not either an employee of the first individual or acting in their professional capacity, which are not either made public at the time of communication or made in the public interest.

It is not an offence for a person to lobby NAMA on their own behalf.

Subsections (5) and (6) make it an offence for a person who believes they have been communicated with in contravention of subs.(1) not to report this to a member of the Garda Síochána.

Protection from civil liability of persons who report certain misconduct

222.—(1) Where a person who is an employee of a participating institution or an officer of NAMA or a director or employee of a NAMA group entity communicates his or her opinion, whether in writing or otherwise, to a member of the Garda Síochána or a member of the Board that—

    (*a*) an offence under this Act or any other enactment has been or is being committed,

    (*b*) any provision of this Act or any other enactment or rule of law has been or is being contravened, or

    (*c*) there has been other serious wrongdoing in relation to NAMA or a NAMA group entity,

then, unless the person acts in bad faith, he or she shall not be regarded as having committed any breach of duty towards any other person, and no person shall have a cause of action against the firstmentioned person in respect of that communication.

(2) Where a person who is an employee of a participating institution, an officer of NAMA or a director or employee of a NAMA group entity communicates his or her opinion, whether in writing or otherwise, to the Minister that a direction given by the Minister under this Act has been or is being contravened, then, unless the person acts in bad faith, he or she shall not be regarded as having committed any breach of duty towards any other person, and no person shall have a cause of action against the first-mentioned person in respect of that communication.

(3) This section applies to a communication—

    (*a*) that would, but for this section, constitute a breach of duty by the person who made it, or

    (*b*) in respect of which another person would, but for this section, have a cause of action against the person who made it.

NOTES AND COMMENTARY

Section 222 protects officers of NAMA and employees of participating institutions from all civil liability that might otherwise arise from any communication they make to a member of the Garda Síochána or a member of the Board of concerns relating to acts of illegality or serious wrongdoing, or to the Minister of concerns relating to contravention of directions given by the Minister under the Act.

Prohibition on penalisation

223.—(1) In this section and in *Schedule 2*:
"employee" means—

    (*a*) an employee of a participating institution,

    (*b*) an officer of NAMA, or

    (*c*) an employee of a NAMA group entity;

"employer" means—

    (*a*) a participating institution,

    (*b*) in relation to an officer of NAMA, both NAMA and the NTMA, or

    (*c*) a NAMA group entity;

"penalisation" includes any act or omission by an employer or a person acting on behalf of an employer that affects an employee to his or her detriment with respect to any term or condition of his or her employment, and in particular includes—

    (*a*) suspension, lay-off or dismissal (including a dismissal within the meaning of the Unfair Dismissals Acts 1977 to 2005), or the threat of suspension, lay-off or dismissal,

    (*b*) demotion or loss of opportunity for promotion,

    (*c*) transfer of duties, change of location of place of work, reduction in wages or change in working hours,

    (*d*) the imposition or administering of any discipline, reprimand or other penalty (including a financial penalty), and

    (*e*) coercion or intimidation.

(2) To avoid doubt, this section and *Schedule 2* have effect in relation to a person who is an officer of NAMA as if both NAMA and the NTMA were employers of the person.

(3) An employer shall not penalise or threaten penalisation against an employee for—

    (*a*) making a complaint to a member of the Garda Síochána or the Minister that a provision of this Act is not being complied with,

    (*b*) giving evidence in any proceedings under this Act, or

    (*c*) giving notice of his or her intention to do any of the things referred to in *paragraph (a)* or *(b)*.

(4) *Schedule 2* has effect in relation to an alleged contravention of *subsection (3)* and matters consequential on such a contravention.

(5) If a penalisation of an employee, in contravention of *subsection (3),*

constitutes a dismissal of the employee within the meaning of the Unfair Dismissals Acts 1977 to 2005, relief may not be granted to the employee in respect of that penalisation both under *Schedule 2* and under those Acts.

NOTES AND COMMENTARY

Section 223 prohibits participating institutions, NAMA, NAMA group entities and the NTMA from penalising or threatening to penalise their employees for making a complaint to a member of the Garda Síochána or the Minister that a provision of this Act is not being complied with or giving evidence in any proceedings under this Act, or giving notice of an intention to do either of the foregoing.

False statements

224.—(1) A person who states to a member of the Garda Síochána or a member of the Board that—

> (*a*) an offence under this Act or any other enactment has been or is being committed,
>
> (*b*) a provision of this Act, a provision of any other enactment or any rule of law has been or is being contravened, or
>
> (*c*) there has been serious wrongdoing by any person in relation to NAMA or a NAMA group entity,

knowing the statement to be false commits an offence.

(2) A person guilty of an offence under this section is liable—

> (*a*) on summary conviction to a fine not exceeding €5,000 or imprisonment for a term not exceeding 12 months or both, or
>
> (*b*) on conviction on indictment to a fine not exceeding €100,000 or imprisonment for a term not exceeding 3 years or both.

NOTES AND COMMENTARY

This section acts as the corollary of the whistleblower protection provisions of ss.222 and 223 which protect employees of participating institutions and NAMA from civil liability and penalisation as an employee for communications made in good faith in relation to concerns of illegality or serious wrongdoing.

Section 224 makes it an offence to state to a member of the Garda Síochána or a member of the Board that an act of illegality or serious wrongdoing has been committed, knowing that statement to be false.

Surcharge on participating institutions

225.—(1) In this section:

"accounting period" shall be construed in accordance with section 27 of the Taxes Consolidation Act 1997;

"surcharge" means the tax referred to in *subsection (3)*;

"underlying loss" means the amount, if any, by which the aggregate of losses incurred by NAMA (including NAMA group entities) exceeds the aggregate of the profits arising to NAMA (including those entities) in the period from the date of its establishment to the date referred to in the direction under *subsection (2)* or the date of the occurrence of the event so referred to.

(2) If—

> (*a*) the Minister decides under *section 227(3)(b)* that the continuation of

NAMA is unnecessary having regard to the purposes of this Act, the Minister shall, or

(*b*)   (i)   10 years have elapsed since the establishment of NAMA, or

(ii)   the Minister proposes to publish or has published a Bill for NAMA's dissolution, restructuring or material alteration,

the Minister may,

direct NAMA to prepare a report and accounts as at a date specified by the Minister or as at the date of the occurrence of an event so specified—

(I)   showing the aggregate profits and losses arising to and incurred by NAMA (including NAMA group entities), respectively, from its activities in the period from the date of its establishment to the date or the occurrence of the event so specified, and

(II)   duly certified by the Comptroller and Auditor General,

and NAMA shall send such report and accounts so certified to the Minister.

(3) Where—

(*a*)   the report and accounts sent to the Minister under *subsection (2)* disclose an underlying loss has been incurred by NAMA (including NAMA group entities), and

(*b*)   the Minister is of the opinion that such underlying loss is unlikely to be otherwise made good,

then the Minister may cause—

(i)   a provision to be included in a Money Bill, or

(ii)   a provision to like effect to be included in any other Bill initiated in Dáil Éireann,

providing for the imposition of a special tax by way of a surcharge on participating institutions in accordance with *subsection (4)*.

(4) The aggregate tax by way of a surcharge to be imposed on participating institutions on their respective profits (within the meaning of section 4 of the Taxes Consolidation Act, 1997) if any—

(*a*)   shall not exceed the amount of the underlying loss, if any, incurred by NAMA (including NAMA group entities),

(*b*)   shall be apportioned to each participating institution on the basis of the book value of the bank assets acquired from each participating institution concerned as a proportion of the total book value of the bank assets acquired from all of the participating institutions,

and the surcharge so apportioned shall be imposed on each institution accordingly and paid by each of them over such period and at such times as provided for by the subsequent Act giving effect to this section and to which *subsection (3)* relates.

(5) Any surcharge due to be paid by a participating institution in accordance with *subsection (4)* may not exceed 100 per cent of the corporation tax, if any, due and payable by that participating institution for the accounting period or periods as the case may be, falling within the period referred to in that subsection.

(6) No surcharge shall become payable until either—

(*a*)   10 years after the passing of this Act, or

(*b*)   NAMA is dissolved or restructured, or there is a material alteration of NAMA's functions,

whichever last occurs.

This provision sets out a mechanism that may be used to pass any losses made by NAMA on to participating institutions in the form of a special tax by way of a surcharge.

This provision is somewhat superfluous as it requires further legislation to be proposed by the Minister and passed by the Oireachtas to enact any such special tax.

This section does, however, ensure that participating institutions are aware of the possibility of such a special tax being imposed at some point in the future.

PART 14

REVIEW OF NAMA

Triennial review of NAMA's progress

226.—(1) As soon as may be after 31 December 2012, and every 3 years after that while NAMA continues in existence, the Comptroller and Auditor General shall assess the extent to which NAMA has made progress toward achieving its overall objectives.

(2) The Comptroller and Auditor General shall present a copy of that report to the Minister as soon as may be and the Minister shall cause a copy of the report to be laid before each House of the Oireachtas.

NOTES AND COMMENTARY

This section is discussed within the commentary to s.227.

Review of achievement of NAMA's purposes

227.—(1) The Minister may at any time require NAMA to report to him or her regarding progress with regard to the achievement of NAMA's purposes.

(2) The Minister shall lay a copy of a report under *subsection (1)* before each House of the Oireachtas as soon as reasonably practicable.

(3) As soon as may be after 31 December 2012, and every 5 years after that while NAMA continues in existence, the Minister—

    (*a*) shall assess the extent to which NAMA has made progress toward achieving its overall objectives, and

    (*b*) shall decide whether continuation of NAMA is necessary having regard to the purposes of this Act.

NOTES AND COMMENTARY

Sections 226 and 227 provide for three different forms of review of NAMA: review by the Comptroller and Auditor General; reporting from NAMA to the Minister; and assessment by the Minister.

Reports of the Comptroller and Auditor General and reports from NAMA to the Minister must be laid before the Houses of the Oireachtas, but there is no similar requirement in relation to the assessment and decisions of the Minister under subs.(3).

Unlike reports by NAMA to the Minister delivered under s.56, reports under s.227(1) do not constitute confidential information.

PART 15

AMENDMENT AND MODIFICATION OF OTHER ENACTMENTS

Operation of certain provisions of Companies Act 1963

228.—(1) A reference to a company in section 60(1) or 72(1) of the Companies Act 1963 shall be taken not to include a NAMA group entity.

(2) Section 286 of the Companies Act 1963 shall not be taken to invalidate or render void a payment made to NAMA or to another person at NAMA's direction.

NOTES AND COMMENTARY

Section 228(1) provides that a reference to a company in ss.60(1) or 72(1) of the Companies Act 1963 shall be taken not to include a NAMA group entity.

Section 60 of the Companies Act 1963 prohibits limited companies from providing financial assistance for the purchase of their own shares.

Section 72(1), as amended by s.231 of the Companies Act 1990, prohibits any reduction of a company's share capital, except as expressly prohibited by that Act.

Section 286 of the Companies Act 1963, as substituted by s.135 of the Companies Act 1990, renders void any payments made as a fraudulent preference within the six months prior to the commencement of a winding-up order.

The Companies Act 1963 is also amended by s.233, as set out in Pt 3 of Sch.3

Operation of certain provisions of Companies (Amendment) Act 1983

229.—A reference to a company in section 41(1), or subsection (1) or (3) of section 45, of the Companies (Amendment) Act 1983 shall be taken not to include a NAMA group entity.

NOTES AND COMMENTARY

Section 229 provides that a reference to a company in s.41(1), or s.45(1) or (3), of the Companies (Amendment) Act 1983 shall be taken not to include a NAMA group entity.

Section 41(1) of the Companies (Amendment) Act 1983 provides as follows:

"Subject to the following provisions of this section, no company limited by shares or limited by guarantee and having a share capital shall acquire its own shares (whether by purchase, subscription or otherwise)."

Section 45(1) of the Companies (Amendment) Act 1983 provides as follows:

"A company shall not make a distribution (as defined by section 51) except out of profits available for the purpose."

Section 45(3) of the Companies (Amendment) Act 1983 provides as follows:

"A company shall not apply an unrealised profit in paying up debentures or any amounts unpaid on any of its issued shares."

Disapplication of section 7 of Official Languages Act 2003

230.—Section 7 of the Official Languages Act 2003 does not apply in relation to this Act. The text of this Act shall be made available electronically in each of the official languages as soon as practicable after its enactment.

NOTES AND COMMENTARY

This provision was not contained in the public consultation draft or the bill as initiated. An amendment proposed by the Minister for Finance in the Report Amendments, and included in the bill as passed by Dáil Eireann, excluded the Act from the provisions of s.7 of the Official Languages Act 2003 altogether. Seanad Eireann passed an amendment to require the eventual electronic publication of the Act in both official languages, and the amended version of the text was retained in the Act.

Section 7 of the Official Languages Act provides as follows (in the English language text of the Act): "As soon as may be after the enactment of any Act of the Oireachtas, the text thereof shall be printed and published in each of the official languages simultaneously".

The net effect of this section is, therefore, that the official Irish language text of the Act is to "be made available electronically" and "as soon as practicable after its enactment" rather than "printed and published" "simultaneously".

An official translation has been made available. In the official translation the Act is known in Irish as "An tAcht fán nGníomhaireacht Náisiúnta um Bainistíocht Sócmhainní 2009", and NAMA is known as "GNBS" or "An Ghníomhaireacht Náisiúnta um Bainistíocht Sócmhainní".

This section reflects the requirements of Art.25.4.4 of the Constitution: "Where the President signs the text of a Bill in one only of the official languages, an official translation shall be issued in the other official language."

The Supreme Court held in *Ó'Beoláin v Fahy* [2001] 2 I.R. 279 that the State bears the responsibility for providing an official translation of each Act of the Oireachtas passed in only one official language.

The Supreme Court, however, also found in *Ó'Murchú v Taoiseach* [2010] IESC 26 that this did not extend to a requirement that an Act of the Oireachtas must be enacted in both official languages or that a translation into the second official language must be available simultaneously with the enactment of an Act.

The Supreme Court instead required in the foregoing cases that the State must make available Irish versions of Acts of the Oireachtas within a reasonable period of time, or as soon as may be practicable.

The Supreme Court also found in *Ó'Murchu* that there was no general constitutional obligation to translate and make available to the public "translations of all and every Statutory Instrument made pursuant to an Act of the Oireachtas", but that an individual may be entitled to claim that the absence of a particular Statutory Instrument in Irish may constitute an inhibition or impediment on them "seeking to vindicate his right to use the first official language in court proceedings". For instance, in *Ó'Beoláin* the State was required to provide an official translation of the Rules of the District Court.

It seems from the foregoing that any party to litigation involving the State or NAMA who chose to exercise their right to conduct that litigation through Irish would be entitled to delay those proceedings until such time as the State issued an official translation of any Statutory Instrument which was of particular importance in that litigation.

Amendment of Building Societies Act 1989

231.—The Building Societies Act 1989 is amended as specified in *Part 1* of *Schedule 3*.

Amendment of Central Bank Act 1942

232.—The Central Bank Act 1942 is amended as specified in *Part 2* of *Schedule 3*.

Amendment of Companies Act 1963

233.—The Companies Act 1963 is amended as specified in *Part 3* of *Schedule 3*.

Amendment of Companies (Amendment) Act 1990

234.—The Companies (Amendment) Act 1990 is amended as specified in *Part 4* of *Schedule 3*.

Amendment of Finance Act 1970

235.—Section 54 of the Finance Act 1970 is amended as specified in *Part 5* of *Schedule 3*.

Amendment of Landlord and Tenant (Amendment) Act 1980

236.—The Landlord and Tenant (Amendment) Act 1980 is amended as specified in *Part 6* of *Schedule 3*.

Amendment of National Treasury Management Agency Act 1990

237.—The National Treasury Management Agency Act 1990 is amended as specified in *Part 7* of *Schedule 3*.

Amendment of Planning and Development Act 2000

238.—The Planning and Development Act 2000 is amended as specified in *Part 8* of *Schedule 3*.

Amendment of Stamp Duties Consolidation Act 1999

239.—The Stamp Duties Consolidation Act 1999 is amended as specified in *Part 9* of *Schedule 3*.

Amendment of Taxes Consolidation Act 1997

240.—The Taxes Consolidation Act 1997 is amended as specified in *Part 10* of *Schedule 3*.

Amendment of Value-Added Tax Act 1972

241.—The Value-Added Tax Act 1972 is amended as specified in *Part 11* of *Schedule 3*.

SCHEDULE 1

POWERS OF STATUTORY RECEIVERS

1. To take immediate possession of, get in and collect any secured asset or any part of it in respect of which he or she is appointed and to make such demands and take such proceedings as may seem expedient for that purpose, and to take possession of the secured assets over which he or she is appointed with like rights.

2. To sell, realise or otherwise dispose of property.

3. To carry on, manage, develop, reconstruct, amalgamate or diversify or concur in carrying on, managing, developing, reconstructing, amalgamating or diversifying any business of the chargor in any manner he or she thinks fit.

4. To appoint and discharge managers, officers, agents, professional advisers, consultants, servants, workmen, employees and others for the purposes specified in this Schedule upon such terms as to remuneration or otherwise as he or she thinks fit and to remove any person so appointed to any such position by the chargor.

5. To raise and borrow money or incur any other liability, either unsecured or on the security of any secured asset either in priority to NAMA's or the relevant NAMA group entity's security or otherwise and generally on any terms and for whatever purpose he or she thinks fit.

6. To grant rights, options or easements over, dispose of, convert into money and realise any secured asset by public auction or private contract and generally in any manner and on any terms he or she thinks fit. The consideration for any such transaction may consist of cash, debentures or other obligations, shares, stock or other valuable consideration and any such consideration may be payable in a lump sum or by instalments spread over any period he or she thinks fit. Fixtures, plant and machinery may be severed and sold separately from the property containing them without the consent of the chargor.

7. To let, hire, lease, licence or grant any interest in any secured asset for any term and at any rent (with or without a premium) he or she thinks fit and to vary the terms, surrender or accept a surrender of any lease or tenancy of any secured asset on any terms which he or she thinks fit (including the payment of money to a lessee or tenant on a surrender).

8. Where the chargor is a company, to require the chargor, or the directors of the chargor, to make calls conditionally or unconditionally upon the shareholders of the chargor in respect of any uncalled capital of the chargor and enforce payment of any call so made by action (in the name of the chargor or the statutory receiver as he or she may think fit) or otherwise.

9. To sell or assign all or any of the book debts in respect of which he or she is appointed in such manner, and generally on such terms and conditions, as he or she thinks fit.

10. To exercise in respect of any secured asset all voting or other powers or rights in such manner as he or she thinks fit.

11. To purchase or acquire any land or any interest in or right over land.

12. To exercise on behalf of the chargor, and without the consent of or notice to the chargor, all the powers conferred on a landlord or a tenant by any legislation from time to time in force in any relevant jurisdiction relating to rents

or agriculture in respect of any part of the secured assets.

13. To exercise on behalf of the chargor and in the name of the chargor all powers and rights of the chargor relevant to effecting and necessary to effect the registration in the Land Registry of any fixed or specific charge created on any registered land, of the crystallisation of any floating charge or his or her appointment as statutory receiver.

14. To settle, adjust, refer to arbitration, allow time for payment, compromise and arrange any claim, contract, account, dispute, question or demand with or by any person who is or claims to be a creditor of the chargor or relating in any way to any secured asset.

15. To bring, prosecute, enforce, defend and abandon any action, suit or proceedings both in his or her own name and in the name of the chargor in relation to any secured asset which he or she thinks fit.

16. To give a valid receipt for any money and execute any assurance or thing that may be necessary or desirable for realising any secured asset.

17. Where the chargor is a company, to form a subsidiary of the chargor, arrange for any such subsidiary to trade or cease to trade as he or she sees fit, in his or her capacity as shareholder and transfer to that subsidiary any secured asset and sell or otherwise dispose of any such subsidiary.

18. To delegate his or her powers.

19. To appoint managers, officers, agents, professional advisers, consultants, servants, workmen, employees and others, for the purpose of exercising his or her powers at such salaries, for such periods and on such terms as he or she determines.

20. To enter into, abandon, perform, repudiate, rescind, vary or cancel any contracts as he or she thinks fit.

21. To lend money or advance credit to any customer of the chargor.

22. To make substitutions of, or improvements to, the chargor's plant and machinery as he or she thinks fit.

23. To effect with any insurer any policy of insurance either in lieu or satisfaction of, or in addition to, the insurances required to be maintained under any security document or loan facility agreement entered into by the chargor which is held by NAMA or a NAMA group entity.

24. To make any election for value-added tax purposes that he or she thinks fit.

25. To run the tax affairs of the chargor in any manner that he or she thinks fit.

26. To conduct and complete all investigations, studies, sampling and testing and all remedial, removal and other actions required by law or by NAMA or a NAMA group entity and comply with all lawful orders and directives of any authority under an environmental law.

27. To take all steps necessary to effect any registration, renewal, application or notification that he or she thinks fit to maintain in force or protect any intellectual property.

28. To redeem any prior security interest and to settle and pass the accounts to which that security interest relates. Any accounts so settled and passed are conclusive and binding on the chargor, and any money so paid shall be taken to be an expense properly incurred by him or her.

29. To effect any repair or insurance and do any other act which the chargor might do in the ordinary conduct of its business to protect or improve any secured asset.

30. To commence and complete any building operation, and to complete any building operation already begun.

31. To arrange for or provide any service proper for the efficient use or management of the secured assets.

32. To apply for and maintain any planning permission, building regulation approval or any other authorisation.

33. To do all other acts and things which he or she may consider desirable or necessary for realising any secured asset or incidental or conducive to any of the rights, powers or discretions conferred on a statutory receiver.

34. To exercise in relation to a secured asset all the rights, powers and authorities that he or she could exercise if he or she were the absolute beneficial owner of the secured asset.

35. To use the name of the chargor when exercising any of the rights, powers or discretions conferred on him or her.

36. Where the chargor is a company, to use the chargor's seal.

37. To do all acts and to execute in the name and on behalf of the chargor any deed, receipt or other document.

38. To draw, accept, make or endorse any bill of exchange or promissory note in the name of and on behalf of the chargor.

39. To make any payment which is necessary or incidental to the performance of his or her functions.

40. To rank and claim in the bankruptcy, insolvency, sequestration or liquidation of any person indebted to the chargor and to receive dividends, and to accede to the trust deeds for the creditors of any such person.

41. Where the chargor is a company, to change the location of the chargor's registered office.

SCHEDULE 2

Complaints to rights commissioner

1. (1) An employee may present a complaint to a rights commissioner that his or her employer has contravened *section 223(3)* in relation to the employee.

(2) Where a complaint under *subparagraph 1* is made, the rights commissioner shall—

    (*a*) give the parties an opportunity to be heard by the commissioner and to present to the commissioner any evidence relevant to the complaint,

    (*b*) give a decision in writing in relation to it, and

    (*c*) communicate the decision to the parties.

(3) A decision of a rights commissioner under *subparagraph (2)* shall do one or more of the following:

    (*a*) declare that the complaint was or, as the case may be, was not well founded;

    (*b*) require the employer to take a specified course of action;

    (*c*) require the employer to pay to the employee compensation of such amount (if any) as is just and equitable having regard to all the circumstances.

(4) The references in *subparagraph (3)* to an employer shall be construed, in a case where ownership of the business of the employer changes after the contravention to which the complaint relates occurred, as references to the person who, by virtue of the change, becomes entitled to that ownership.

(5) A rights commissioner shall not entertain a complaint under this paragraph if it is presented to him or her after the expiration of the period of 6 months beginning on the date of the contravention to which the complaint relates.

(6) Notwithstanding *subparagraph (5)*, a rights commissioner may entertain a complaint under this paragraph presented to him or her after the expiration of the period referred to in *subparagraph (5)* (but not later than 6 months after such expiration) if he or she is satisfied that the failure to present the complaint within that period was due to reasonable cause.

(7) A complaint shall be presented by giving notice of it in writing to a rights commissioner and the notice shall contain such particulars and be in such form as may be specified from time to time by the Minister.

(8) A copy of a notice under *subparagraph (7)* shall be given to the other party concerned by the rights commissioner concerned.

(9) Proceedings under this paragraph before a rights commissioner shall be conducted otherwise than in public.

(10) A rights commissioner shall furnish the Labour Court with a copy of each decision given by the commissioner under *subparagraph (2)*.

Appeals from decisions of rights commissioner

2. (1) A party concerned may appeal to the Labour Court from a decision of a rights commissioner under *paragraph 1* and, if the party does so, the Labour Court—

(*a*) shall give the parties an opportunity to be heard by it and to present to it any evidence relevant to the appeal,

(*b*) shall make a determination in writing in relation to the appeal affirming, varying or setting aside the decision, and

(*c*) shall communicate the determination to the parties.

(2) An appeal under this paragraph shall be initiated by the party concerned giving within 6 weeks (or such greater period as the Court may determine in the particular circumstances) from the date on which the decision to which it relates was communicated to the party, a notice in writing to the Labour Court containing such particulars as are determined by the Labour Court under *subparagraph (4)* and stating the intention of the party concerned to appeal against the decision.

(3) A copy of a notice under *subparagraph (2)* shall be given by the Labour Court to any other party concerned as soon as practicable after the receipt of the notice by the Labour Court.

(4) The Labour Court shall determine the following matters, or the procedures to be followed in relation to them:

(*a*) the procedure in relation to all matters concerning the initiation and the hearing by the Labour Court of appeals under this paragraph;

(*b*) the times and places of hearings of such appeals;

(*c*) the representation of the parties to such appeals;

(*d*) the publication and notification of determinations of the Labour Court;

(*e*) the particulars to be contained in a notice under *subparagraph (2)*;

(*f*) any matters consequential on, or incidental to, the foregoing matters.

(5) The Minister may, at the request of the Labour Court, refer a question of law arising in proceedings before it under this paragraph to the High Court for its determination. The determination of the High Court in relation to such a question shall be final and conclusive.

(6) A party to proceedings before the Labour Court under this paragraph may appeal to the High Court from a determination of the Labour Court on a point of law. The determination of the High Court on such an appeal shall be final and conclusive.

Paragraphs 1 and 2: supplemental provisions

3. (1) Section 39(17) of the Redundancy Payments Act 1967 shall apply in relation to proceedings before the Labour Court under *paragraph 2* as it applies to matters referred to the Employment Appeals Tribunal under that section with—

(*a*) the substitution in that provision of references to the Labour Court for references to the Tribunal, and

(*b*) the substitution in paragraph (*e*) of that provision of "€3,000" for "£150".

(2) Where a decision of a rights commissioner in relation to a complaint under this Schedule has not been carried out by the employer concerned in accordance with its terms, the time for bringing an appeal against the decision has expired and no such appeal has been brought, the employee concerned may bring the

complaint before the Labour Court and the Labour Court shall, without hearing the employer concerned or any evidence (other than in relation to the matters aforesaid), make a determination to the like effect as the decision.

(3) The bringing of a complaint before the Labour Court under *subparagraph (2)* shall be effected by giving to the Labour Court a written notice containing such particulars (if any) as may be determined by the Labour Court.

(4) The Labour Court shall publish, in a manner it considers appropriate, particulars of any determination made by it under *subparagraph (4)(a), (b), (c), (e)* and *(f)* of *paragraph 2* (not being a determination in relation to a particular appeal under that paragraph) and *subparagraph (3)*.

Enforcement of determinations of Labour Court

4. (1) If an employer fails to carry out a determination of the Labour Court in relation to a complaint under *paragraph 1* in accordance with its terms within 6 weeks from the date on which the determination is communicated to the parties, the Circuit Court shall, on application to it in that behalf by—

    (*a*) the employee concerned,

    (*b*) with the consent of the employee, any trade union of which the employee is a member, or

    (*c*) the Minister, if the Minister considers it appropriate to make the application having regard to all the circumstances,

without hearing the employer or any evidence (other than in relation to the matters aforesaid), make an order directing the employer to carry out the determination in accordance with its terms.

(2) The reference in *subparagraph (1)* to a determination of the Labour Court is a reference to a determination in relation to which, at the expiration of the time for bringing an appeal against it, no such appeal has been brought or, if such an appeal has been brought it has been abandoned and the references to the date on which the determination is communicated to the parties shall, in a case where such an appeal is abandoned, be read as references to the date of such abandonment.

(3) In an order under this paragraph providing for the payment of compensation, the Circuit Court may, if in all the circumstances it considers it appropriate to do so, direct the employer concerned to pay to the employee concerned interest on the compensation at the rate referred to in section 22 of the Courts Act 1981, in respect of the whole or any part of the period beginning 6 weeks after the date on which the determination of the Labour Court is communicated to the parties and ending on the date of the order.

(4) An application under this paragraph shall be made to the Circuit Court sitting in the Circuit in which is situated the place of work (within the meaning of the Safety, Health and Welfare at Work Act 2005) at which the employee is normally employed by the employer.

Provisions relating to winding up and bankruptcy

5. (1) There shall be included among the debts which, under section 285 of the Companies Act 1963 (as amended by section 10 of the Companies (Amendment)

Act 1982 and section 134 of the Companies Act 1990) are, in the distribution of the assets of a company being wound up, to be paid in priority to all other debts, all compensation payable by virtue of a decision under *paragraph 1(2)(b)* or a determination under *paragraph 2(1)* by the company to an employee, and that Act shall have effect accordingly. Formal proof of the debts to which priority is given under this subparagraph shall not be required except in cases where it may otherwise be provided by rules made under that Act.

(2) There shall be included among the debts which, under section 81 of the Bankruptcy Act 1988 are, in the distribution of the property of a bankrupt or arranging debtor, to be paid in priority to all other debts, all compensation payable by virtue of a decision under *paragraph 1(2)(b)* or a determination under *paragraph 2(1)* by the bankrupt or arranging debtor, as the case may be, to an employee, and that Act shall have effect accordingly. Formal proof of the debts to which priority is given under this subparagraph shall not be required except in cases where it may otherwise be provided under that Act.

SCHEDULE 3

AMENDMENTS OF OTHER ACTS

PART 1

AMENDMENT OF BUILDING SOCIETIES ACT 1989

Item	Provision amended	Amendment
1	Section 2(1)	After the definition of "society", insert— " 'special investment shares' shall be construed in accordance with section 18(1A);".
2	Section 14(6)	Substitute "With the exception of any alteration to the rules that make changes necessary to or consequential on the issue of special investment shares, an alteration" for "An alteration".
3	Section 17(3)	After paragraph (*a*), insert— "(*aa*) the acceptance of payments by way of subscription for special investment shares;".
4	Section 18(1)(*b*)(i)	After "deferred", insert ", special investment".
5	Section 18(1)	After subsection (1), insert— "(1A) Special investment shares shall be issued only to the Minister for Finance or to such other person as he or she may nominate, and that Minister may specify the terms and conditions on which special investment shares may be issued, including terms and conditions— (*a*) that entitle the holder of the shares to such voting rights on resolutions as the terms of issue provide in accordance with section 69(3A), (*b*) that entitle the holder of the shares to appoint such number of directors of the society as the terms of issue provide in accordance with section 50(18), and (*c*) that the Minister for Finance considers necessary in the context of the Minister's agreement to subscribe for such shares and for the purposes of the Credit Institutions (Financial Support) Act 2008, including terms and conditions relating to— (i) the capital status and priority of the shares, (ii) the redemption, repurchase or other realisation of the shares, (iii) the dividends, if any, to be paid on the shares, and (iv) the transferability of the shares, but nothing in this Act or the society's rules shall be construed as limiting or affecting such terms and conditions, or the enforceability of, or rights arising from, such terms and conditions.".
6		After section 18, insert— "*Relationship framework.* 18A.—(1)(*a*) The Minister for Finance may from time to time— (i) specify in writing a relationship framework to govern the relationship between a building society that issues one or more special investment shares to the Minister for Finance or that Minister's nominee, and that Minister or nominee, and (ii) amend or revoke any such relationship framework.

Item	Provision amended	Amendment
		(*b*) Such a relationship framework shall recognise the separation of the building society concerned from that Minister or nominee and limit the extent of any intervention by that Minister or nominee in the conduct of the building society's business to that necessary to protect the public interest. (*c*) The relationship framework shall at all times comply with regulatory requirements. (2) The building society concerned, the Minister for Finance and any nominee of that Minister shall act in accordance with any relationship framework specified under subsection (1). (3) Parts 2 and 3 of the Competition Act 2002 shall not apply to the issue to the Minister for Finance, or that Minister's nominee, of one or more special investment shares. (4) Section 7 of the Credit Institutions (Financial Support) Act 2008 shall not apply to the issue to the Minister for Finance, or that Minister's nominee, of one or more special investment shares.".
7	Section 50(1)	Substitute "subsections (11), (16) and (18) and section 69(3A)(*c*)" for "subsections (11) and (16)".
8	Section 50	Insert after subsection (17)— "(18) Where the terms and conditions of issue so provide, a member who holds special investment shares shall be entitled, from time to time, by notice in writing to the society, to appoint such number of directors of the society as may be specified in the terms of issue of such shares, to remove any director so appointed and to replace the person removed with another person. (19) A provision in the memorandum or rules of a society shall not operate to— (*a*) prevent the appointment of directors pursuant to subsection (18), or (*b*) have the effect of requiring a director appointed by a member holding special investment shares to be a member of the society, to hold shares in or a deposit with the society or to resign or retire from office other than in accordance with subsection (18). (20) Where the terms and conditions of issue so provide, a member who holds special investment shares shall be entitled, by ordinary resolution, to remove a director before the expiration of his or her period of office notwithstanding anything in the rules or in any agreement between the society and the director.".
9	Section 69(1)(*a*)	Substitute— "(*a*) on a resolution other than a conversion resolution— (i) all the members who at the end of the last financial year of the society before the date of the meeting or the postal ballot, as the case may be, had held continuously shares to the value of not less than €125 for the preceding period of 6 months and continue to hold such shares on the voting date, and (ii) any member holding special investment shares; and".
10	Section 69(3)	Substitute "Subject to subsection (3A), on" for "On".

Item	Provision amended	Amendment
11	Section 69	After subsection (3), insert— "(3A) At any time when special investment shares are in issue and their terms so provide— (*a*) no resolution may be passed without the consent in writing of the member holding such shares, (*b*) where the member holding such shares votes in favour of a resolution, that resolution shall be treated for all purposes as having been passed by a majority of the members entitled to vote on such resolution, and (*c*) notwithstanding any other provision of this Act or any provision of the society's rules— (i) a resolution in writing signed by the member holding such shares shall be as valid and effective for all purposes as if the resolution had been passed at a general meeting of the society duly convened and held, and (ii) a resolution mentioned in subparagraph (i), if described as a special resolution or conversion resolution, shall be deemed to be such a resolution.".
12	Section 70(2)	Substitute "Subject to section 69(3A), a resolution" for "A resolution".
13	Section 71(1)	Substitute "Subject to section 69(3A), a resolution" for "A resolution".
14		After section 71, insert— "*Resolutions for special investment shares.* 71A.—(1) Where a building society proposes to issue special investment shares and its board of directors in good faith forms the opinion that the issue of such shares will assist in securing the financial position of the building society, the board of directors may, notwithstanding any provision in the society's rules, propose a resolution to approve of the issue of such shares and a special resolution to alter the society's memorandum and rules to give effect to all necessary and consequential changes relating to the issue of such shares. (2) Where the resolution and special resolution mentioned in subsection (1) are to be considered at a meeting, then, notwithstanding any other provision of this Act or any provision of the rules, the board of directors of the society concerned may reduce the period of notice otherwise required to be given for the meeting to a period not shorter than 5 days, if that board is of the view that the circumstances warrant it. (3) Where the resolution and special resolution mentioned in subsection (1) are to be voted on by postal ballot, then, notwithstanding any other provision of this Act or any provision of the rules, the board of directors of the society concerned may reduce the period of notice otherwise required to a period not shorter than 5 days before the date which the board specifies as the date for the postal ballot, if that board is of the view that the circumstances warrant it.".
15	Section 73(1)(*b*)	Substitute— "(*b*) of making ineffective a demand for a poll on any such question which is made by— (i) not less than 10 members having the right to vote at the meeting, or (ii) a member holding special investment shares.".

PART 2

AMENDMENT OF CENTRAL BANK ACT 1942

Item	Provision amended	Amendment
1	Section 18B(2)	Delete subsection.
2		After section 18B, insert— "*Membership of Board and Regulatory Authority.* 18BA.—(1) Nothing in this Act shall be read so as to prevent any member of the Board from being a member of the Regulatory Authority. (2) Where more than half of the members of the Board are also members of the Regulatory Authority, then paragraph 2 of Schedule 1 shall apply as if it read 'A quorum for all meetings of the Board is 7'.".
3		After section 19A, insert— "*Decisions about certain issues involving Treaties governing European Communities and ESCB Statute.* 19B.— Where the Board is considering a budgetary or funding issue relating to the Bank or the Regulatory Authority that may have implications for the independence of the Bank or the performance by the Governor of the functions conferred on the Governor and the Bank by or under the treaties governing the European Communities (within the meaning given by section 1 of the European Communities Act 1972) or the ESCB Statute— (*a*) the Governor has the sole right to determine the issue, and (*b*) the Governor's decision is final.".
4	Section 25(2)	Delete subsection.
5	Section 25(3)	Delete "otherwise than by virtue of being a member of the Regulatory Authority".
6	Section 25(4)(*b*)	Substitute— "(*b*)in order to enable the Board or the Board and the Regulatory Authority to function effectively, or (*c*) in order to facilitate a restructuring of the Board and the Authority so as to enable a closer working relationship between them.".
7	Section 33E(1)	Substitute "The Regulatory Authority comprises no fewer than 8 and no more than 12 members" for "The Regulatory Authority comprises no fewer than 8 and no more than 10 members".
8	Section 33E(1)(*c*)	Substitute "no fewer than 6 and no more than 10 are persons appointed by the Minister for Finance" for "no fewer than 6 and no more than 8 are persons appointed by the Minister for Finance".
9	Section 33E	After subsection (1), insert— "(1A) Nothing in this Act shall be read so as to prevent any member of the Regulatory Authority from being a member of the Board.".
10	Section 33I	After subsection (1), insert—

Item	Provision amended	Amendment
		"(1A) Where the Minister appoints or has appointed the Governor as a member of the Authority, then nothing in this Act shall be read so as to prevent the appointment of the Governor as its Chairperson.".
11	Schedule 2, Part 1	At the end, insert— " <table><tr><td></td><td>*National Asset Management Agency Act 2009*</td><td>Part 12</td></tr></table> ".
12	Schedule 3, paragraph 5(3)(*b*)	Substitute— "(*b*)in order to enable the Regulatory Authority or the Authority and the Board to function effectively, or (*c*) in order to facilitate a restructuring of the Authority and the Board so as to enable a closer working relationship between them.".

PART 3

AMENDMENT OF COMPANIES ACT 1963

Item	Provision amended	Amendment
1	Section 216	After subsection (1), insert— "(2) The court shall not make an order for the winding up of a company unless— (*a*) the court is satisfied that the company has no obligations in relation to a bank asset that has been transferred to the National Asset Management Agency or a NAMA group entity, or (*b*) if the company has any such obligation— (i) a copy of the petition has been served on that Agency, and (ii)the court has heard that Agency in relation to the making of the order. (3) In subsection (2) 'bank asset' and 'NAMA group entity' have the same respective meanings as in the *National Asset Management Agency Act 2009*.".

PART 4

AMENDMENTS OF COMPANIES (AMENDMENT) ACT 1990

Item	Provision amended	Amendment
1	Section 2	After subsection (4), insert— "(5) The court shall not make an order under this section unless— (*a*) the court is satisfied that the company has no obligations in relation to a bank asset that has been transferred to the National Asset Management Agency or a NAMA group entity, or (*b*) if the company has any such obligation—

Item	Provision amended	Amendment
		(i) a copy of the petition has been served on that Agency, and (ii) the court has heard that Agency in relation to the making of the order. (6) In subsection (5) 'bank asset' and 'NAMA group entity' have the same respective meanings as in the *National Asset Management Agency Act 2009*.".
2	Section 4	After subsection (6), insert— "(7) The court shall not make an order under this section unless— (*a*) the court is satisfied that the related company has no obligations in relation to a bank asset that has been transferred to the National Asset Management Agency or a NAMA group entity, or (*b*) if the related company has any such obligation— (i) a copy of the petition has been served on that Agency, and (ii) the court has heard that Agency in relation to the making of the order. (8) In subsection (7) 'bank asset' and 'NAMA group entity' have the same respective meanings as in the *National Asset Management Agency Act 2009*.".

PART 5

AMENDMENT OF FINANCE ACT 1970

Item	Provision amended	Amendment
1	Section 54	After subsection (7D), insert— "(7E) The Minister— (*a*) may engage in such transactions of a normal banking nature with any person as he or she considers appropriate— (i) in connection with the performance of his or her functions under the *National Asset Management Agency Act 2009*, and (ii) for the purpose of the better management of any indebtedness incurred by the Minister under that Act, and (*b*) may for the purpose of those transactions issue such funds from the Exchequer as he or she considers appropriate. The expenses and other costs incurred by the Minister in connection with or arising out of those transactions shall be charged on the Central Fund or the growing produce of that Fund.".

PART 6

AMENDMENTS OF LANDLORD AND TENANT (AMENDMENT) ACT 1980

Item	Provision amended	Amendment
1	Section 17(2)(*a*)(v)	Substitute "management, or" for "management.".
2	Section 17(2)(*a*)	After subparagraph (v), insert— "(vi) the landlord (being the National Asset Management Agency) will require possession, within 5 years after the termination of the existing tenancy, for any purpose for which that Agency is entitled to acquire (by purchase or otherwise) property under the *National Asset Management Agency Act 2009*.".

PART 7

AMENDMENTS OF NATIONAL TREASURY MANAGEMENT AGENCY ACT 1990

Item	Provision amended	Amendment
1		After section 4A, insert— *"Further powers of NTMA.* 4B.—(1) The Agency shall have all powers necessary or expedient for the performance of any function conferred on it by the *National Asset Management Agency Act 2009*. (2) The performance by the Agency of a function under the *National Asset Management Agency Act 2009* is not a function of the Agency under this Act.".
2	Section 12	After subsection (3), insert— "(4) The audited accounts prepared in pursuance of this section shall include a record of any expenses incurred by the Agency in the performance of functions under the *National Asset Management Agency Act 2009*.".
3	Schedule 1	After paragraph (*ge*), insert— "(*gf*) section 54(7E) (inserted by the *National Asset Management Agency Act 2009*) of the Finance Act 1970;".
4	Schedule 1	After paragraph (*t*), insert— "(*u*) section 47 of the *National Asset Management Agency Act 2009*.".

PART 8

AMENDMENT OF PLANNING AND DEVELOPMENT ACT 2000

Item	Provision amended	Amendment
1	Section 40(3)	Substitute "In this section and sections 42 and 42A," for "In this section and in section 42,".
2		After section 42, insert—

Item	Provision amended	Amendment
		"*Power to extend appropriate period on application of NAMA.* 42A.—(1) Notwithstanding section 42, on application by the National Asset Management Agency to it in that behalf a planning authority shall, as regards a particular permission as and from the expiry of that permission, extend the appropriate period by such additional period not exceeding 5 years as the authority considers requisite to enable the development to which the permission relates to be completed provided that each of the following requirements is complied with: (*a*) either— (i) the authority is satisfied that— (I) the development to which the permission relates was commenced before the expiration of the appropriate period sought to be extended, (II) substantial works were carried out pursuant to the permission during that period, and (III) the development will be completed within a reasonable time, or (ii) the authority is satisfied that— (I) there were considerations of a commercial, economic or technical nature beyond the control of the applicant which substantially militated against either the commencement of development or the carrying out of substantial works pursuant to the planning permission, and (II) there have been no significant changes in the development objectives in the development plan or in regional development objectives in the regional planning guidelines for the area of the planning authority since the date of the permission such that the authority would not, as a result of those changes, grant an application for permission for the development as being in material contravention of the proper planning and sustainable development of the area of the authority, (*b*) the application is in accordance with such regulations under this Act as apply to it, (*c*) any requirements of, or made under those regulations are complied with as regards the application, and (*d*) subject to subsection (7), the application is duly made prior to the end of the appropriate period. (2)(*a*) Where an application is duly made under this section to a planning authority and any requirements of, or made under, regulations under section 43 are complied with as regards the application, the planning authority shall make its decision on the application as expeditiously as possible.

Item	Provision amended	Amendment
		(b) Without prejudice to the generality of paragraph (a), it shall be the objective of the planning authority to ensure that it shall give notice of its decision on an application under this section within the period of 8 weeks beginning on— (i) in case all of the requirements referred to in paragraph (a), are complied with on or before the day of receipt by the planning authority of the application, that day, and (ii) in any other case, the day on which all of those requirements stand complied with. (3) A decision to extend an appropriate period shall be made once and once only under this section and a planning authority shall not further extend the appropriate period. (4) Particulars of any application made to a planning authority under this section and of the decision of the planning authority in respect of the application shall be recorded on the relevant entry in the register. (5) Where a decision to extend is made under this section, section 40 shall, in relation to the permission to which the decision relates, be construed and have effect, subject to, and in accordance with, the terms of the decision. (6) In satisfying itself under subsection (1)(a)(ii), a planning authority shall have regard to any guidelines issued by the Minister under section 28, notwithstanding that they were so issued after the date of the grant of permission in relation to which an application is made under this section. (7) In relation to a permission where the expiry of the appropriate period occurs during the period beginning on or after 1 January 2009 and ending on or before 31 December 2011, NAMA may make an application to extend the appropriate period— (a) before the expiry of the appropriate period, or (b) at any time during the period of 2 years beginning on the date of expiry of the appropriate period.".

PART 9

AMENDMENT OF STAMP DUTIES CONSOLIDATION ACT 1999

Item	Provision amended	Amendment
1		After section 108A, insert— "*National Asset Management Agency.* 108B.—(1) In this section: 'acquired bank asset', 'bank asset' and 'participating institution' have, respectively, the meanings given by section 4(1) of the Act of 2009; 'Act of 2009' means the *National Asset Management Agency Act 2009*; 'NAMA' means the National Asset Management Agency;

Item	Provision amended	Amendment
		'NAMA-subsidiary', in relation to an instrument referred to in subsection (3), means a body corporate which at the time of execution of the instrument is associated with NAMA in accordance with the provisions of section 79.

(2)(*a*) Where NAMA directly owns any part of the ordinary share capital, within the meaning of section 79, of another body corporate (in this subsection referred to as the 'first body corporate'), then NAMA shall be deemed to be associated with the first body corporate in accordance with the provisions of section 79.

(*b*) Where the first body corporate is associated, directly or indirectly, with another body corporate (referred to in this paragraph as the 'second body corporate') in accordance with the provisions of section 79, then NAMA shall be deemed to be associated with the second body corporate in accordance with the provisions of section 79.

(3) Stamp duty shall not be chargeable under or by reference to any Heading in Schedule 1 on an instrument—

(*a*) for the sale, transfer, lease or other disposition of any property, asset or documentation to NAMA or a NAMA-subsidiary by NAMA, a NAMA-subsidiary or a participating institution,

(*b*) for the transfer, to a NAMA-subsidiary or a participating institution, of securities issued in accordance with the Act of 2009 for the purposes of *section 47(2)(b)*, *48(2)(b)* or *49* of that Act,

(*c*) for the transfer to a NAMA-subsidiary by NAMA or a NAMA-subsidiary of securities issued in accordance with the Act of 2009 for the purposes of *section 47(2)(a)* or *48(2)(a)* of that Act,

(*d*) for the transfer to a participating institution of a bank asset, security or other property by NAMA or a NAMA-subsidiary in connection with *section 125* of the Act of 2009, or

(*e*) for the transfer or other disposition to NAMA or a NAMA-subsidiary of any property in settlement or part settlement of an acquired bank asset.

(4) Section 12(2) shall not apply to an instrument to which subsection (3) applies.

(5) This section applies as respects instruments executed on or after the establishment day (within the meaning of *section 4* of the Act of 2009).".

PART 10

AMENDMENTS OF TAXES CONSOLIDATION ACT 1997

Item	Provision amended	Amendment
1	Section 172A(1)(*a*), definition of "relevant distribution"	In subparagraph (i)(II), substitute "Commission," for "Commission, or".
2	Section 172A(1)(*a*), definition of "relevant distribution"	After subparagraph (i)(III), insert— "(IV) the National Asset Management Agency, or a company referred to in section 616(1)(*g*), and".
3		After section 230A, insert— "*NAMA profits exempt from corporation tax.* 230AA.—Notwithstanding any provision of the Corporation Tax Acts, profits arising to the National Asset Management Agency shall be exempt from corporation tax.".
4	Section 246(3)	After paragraph (*e*), insert— "(*ea*) interest paid to— (i) the National Asset Management Agency or a company referred to in section 616(1)(*g*), (ii) the State acting through the National Asset Management Agency or through a company referred to in section 616(1)(*g*), or (iii) the National Treasury Management Agency by the National Asset Management Agency or by a company referred to in section 616(1)(*g*), (*eb*) interest paid by— (i) the National Asset Management Agency, (ii) a company referred to in section 616(1)(*g*), or (iii) the State acting through the National Asset Management Agency, or through a company referred to in section 616(1)(*g*), to a person who, by virtue of the law of a relevant territory, is resident for the purposes of tax in the relevant territory, except, in a case where the person is a company, where such interest is paid to the company in connection with a trade or business which is carried on in the State by the company through a branch or agency,".
5	Section 256(1), definition of "relevant deposit", paragraph (*a*)	After subparagraph (iiic), insert— "(iiid) the National Asset Management Agency, (iiie) the State acting through the National Asset Management Agency,".
6	Section 396(1)	Substitute "Subject to section 396C, where in any accounting period" for "Where in any accounting period".

Item	Provision amended	Amendment
7		After section 396B, insert—

"*Relief from Corporation Tax for losses of participating institutions.*

396C.—(1)(*a*) In this section—

'available losses', in relation to an accounting period of a participating institution, means losses, carried forward from preceding accounting periods, for which relief is available under section 396(1) in that accounting period or succeeding accounting periods;

'group company', for an accounting period in relation to a participating institution (in this definition referred to as the 'first-mentioned institution'), means a company which is a participating institution that has an accounting period that coincides with the accounting period of the first-mentioned institution where, throughout the accounting period of the first-mentioned institution—

(*a*) the company is a subsidiary of the firstmentioned institution,

(*b*) the first-mentioned institution is a subsidiary of the company, or

(*c*) both the company and the first-mentioned institution are subsidiaries of a third company;

'participating institution' and 'subsidiary' have the same meanings respectively as in *section 4* of the *National Asset Management Agency Act 2009*;

'relevant amount' for an accounting period in relation to a participating institution means 50 per cent of the amount, if any, by which the aggregate of the trading income, if any, of the participating institution and its group companies for the accounting period exceeds the aggregate of the trading losses, if any, incurred by the participating institution and its group companies in that accounting period;

'relevant limit' in relation to an accounting period of a participating institution means an amount determined by the formula—

$$\frac{A \times B}{C}$$

where—

A is the relevant amount for the accounting period in relation to the participating institution,

B is the aggregate amount of the trading income, if any, of the participating institution for the accounting period before any relief for available losses, and

C is the aggregate amount of the trading income, if any, of the participating institution and its group companies for the accounting period before any relief for available losses.

(*b*) For the purposes of this section—

(i) an accounting period of a company coincides with an accounting period of another company if the first-mentioned accounting period begins on the same day and ends on the same day as the secondmentioned accounting period, and

224

Item	Provision amended	Amendment
		(ii) references to trading income or trading losses are references to trading income or trading losses, as the case may be, arising— (I) to a company resident in the State, or (II) through or from a branch or agency in the State of a company that is not so resident. (2) Where for any accounting period a participating institution makes a claim under subsection 396(1) for relief in respect of available losses incurred, or deemed under subsection (3) to have been incurred, in a trade carried on by that institution, the amount of the losses which may be set off against trading income of the trade in that accounting period shall not exceed the relevant limit of the participating institution for that period. (3)(*a*) Subject to subsection (2) and paragraphs (*b*) and (*c*), where in relation to an accounting period— (i) a participating institution has an amount of available losses (referred to in this subsection as the 'excess available losses') in respect of which it cannot obtain relief for that period, and (ii) a group company in relation to that institution, having claimed all relief under section 396(1), if any, to which it would otherwise be entitled (including by reference to other claims made under this subsection), could obtain relief, or more relief, under section 396(1) for that accounting period if some or all of the excess available losses of the participating institution were deemed to have been incurred by the group company, then, on the making of a claim in that regard by the group company, the participating institution may surrender to the group company an amount of those excess available losses that does not exceed the amount for which the group company could obtain relief for that accounting period, having claimed all other relief under section 396(1) to which it is entitled, and— (I) that group company shall be deemed for the purposes of section 396(1) to have incurred those losses and shall set off the amount so surrendered against its trading income for the accounting period, which income shall be treated as reduced by that amount, and (II) the available losses of the surrendering company shall be deemed for all purposes of the Corporation Tax Acts to be reduced by the amount surrendered. (*b*) More than one group company may make a claim under this subsection relating to the same participating institution and to the same accounting period of that institution but, whether by reference to this section or any other section of the Corporation Tax Acts or any combination thereof, relief shall not be given more than once in respect of an amount of available losses. (*c*) A claim for relief under this subsection— (i) shall be made in the return required to be made under section 951 for the accounting period of the group company which is claiming the relief,

Item	Provision amended	Amendment
		(ii) shall require the consent of the participating institution notified to the inspector in such form as the Revenue Commissioners may require, and (iii) shall be made within 2 years from the end of the accounting period to which the claim relates. (4)(*a*) Subject to subparagraph (*b*), where the inspector ascertains that any relief claimed in accordance with this section is or has become excessive, he or she may make an assessment to corporation tax under Case I of Schedule D in the amount which in his or her opinion ought to be charged. (*b*) Subparagraph (*a*) is without prejudice to the making of an assessment under section 919(5)(*b*)(iii) and to the making of all such other adjustments by means of discharge or repayment of tax or otherwise as may be required where a company has obtained too much relief. (5) This section has effect for accounting periods commencing on or after the passing of the *National Asset Management Agency Act 2009*.".
8	Section 495(10)	Substitute— "(10) Subject to section 507, the company shall not at any time in the relevant period— (*a*) control (or together with any person connected with it control) another company or be under the control of another company (or of another company and any person connected with that other company) unless such control is exercised by the National Asset Management Agency, or by a company referred to in section 616(1)(*g*), or (*b*) be a 51 per cent subsidiary of any company other than the National Asset Management Agency or a company referred to in section 616(1)(*g*), or itself have a 51 per cent subsidiary, and no arrangements shall be in existence at any time in that period by virtue of which the company could fall within paragraph (*a*) or (*b*).".
9	Section 530(1)	After the definition of "meat processing operations", insert: " 'NAMA' and 'NAMA group entity' have the same meanings, respectively, as they have in the *National Asset Management Agency Act 2009*;".
10	Section 530(1), definition of "relevant contract"	After "of employment", insert ", or a contract between NAMA and a NAMA group entity or a contract between a NAMA group entity and another NAMA group entity".
11	Section 616(1)	After paragraph (*f*), insert: "(*g*) Notwithstanding paragraph (*b*)— (i) a company (in this paragraph referred to as the 'first-mentioned company') shall be an effective 75 per cent subsidiary of the National Asset Management Agency where that Agency directly owns any part of the ordinary share capital of that company, and

Item	Provision amended	Amendment
		(ii) any other company which is an effective 75 per cent subsidiary of the first-mentioned company shall be an effective 75 per cent subsidiary of the National Asset Management Agency.".
12	Section 623(2)	Substitute "Subject to subsection (2A), this section applies where—" for "This section applies where—".
13	Section 623	After subsection (2), insert— "(2A) (*a*) This section does not apply to a bank asset where that asset is acquired on or after the establishment day by— (i) NAMA, or (ii) a company to which section 616(1)(*g*) relates from that Agency or a company to which that paragraph relates. (*b*) In this subsection 'bank asset', 'establishment day' and 'NAMA' have the same meanings, respectively, as they have in the *National Asset Management Agency Act 2009*.".
14		After section 644AA, insert— "*Treatment of profits or gains from land rezonings.* 644AB.—(1) In this section— 'basis period' has the same meaning as in section 127(1); 'company' has the same meaning as in section 4; 'construction operations', in relation to land, means operations of any of the descriptions referred to in the definition of 'construction operations' in section 530(1); 'development land-use' means residential, commercial or industrial uses or a mixture of such uses; 'distribution' has the same meaning as in section 130(2); 'non-development land-use' means a land-use which is agricultural, open space, recreational or amenity use or a mixture of such uses; 'qualifying land' means land which is disposed of at any time in the course of a business, being land— (*a*) disposed of to an authority possessing compulsory purchasing powers where the Revenue Commissioners are satisfied that the disposal would not have been made but for the exercise of those powers or the giving by the authority of formal notice of its intention to exercise those powers, or (*b*) disposed of by a company referred to in section 616(1)(*g*); 'rezoning' means a change in the zoning of land in a development plan or local area plan made or varied on or after 30 October 2009 under Part II of the Planning and Development Act 2000 from non-development land-uses to development land-uses or from one development land-use to another development land-use including a mixture of such uses. (2) This section applies to— (*a*) profits or gains arising from dealing in, or developing, land in the course of a business consisting of or including dealing in or developing land which is, or is regarded as, a trade within Schedule D or part of such a trade, or

Item	Provision amended	Amendment
		(*b*) any gain of a capital nature arising directly or indirectly from the disposal of land which, by virtue of section 643, constitutes profits or gains chargeable to tax under Case IV of Schedule D, to the extent to which the profits or gains are attributable to the rezoning of that land. (3) Notwithstanding any provision to the contrary in the Corporation Tax Acts, but subject to this section, a company shall not be chargeable to corporation tax in respect of profits or gains to which this section applies and, accordingly, such profits or gains shall not be regarded as profits or gains of the company for the purposes of corporation tax. (4) Notwithstanding any other provision of the Tax Acts and subject to subsections (6) and (7), to the extent to which profits or gains of a basis period for a year of assessment consist of profits or gains to which this section applies— (*a*) those profits or gains shall be chargeable to income tax for such year at the rate of 80 per cent, and (*b*) those profits or gains shall be disregarded for all the purposes of the Tax Acts, other than those relating to the assessment, collection and recovery of income tax and of any interest or penalties on that tax. (5)(*a*) To the extent that a loss is attributable to the rezoning of land referred to in subsection (2), that loss— (i) may be carried forward and may only be deducted from or set off against the amount of profits or gains to which this section applies for any subsequent year of assessment, and (ii) in the case of a company, shall be disregarded for the purposes of the Corporation Tax Acts. (b) Any relief under this subsection shall be given as far as possible against the profits or gains for the first subsequent year of assessment and, in so far as it cannot be so given, from the profits or gains for the next year of assessment and so on for succeeding years. (6) Where an individual is chargeable to tax in accordance with subsection (4) in respect of profits or gains, the profits or gains shall not be included in reckonable income— (*a*) within the meaning of section 2(1) of the Social Welfare Consolidation Act 2005, or (*b*) within the meaning of section 1 of the Health Contributions Act 1979, for the purposes of those Acts or any regulations made under those Acts. (7) For the purposes of the Tax Acts in computing the profits or gains to which this section applies, no account shall be taken, in determining those profits or gains, of that part, if any, of profits or gains which are attributable to— (*a*) construction operations on the land, or (*b*) qualifying land. (8) Where, in order to give effect to the provisions of subsections (2), (4) and (7), an apportionment of profits and gains, amounts receivable or expenses incurred is required to be made, such apportionment shall be made in a manner that is just and reasonable.

Item	Provision amended	Amendment
		(9) Where a distribution is made by a company in part out of profits or gains to which this section applies and in part out of other profits or gains, then the distribution shall be treated as if it consisted of 2 distributions respectively made out of the profits or gains to which this section applies and out of other profits or gains. (10) So much of any distribution as has been made out of profits or gains to which this section applies shall not be regarded as income for any purpose of the Income Tax Acts or be included in reckonable income— (*a*) within the meaning of section 2(1) of the Social Welfare Consolidation Act 2005, or (*b*) within the meaning of section 1 of the Health Contributions Act 1979, for the purposes of those Acts or any regulations made under those Acts. (11) This section shall apply as respects the year of assessment 2010 and subsequent years of assessment.".
15		After section 649A, insert— "*Windfall gains from rezonings: rate of charge.* 649B.—(1) In this section— 'development land-use' means residential, commercial or industrial uses or a mixture of such uses; 'loss arising on rezoning' means a loss realised on or after 30 October 2009 on a disposal of land to the extent to which that loss is attributable solely to a decrease in the market value of the land arising on a rezoning, and which loss has not otherwise been effectively relieved; 'non-development land-use' means a land-use which is agricultural, open space, recreational or amenity use or a mixture of such uses; 'rezoning' means a change in the zoning of land in a development plan or local area plan made or varied on or after 30 October 2009 under Part II of the Planning and Development Act 2000 from non-development land-uses to development land-uses or from one development land-use to another development land-use including a mixture of such uses. 'windfall gain' means any increase in the market value of land which is attributable to rezoning. (2) This section applies to a relevant disposal, made on or after 30 October 2009, where the disposal consists of land that— (*a*) has been the subject of rezoning since its acquisition by the person making the disposal, (*b*) was acquired from a connected person and the acquisition cost for the purposes of the Capital Gains Tax Acts was other than market value, where the rezoning took place during the ownership period of either person, or (*c*) was the subject of a sequence of transfers between connected persons, if the rezoning took place during the period between the date of disposal and the latest date at which the acquisition cost, at any step in the sequence, was market value.

Item	Provision amended	Amendment
		(3) Notwithstanding section 28(3), the rate of capital gains tax in respect of a chargeable gain, being the lesser of the gain arising on the disposal and the windfall gain, accruing to a person on a relevant disposal to which this section applies shall be 80 per cent. (4) This section shall not apply to a disposal of land to which subsection (2) relates where— (*a*) the land is disposed of to an authority possessing compulsory purchasing powers, but only if the Revenue Commissioners are satisfied that the disposal would not have been made but for the exercise of those powers or the giving by the authority of formal notice of its intention to exercise those powers, or (*b*) the disposal is a disposal by a company referred to in section 616(1)(*g*), and, accordingly, the rate of capital gains tax in respect of a chargeable gain on a relevant disposal referred to in paragraphs (*a*) to (*c*) shall be the rate specified in section 28(3). (5) Notwithstanding any provision to the contrary in the Capital Gains Tax Acts, any loss accruing on any disposal shall not be deducted from a chargeable gain to which this section applies except a loss arising on a rezoning. (6) This section shall apply to relevant disposals made on or after 30 October 2009.".
16	Section 730D(2)(*b*)(v)	Delete "or".
17	Section 730D(2)(*b*)(vi)	After "Court," insert "or".
18	Section 730D(2)(*b*)	After subparagraph (vi), insert—
		"(vii) the National Asset Management Agency,".
19	Section 730E(3)(*e*)(v)	Delete "or".
20	Section 730E(3)(*e*)(vi)	After "Court," insert "or".
21	Section 730E(3)(*e*)	After subparagraph (vi), insert— "(vii) the National Asset Management Agency,".
22	Section 730E(3)(*f*)	Substitute "paragraph (*e*)" for "subparagraph (i) to (v), or (vi) of paragraph (*e*)".
23	Section 739D(6)	After paragraph (*k*), insert— "(*ka*) is the National Asset Management Agency and has made a declaration to that effect to the investment undertaking,".
24	Section 980	After subsection (11), insert— "(12) The enforcement of a debt security by the National Asset Management Agency or by a company to which section 616(1)(*g*) relates does not constitute consideration for the purposes of this section.

Item	Provision amended	Amendment
		(13) Subsection (9) does not apply to the National Asset Management Agency or to a company to which section 616(1)(g) relates. (14) This section does not apply to a disposal by a company that would be a company to which section 616(1)(g) relates if the reference in that section to a 75 per cent subsidiary were a reference to a 51 per cent subsidiary. (15) For the purposes of this section, the enforcement of a debt security by the National Asset Management Agency or by a company to which section 616(1)(g) relates shall not be treated as a disposal of an asset.".
25	Schedule 13	After paragraph 173, insert— "174. The National Asset Management Agency or a company to which section 616(1)(g) relates.".
26	Schedule 15, Part 1	After paragraph 42, insert— "43. The National Asset Management Agency.".

PART 11

AMENDMENTS OF VALUE-ADDED TAX ACT 1972

Item	Provision amended	Amendment
1	Section 4B(2)	Substitute "Subject to subsections (3), (5), (7) and (8)" for "Subject to subsections (3), (5) and (7)".
2	Section 4B(5)	Substitute "Subject to subsection (8), where a taxable person" for "Where a taxable person".
3	Section 4B(7)	After paragraph (b), insert— "(c) Where a relevant supply is a supply of immovable goods to which this subsection would apply, the recipient shall be treated thereafter, for the purposes of this subsection in respect of those immovable goods, as if it were a person connected (within the meaning of section 7A) to the person who developed those immovable goods. (d) In this subsection and in subsection (8)— 'recipient' has the meaning assigned to it by section 8(1C); 'relevant supply' has the meaning assigned to it by section 8(1C).".
4	Section 4B	After subsection (7), insert— "(8)(a) Where a relevant supply occurs and where that supply would otherwise be exempt in accordance with subsection (2) the recipient may opt to tax that supply (in this subsection referred to as an 'option for taxation'), and where that option is exercised, tax shall, notwithstanding subsection (2), be chargeable on that supply, and in that case subsection (5) shall not apply. The option for taxation shall not apply to relevant supplies that are exempt in accordance with section 4(9) or subsection (2) or (6)(b) of section 4C.

Item	Provision amended	Amendment
		(*b*) The option for taxation shall be deemed to be exercised by the recipient in relation to a relevant supply which would otherwise be exempt in accordance with paragraphs (*b*), (*c*), (*d*) and (*e*) of subsection (2).".
5	Section 8	After subsection (1B), insert— "(1C)(*a*) Where a relevant supply occurs, then the recipient shall in relation to that supply be an accountable person and shall be liable to pay the tax chargeable in relation to that supply as if that recipient made that supply of goods in the course or furtherance of business. (*b*) Where paragraph (*a*) applies the supplier shall not be accountable for or liable to pay the tax in relation to the relevant supply. (*c*) In this subsection— 'NAMA' has the meaning assigned to it by the *National Asset Management Agency Act 2009*; 'NAMA entity' means a person or body of persons to which NAMA is connected within the meaning of section 7A; 'relevant supply' means a supply of goods being a transfer of ownership of goods effected by a vesting order made in accordance with *section 153* of the *National Asset Management Agency Act 2009*; 'recipient' in relation to a relevant supply means NAMA and any NAMA entity; 'supplier' in relation to a relevant supply means the chargor referred to in *section 153* of the *National Asset Management Agency Act 2009*.".
6	Section 12(1)(*a*)(iiic)	Substitute "section 4B(6)(*a*), 4(8) or 8(1C)" for "section 4B(6)(*a*) or 4(8)".
7	Section 12E	After subsection (9), insert— "(9A) (*a*) Subsection (9) shall not apply where— (i) a connected supply occurs and the seller enters into a written agreement with the purchaser to the effect that that purchaser shall be responsible for all obligations under this section in relation to the capital good from the date of the supply or transfer of that capital good, as if— (I) the total tax incurred and the amount deducted by that seller in relation to that capital good were the total tax incurred and the amount deducted by that purchaser, and (II) any adjustments required to be made under this section by that purchaser were made, and (ii) the seller issues a copy of the capital good record in respect of the capital good referred to in subparagraph (i) to the purchaser.

Item	Provision amended	Amendment
		(*b*) Where paragraph (*a*) applies the purchaser shall be responsible for the obligations referred to in paragraph (*a*)(i) and shall use the information in the copy of the capital good record issued by the seller in accordance with paragraph (*a*)(ii) for the purposes of calculating any tax chargeable or deductible in accordance with this section in respect of that capital good by that purchaser from the date on which the supply or transfer referred to in paragraph (*a*)(i) occurs. (*c*) In this subsection— 'connected supply' means a supply or transfer of a capital good which is a supply or transfer on which a seller would, but for the application of this subsection be obliged to calculate an amount of tax due in accordance with subsection (9); 'purchaser' means the person to whom the supply or transfer referred to in subsection (9) is made; 'seller' means the capital goods owner referred to in subsection (9) who makes the supply or transfer of the capital good referred to in that subsection.".

INDEX

239